CW00750290

Laduma!

Laduma!

Soccer, Politics and Society in South Africa

PETER ALEGI

UNIVERSITY OF KWAZULU-NATAL PRESS

Laduma! Soccer, Politics and Society in South Africa

ISBN 1 86914 040 0

© Peter Alegi 2004

All rights reserved. No part of this publication may be reproduced or transmitted in any form or by any means, electronic or mechanical, including photocopying, recording or any information storage and retrieval system, without prior permission in writing from University of KwaZulu-Natal Press.

Published by University of KwaZulu-Natal Press
Private Bag X01
Scottsville 3209
South Africa
Email: books@ukzn.ac.za
Website: www.ukznpress.co.za

Editor: Andrea Nattrass
Cover designer: Sumayya Essack
Typesetter: Alpha Typesetters cc

Cover image: Orlando Pirates vs Black Swallows, 3 November 1975 (Courtesy of National Library of South Africa)

Printed and bound by Interpak Books, Pietermaritzburg

Contents

List of Illustrations

I wish to thank the individuals and organisations for their permission to use the various photographs and illustrative materials which have greatly enhanced the visual quality of *Laduma!* In a few instances, despite concerted effort, it was not possible to track down the relevant copyright holders. Any feedback in this regard would be welcomed.

Preface

The inspiration to write a history of black South African soccer or football – I use the terms interchangably – came to me on a hot February afternoon in 1993, while coaching in Khayelitsha Site B, outside Cape Town. My Ikhusi Primary School under-12 boys' soccer team was playing against rival Umangaliso Primary on our home field – a tiny sand patch with a sewer pipe discharging filthy liquids onto the ground.

Suddenly, I realised that there were at least a hundred people who had emerged from their shacks and become captivated by our game. Men, women and children cheered, shouted, laughed, and encouraged the young athletes from behind the barbed-wire fence surrounding the school grounds. In the context of grinding township poverty and a desperate lack of amenities, this simple school soccer match provided the day's popular entertainment.

Was this a novel phenomenon? Or did football have an important role in the social lives of black South Africans in the darkest days of segregation and apartheid? Eagerly, I visited the South African Library (now the National Library of South Africa) in Cape Town to learn more about South African soccer. But I was astonished to discover that there were no scholarly books on this subject. Upon entering graduate school later that year, I began to lay the foundations for this book which gets its *Laduma!* title from a Zulu expression (meaning 'to thunder' or 'to be famous') that is used by soccer television commentators when a goal is scored.

The research for *Laduma!* generated considerable interest in South Africa and, as a white male university researcher from Italy working in the United States, I was graciously received in South African academic and sporting circles. In both formal interviews and informal conversations, an excitement permeated individuals' responses to inquiries about football. Vince Belgeums who had launched his professional career in the early 1960s at the tender age of sixteen started our interview by thanking me for coming all the way from America to talk with him. Gripped by emotion, he said that nobody had ever bothered to ask about his football past, an aspect of his life that had meant so much to him as a young black man living in apartheid South Africa.

On another occasion, an interviewee took time off work and graced us with his presence at a university seminar; his poignant testimony greatly enriching our academic discussion. Faculty, staff, and students at various campuses around the country where I presented preliminary research findings found the work stimulating and full of potential.

The popular appeal of sport in black and white communities in South Africa led to an invitation from a local radio station to discuss my project on the air. Finally, a brief address I gave at the South African Football Association's inaugural national coaching certification course in July 1995 suggests the ways in which my research became more subject-driven over time. I took the podium after then *Bafana Bafana* coach Clive Barker and spoke on the pre-apartheid history of the game. My talk sparked a vigorous debate among the attendees about South African playing styles. Patrick 'Ace' Ntsoeloengoe, Cedric 'Sugar Ray' Xulu, and other leading practitioners of the post-1960 period who were in the room highlighted the need for me to investigate not only the social dimension of the game, but also its technical and tactical performance on the field of play.

My experience playing, coaching, and watching football in the 1990s everywhere from sandpatches to ramshackle grounds in black townships, and on lush grass pitches in suburban clubs and larger stadiums, encouraged me to think like a South African athlete as much as a professional historian. In researching and writing this book, therefore, I tried to strike a sensitive balance between football's organisational history, the relationship of the sport to South African society and political economy, and changes in the game within the boundaries of the playing fields.

I hope that those who read this book – ardent soccer fans and scholars of African history alike – will find it revealing and that it will spark further research into the history and political economy of African sport.

Peter Alegi
February 2004

Foreword

It is essential for any country claiming to have a football culture to also have a history of that culture. South Africa likes to believe that it possesses a unique soccer culture and an abiding passion for football. Sadly, prior to this point, we knew little of the roots of the game in the country. Peter Alegi's work, *Laduma!*, goes a long way to filling this gaping hole and giving South African soccer a sense of its sporting heritage.

Football in South Africa has long been a vital part of the fabric of society, a powerful vehicle that provided a bright distraction from the turmoils of segregation and apartheid and gave rise to hopes and ambitions that ordinarily would have been dampened by the discriminatory political system.

Leaders and heroes were created by football – role models who inspired thousands of people. As *Laduma!* reveals, soccer can rightfully claim to have had a major hand in the social liberation of South Africa's people. It was on the playing fields, in supportive administrative positions, and in the role of spectators and fans that many black South Africans could give expression to their abilities and creativity. From these sporting arenas the strength was found to continue the fight against oppression.

Unfortunately, the remarkable stories, trials, tribulations, contributions and achievements have been largely forgotten over the years and the importance of this heritage has been eroded. South Africa has been to two soccer World Cups since its return to international competition in 1992, and yet a general apathy with regard to the history of sport and its role in the development of South African society has ensured that this country does not possess a formal history of its football.

Peter Alegi's passionate and meticulous research ensures that a lost legacy is highlighted and that the roots of the game have now been properly recorded. *Laduma!* reveals a fascinating history, exceptional in the world game – a history that is intertwined with the dramatic and turbulent past of an exciting young democracy.

Almost every season, South African soccer delivers up another new icon – who is all too quickly forgotten with the quick passing of time. *Laduma!* is interwoven with the names of long-forgotten heroes whose roles in the development of the South African game deserve to be remembered.

South African soccer sits at an important juncture with the real possibility of hosting a future World Cup. But to push forward to an exciting future, it is vital not to forget the past. Peter Alegi has captured the role that football played in the history of black society and how soccer has developed into the popular culture that today dominates our newspapers and airwaves. Hopefully *Laduma!* will inspire others to add to this rich tapestry of our sporting heritage.

Mark Gleeson
Cape Town

Mark Gleeson is a long-standing soccer writer and commentator, having covered South African and African football extensively for the last two decades. He started the bi-weekly magazine *Kick Off* and is the correspondent on African soccer for Reuters and the London-based magazine *World Soccer*.

Acknowledgements

Laduma! would never have been published without the gracious and generous help of many individuals and institutions. The main sources of funding for my research in South Africa came from a Fulbright-IIE Fellowship and a Ford Foundation Pre-Dissertation grant. Additional funds for graduate study at Boston University came in the form of a Foreign Language and Areas Studies Fellowship and tuition awards from the African Studies Center, as well as Teaching Fellowships and a Saul Englebourg grant from the Department of History.

I am indebted to Diana Wylie, my extraordinary dissertation supervisor, and James McCann, Jean Hay, Houchang Chehabi, and Konrad Tuscherer, who strongly supported this unorthodox project while saving me from many unnecessary errors. My Zulu teachers Bhekinkosi Sikhakhane and Sandra Sanneh taught me necessary language skills. Gretchen Walsh, African Studies librarian at Boston University, helped with long-distance research. Robert Harms, Ann Biersteker, John Nauright, Douglas Booth, Charles Korr, Jeanne Penvenne, and Paul Darby provided valuable assistance and encouragement at critical times.

In South Africa, my research benefited from the efficient support of staff workers at the National Archives in Pretoria, Cape Town, Durban, and Pietermaritzburg; the National (South African) Library; the Manuscripts and Archives division of the University of Cape Town; the University of South Africa's Documentation Centre for African Studies; the Cullen Library at the University of the Witwatersrand, and the Alan Paton Centre at the University of KwaZulu-Natal, Pietermaritzburg. Francis Wilson and Archie Mafeje gave me permission to use documents on football in the Monica Wilson papers. Alan Tomlinson sent documents from the Sir Stanley Rous collection at the University of Brighton. David Morala Notoane, Conrad Stuurman, Joe Mthimka, Sean Field, and Ignatius Zuma helped with the interviews.

Many people in South Africa gave more than expected and asked for nothing in return. Scholars Philip Bonner, Saleem Badat, Albert Grundlingh, Cecil Manona, Paul Maylam, Goolam Vahed, Gary Minkley, Ciraj Rassool, Leslie Witz, Bill Freund, Sifiso Ndlovu, David Coplan, Christopher Merrett, Clive Glaser, Bobby Eldredge, and Verne Harris contributed knowledge, time, and resources at various stages of the project. I gained a deeper understanding of South African soccer from journalists Rodney Reiners, Richard Maguire, Mark Gleeson, Clinton Asary, and from members of Santos Football Club. I am grateful to Maguire and Gleeson for sharing precious research materials and unpublished manuscripts. Bernard Mahloko took me to Orlando Stadium to see Pirates for the first time and Louis Jeevanantham organised my visit to Esselenpark School of Excellence and the SAFA Coaching Course in 1995. My experience coaching with the Sports' Coaches Outreach (SCORE) programme in 1993 provided the initial spark for this project.

I wish to express my deep gratitude to the families of Rodney and Ayesha Reiners, Bernard and Felicity Hartze, Poobie and Pam Govindasamy, Saleem and Shireen Badat, and Ronnie Chetty for welcoming me into their homes. I must also thank the numerous South Africans I met at football grounds across the country who shared their stories and their passionate interest in recovering football's past.

Several experts helped to steer the manuscript's transformation from a dissertation into a book. Anonymous reviewers for Heinemann and the University of KwaZulu-Natal Press helped sharpen the book's intellectual architecture and analysis. Comments by Emmanuel Akyeampong, Charles Ambler, and Ben Carton strengthened several chapters. Earlier versions of parts of Chapters 5 and 6 were published in the *International Journal of African Historical Studies* and in the edited volume *Africa's Young Majority*. Meetings of the Northeast Workshop for Southern Africa at the University of Vermont provided an ideal setting in which to refine my arguments. Tom Appleton read the entire manuscript, Ron Huch and John Wade, chairs of the Department of History at Eastern Kentucky University, gave me much-needed release time and paid for photographic and indexing costs. Special recognition goes to Glenn Cowley, a courageous and visionary publisher, Andrea Nattrass, my superb editor, and the entire team from the University of KwaZulu-Natal Press for their professionalism in bringing this book to fruition.

Finally, many friends and family members encouraged me through the exigencies of research and writing. I am most grateful to Yusufu Lawi, Derick Fay, Robert Vinson, Robert Topmiller, Ignazio Pediconi, Simone Poliandri, Simone Santercole, the Foley family, my parents, Peter and Nicoletta, and the families of Gregory and Daniel Alegi. I dedicate this book to Catherine and to our beautiful daughters Sophie and Anna.

Abbreviations Used

ABCFM	American Board of Commissioners for Foreign Missions
ABM	American Board Mission
ANC	African National Congress
BMSC	Bantu Men's Social Centre
BP	British Petroleum
CAF	Confédération Africaine de Football
CCIRS	Co-ordinating Committee for International Recognition of Sport
CPSA	Communist Party of South Africa
DDAFA	Durban and District African Football Association
DDNFA	Durban and District Native Football Association
DIFA	Durban Indian Football Association
DOCC	Donaldson Orlando Community Centre
FASA	Football Association of South Africa
FSAW	Federation of South African Women
FIFA	Fédération Internationale de Football Association
FPL	Federation Professional League
JAFA	Johannesburg African Football Association
JBFA	Johannesburg Bantu Football Association
JMTFA	Johannesburg Municipal Townships Football Association
ICU	Industrial and Commercial Workers' Union
NAD	Native Affairs Department
NASL	North American Soccer League
NEAD	Non-European Affairs Department
NFL	National Football League
NPSL	National Professional Soccer League
NRC	Native Recruiting Corporation
ODBFA	Orlando and District Bantu Football Association
SAAFA	South Africa African Football Association
SAB	South African Breweries
SABC	South African Broadcasting Corporation
SABFA	South African Bantu Football Association
SACTU	South African Congress of Trade Unions
SAFA	South African Football Association
SAIFA	South African Indian Football Association
SAIRR	South African Institute of Race Relations

SANFA	South African National Football Association
SASA	South African Sports Association
SACOS	South African Council of Sport
SASF	South African Soccer Federation
SASL	South African Soccer League
SONREIS	Support Only Nonracial Events In Sport
TAFA	Transvaal African Football Association
UFASI	Union des Fédérations et Associations Sportives Indigénes
UMHK	Union Miniére du Haute Katanga
UTC	United Tobacco Company
WDNFA	Witwatersrand and District Native Football Association

Introduction

South Africa has been described as 'the most sports-mad country in the world', and no sport has been watched, played, and discussed more than football.[1] Recognising that millions of South Africans are captivated by the game, Nelson Mandela attended a match between South Africa and Zambia at a sold-out Ellis Park Stadium in Johannesburg just hours after his presidential inauguration on 10 May 1994. Since that festive afternoon, the national team, affectionately known as *Bafana Bafana* ('The Boys' in Zulu and Xhosa), has become a source of national pride, winning the 1996 African Nations Cup and qualifying for the prestigious World Cup finals in 1998 and 2002.

However, the significance of the game in black[2] social life is not a recent phenomenon, as the impressive growth over time of South African football clearly demonstrates. The number of African football teams in Durban increased from fewer than 10 in 1916 to 47 with more than 1 500 players in 1935, and to 264 with at least 5 000 players in 1959.[3] A similar pattern unfolded in Johannesburg during the same period: from 12 teams in 1917 to more than 230 teams with 4 000 to 5 000 players in 1939, and nearly 600 teams with about 10 000 players in 1959.[4]

The number of registered players (of all races) in 2004 reached 1,8 million and football's huge popularity among black South Africans stimulated unprecedented financial investments in the elite professional game. Corporate sponsorships rose from R15 million in 1996 to R70 million in 1998, and reached R640 million in 2002.[5] The game's political and economic importance led to a well-organised but unsuccessful South African bid to host the 2006 FIFA World Cup finals. In a highly controversial vote in July 2000, the world governing body FIFA awarded the 2006 World Cup finals to Germany. However, in the light of FIFA's recent decision to rotate the World Cup on a continental basis, beginning with Africa in 2010, South Africa is highly likely to host the event in the near future.[6]

By investigating the history of football from the formation of the Union of South Africa in 1910 to the Soweto uprising of 1976, *Laduma!* analyses the ways in which Africans transformed the British sport of football into a leading form of urban popular culture.[7] It examines the creation and maintenance of a sphere of social action that influenced class and generational divisions, shaped masculine identities, and served as a mobilising force for neighbourhood, township, and political organisations. This study is valuable and relevant in its own right: football matters to the people. For scholars, the social history of football sheds new light on key themes in the modern historiography of South Africa, as well as north of the Limpopo River.

Life is great.

SPORT AND LEISURE

Laduma! expands on the work of E.P. Thompson, Fred Cooper, Keletso Atkins, and Phyllis Martin,[8] which revealed how everyday struggles over leisure space and the meaning and use of free time were crucial avenues for contesting, negotiating, and shaping capitalist and colonial attempts to impose strict controls over workers' lives. In twentieth-century South Africa, the unwillingness of white taxpayers, employers, and white minority governments to pay for African social welfare resulted in the gross neglect of African sport. This trend was especially pronounced between the end of the South African War and the beginning of the Great Depression. The 'benevolent paternalism' of the 1930s and 40s and then the apartheid regime's high-modernist urban planning and social engineering of the 1950s and 60s,[9] led to the construction of some rudimentary football grounds in new, racially exclusive 'Native Locations' and townships. An analysis of the relationship between football and broader struggles for space and time should deepen our understanding of how local and national power was negotiated and contested in segregation- and apartheid-era South Africa.

By examining football's effects on internal divisions in African communities and its role in the formation of meaningful social identities and organised political movements *Laduma!* extends the recent work on sport and leisure by John Nauright and Douglas Booth on South Africa, and Laura Fair on Zanzibar.[10] As a popular cultural resource in industrialising South Africa, soccer reinforced and elided internal cleavages based on age, gender, race, class, region, and ethnicity. The sociability of football teams, leagues, and supporters' groups created bonds of solidarity that inspired collective action. Football functioned as a mobilising force that shaped urban social identities and influenced political organisations. Sport became bound up with both informal and formal politics. Football clubs expressed street, neighbourhood, and township identities as well as territorial rivalries often linked to the activities of gangs and migrant workers' associations.[11] Recognising football's magnetic attraction among ordinary working people, criminals and activists alike used the game to construct patronage networks and alliances, and to legitimise their activities at the grassroots level. After the Second World War and the rise of apartheid, football's mass popularity brought it into close contact with formal resistance politics (in the 1950s and 60s). The sport boycott movement that played an important role in the fall of apartheid relied heavily on the support of soccer players, fans, and organisations. International football sanctions were among the first international indictments of the apartheid regime.

AFRICANISATION OF SOCCER
Laduma! breaks new ground through its examination of the historical process of the Africanisation or vernacularisation of British football, creating an opportunity to assess the agency of black South Africans in shaping their own sporting and leisure history. While the interests and actions of local and national governments, white humanitarians, and private companies are of considerable importance, the main focus here is on African workers, entrepreneurs, and political leaders. That Africans were not passive dupes in their acceptance of modern sport is abundantly clear. The game was fun, inexpensive, and relatively easy to play. Furthermore, crucial cultural continuities linked traditional and modern sport. Enduring values of physical prowess, assertive masculinity, theatrical performance, and martial competition, as well as the infusion of magical preparatory rituals and the spectators' practice of praise-naming, demonstrate the percolation of agrarian influences into an urban cultural form of the industrial era.

The articulation of distinctive playing styles and the impact of the black popular press further highlight subaltern agency. Football influenced personal development and men's conceptions of self. It fostered friendships and camaraderie among team members and fans. It offered excitement, unpredictability, and experiences outside daily work routines (such as travel and new adventures); sport created popular discourse and generated emotional attachment. The 'intrinsic value' of football provided valuable entertainment and granted temporary relief from police harassment and grinding poverty. The meritocratic principles upon which sport is predicated helped to transform football into a field of action where black South Africans pursued and maintained social visibility, status, and prestige. Male-dominated football teams, contests, and organisations enabled people denied basic political and human rights to adapt to industrial conditions, cope with urban migration, and build alternative institutions and networks on a local, regional, and national scale.

DEFINITIONS OF GENDER AND MASCULINITY

The importance of sport to definitions of gender and masculinity is another way in which *Laduma!* departs from the existing scholarship. Football teams and competitions emphasising physical force, toughness, skill, and courage enabled older, agrarian martial and athletic masculinities undermined by colonial conquest to re-emerge in the industrial milieu. Fans and players transformed football into a public stage for the articulation of reconstructed young male identities, such as the gang and school masculinities analysed by historian Clive Glaser.[12] Age as much as gender considerations shaped male identities. Football administration and refereeing provided space for an adult patriarchal masculinity devoted to exercising authority, resolving conflicts through negotiation and compromise, and fostering the unity and prosperity of the collective.[13] In other words, sport expressed multiple and competing masculinities.[14]

The ways in which women's identities were reshaped by football is not clear and scholarly research on African women's sport is extremely rare.[15] Women filled both conservative and progressive roles. Many mothers and wives supported the efforts of their sons and husbands with their labour and moral encouragement; football matches were an opportunity for younger, unmarried women to have fun and socialise with men, while other women sold liquor and various goods to spectators. Women became more actively involved in football in the 1960s, attending matches in greater numbers and taking leading roles in supporters' organisations.

CHAPTER OUTLINE

This book is divided into eight narrative chapters and an epilogue arranged thematically and chronologically. Chapter 1 looks at indigenous sport and competition in pre-colonial times. It illustrates how stick fighting, cattle raiding, racing and hunting, as well as dancing traditions prior to Britain's nineteenth-century imperial expansion influenced in specific ways the rapid diffusion of football among African workers, traders, and students during the industrial period. Chapter 2 charts the origins of colonial football in South Africa. British ideas about race, class, gender, and empire drove this process, which led to the appropriation of rugby and cricket by whites, and football and boxing by blacks.

Chapter 3 focuses on the early development of the first metropolitan African football association – the Durban and District African Football Association. It discusses class and generational divisions, transformations in masculinity, as well as struggles over space in the inter-war period. Chapter 4 shifts the spotlight to

Soccer at Langa Stadium (25 November 1972).

Johannesburg in the 1930s, in particular, looking at football on the gold mines. It also explores the impact of the state and philanthropic organisations on both the expansion of the game and the conceptualisation and use of leisure time. Chapter 5 analyses the indigenisation or Africanisation of football through the increasing role of religious specialists and magic, rituals of spectatorship, including nicknaming, as well as the emergence of different styles of play.

Chapter 6 highlights the important role of football clubs in defining and cementing neighbourhood and township identities and bonds. A case study of the Orlando Pirates Football Club shows the creation of a social institution guided by a pray-and-play ethos, fraternal solidarity, and civic responsibility. Stiffening competition, generational tensions, and persistent struggles for access to playing grounds deeply affected a club trying to survive in the midst of dramatic shifts in the social, economic, and political conditions of post-war South Africa.

Chapter 7 explores two themes in the first decade of apartheid: the direct connections between football and nationalism, and inter-racialism, and the relationship between sport and entrepreneurship. Chapter 8 analyses the rise of integrated professional soccer in the 1960s and the increasing international pressure on South Africa to abandon apartheid in sport. Finally, the Epilogue highlights the most important developments in domestic football between 1971 and 1992 in order to bring the story closer to the present.

Laduma!'s attempt at crafting a social and political history of soccer in South Africa is necessarily selective and makes no claim to be either exhaustive or definitive. Nevertheless, this book charts a new path. It is a tribute to the skill, courage, and passion of players, organisers, and fans who enriched the lives of people with little else to cheer about. Football gave South Africans a sense of their own humanity. As Chapter 1 shows, pre-colonial indigenous athletic traditions shaped the encounter with modern British sporting culture in fundamental ways.

—— CHAPTER 1 ——

South African Athletic Traditions

Throughout pre-colonial Africa, ritualistic dances and games were long performed with a seriousness akin to sport in modern industrial societies, and for purposes not altogether different: the striving for status, the assertion of identity, the maintenance of power in one form or another, and the indoctrination of youth into the culture of their elders.[1]

In his autobiography, *Long Walk to Freedom*, former South African president Nelson Mandela highlighted the role of athleticism in Xhosa male youth culture. As a youth in rural Transkei, Mandela had 'no higher ambition than to eat well and become a champion stick-fighter'.[2] 'From an early age, I spent most of my free time in the veld playing and fighting with the other boys of the village,' Mandela said. 'I learned to stick-fight – essential knowledge to any rural African boy – and became adept at its various techniques, parrying blows, feinting in one direction and striking in another, breaking away from an opponent with quick footwork.'[3]

An appreciation of physical competition and the development of special kinetic skills prepared Mandela for his encounter with modern sport, including soccer, at Eastern Cape mission schools. His youthful passion for stick fighting later found an outlet in boxing. Mandela fought in the heavyweight division after migrating to Johannesburg in the early 1940s. 'I never did any real fighting after I entered politics. My main interest was in training,' Mandela remembered. 'I found the rigorous exercise to be an excellent outlet for tension and stress. After a strenuous workout, I felt both mentally and physically lighter. It was a way of losing myself in something that was not the struggle. After an evening's workout I would wake up the next morning feeling strong and refreshed, ready to take up the fight again.'[4]

Mandela's transition from rural stick fighting to urban boxing captures how agrarian notions of physical prowess, masculine identity, theatrical performance, and martial competition endured in modern sport. These cultural residuals found in boxing, football, athletics and, to a lesser extent, rugby and cricket, linked past and present in the second half of the nineteenth century. In mission schools, mines, and cities, black South Africans, fascinated by the cultural practices of the colonisers and able to draw from established agrarian sporting traditions, adopted modern sport.

Young *kholwa* (Christian) African men who migrated to the new mining centres of Kimberley and Johannesburg in search of wage employment used sport to prove their capacity to assimilate Victorian ways and to distinguish themselves from the lower ranks of the African population.[5] At this time, rural migrant workers also became interested in modern sport. But, initially, the temporary nature of migrant labour contracts and young rural men's low status in a neo-industrial society led most Africans to rituals of spectatorship rather than membership in sporting clubs and competitions.

AGRARIAN TRADITIONS OF PHYSICAL PROWESS
In the pre-colonial period, patriarchal South African societies developed gender- and age-based athletic contests and recreations. Initiations, weddings, funerals, and less formal social gatherings (usually run by the youth) presented an opportunity for public spectacles of physical prowess among the Nguni (Zulu, Xhosa, Swazi, Ndebele) and Sotho-Tswana, the two main groups each sharing a similar social organisation, division of labour, and closely related languages.[6]

Outdoor sport was largely, although never exclusively, the domain of boys and young men (initiated but unmarried).[7] Stick fighting, hunting, competitive dancing, foot races, and cattle racing developed physical strength, honed bodily movements, facilitated competition and creativity, and called upon collective understandings needed for combat, hunting game, and herding and raiding cattle.[8] Xhosa, Zulu, and Sotho girls initially shared recreations with boys, sometimes even stick fighting, but then developed separate amusements (role-playing, imitating adults, singing and dancing) around the time they reached puberty. The demands for girls' labour in the homestead sharply curtailed female youths' freedom to play; while the organisation of rural production afforded boys substantial freedom from parental supervision and encouraged the development of a male athletic culture.

Interviews with migrants conducted by researchers in Lesotho revealed how informants 'stressed the importance of their boyhood herding to the development of their characters. It was then, in the struggle for dominance within herding groups, in the physical privation, in the rivalry amongst different groups, that the fighting skills, the physical toughness and the aggression which one needs to deal successfully with the world were developed.'[9] After initiation the intertwined relationship between youth, violence, and social identity in African patriarchal societies gave way to a mature masculinity (*ubudoda* in Zulu and Xhosa) that valued negotiation, compromise, 'one's effectiveness as a family head', and respect for tradition and custom.[10] Young men remained active in indigenous sports such as hunting and cattle racing. Older men watched and sometimes advised boys involved in competitive dancing and stick fighting.

YOUTHS' SPORT: STICK FIGHTING

For African male youths, stick fighting *was* sport. Stick-fights were public spectacles serving leisure and socialisation objectives. These enjoyable contests created an arena in which youth demonstrated physical strength, forged an assertive masculine identity, and enhanced their reputation as warriors. The uncertain outcome of competition afforded an opportunity for meritorious youth to gain status within an age group or district, and to do so within the legitimising framework of dominant social norms and cultural practices. Stick-fights provided an arena for playing out male youth hierarchies.[11]

The importance of individual athletic performance and competition in indigenous sporting traditions underpinned the later development of ways of playing football that emphasised personal style and spectacular displays of skill. The use of praise names – *izibongo* (Zulu) or *lithoko* (Sotho) – was another powerful symbol of the personal and social significance of stick fighting. Either self-composed or, more often, conferred by their peers, praise names 'were used to excite and delight. They were a fairly faithful and inspired record of your career and character. In youth they told your measure of promise, your inclinations and your dormant but dominant qualities.'[12] Praise names expressed individual identities in a 'ritual language that attempted to "fix" and stabilize a sense of self in a process of restless adolescent gendering'.[13] The social upheaval linked to industrialisation and the creation of a racist state saw rural migrant workers carrying the tradition of praising and praise names to cities and towns, where the practice was then incorporated into African rituals of spectatorship and the making of a subaltern football culture.[14]

Like football matches in modern times, a festive atmosphere enveloped the public spectacle of formal stick-fighting bouts. Women brewed beer, young men presided over the fights; 'trainers' and spectators cheered the combatants on. Fights had no time limit and were usually staged in a cleared space in the fields near the homestead. In Zululand the contests began with one youth calling out an opponent: '[t]he challenge was *inselelo*, "I challenge you to fight." If accepted, the reply would be "*Woz'uzithathe izinduku*" (sticks understood), meaning "come and take them", that is, "come and see if you can master me and deprive me of my sticks".'[15] As the combatants taunted each other they interacted with the audience. The fight ended when one of the fighters was knocked down and symbolically stabbed.

Xhosa male youth associations (*umtshosho*) – organised on a fiercely territorial basis – transformed stick fighting into a central aspect of their regular activities. Jousting with sticks provided an arena for the display of individual masculine prowess and expressed territorial rivalries between *umtshosho* groups.[16] These Xhosa youth associations operated independently from adults, though in accordance with broader cultural values and norms.[17] This agrarian tradition of independent leisure continued after the formation of football clubs and leagues in the industrial era, a process that reveals how 'autonomy is crucial to the definition of leisure' in the African context.[18] Rural isolation and conscious attempts to maintain traditional cultural institutions and practices in the Transkei saw stick fighting endure as the dominant youth sport until recently. Research has shown that 'stick-fighting traditionalist youth associations based on locality remained a major feature of rural life in the Transkei and Ciskei at least till the 1960s and played a central role in the socialization of youths up to marriage'.[19] Even after football replaced stick fighting as the most popular sport in the Eastern Cape in the 1970s, the organisation of teams remained rooted in territory: 'The soccer mania in Shixini [Willowvale district, Transkei] is structured in terms of existing neighborhoods, sub-ward boundaries, rivalries and alliances, and in this way is related to the wider society in a similar manner to the earlier youth associations'.[20]

In pre-colonial times, stick-fights involving clusters of homesteads, or districts, drew large crowds and could affect the prestige of a family, homestead, and area. District fights collapsed individual and collective interests into one. In parts of Zululand, stick-fights contained rising tensions between districts in the wake of the Anglo-Zulu War of 1879 and the dismemberment of the Zulu kingdom in the 1880s. According to Jonathan Clegg, 'in Zululand, "playing" between districts in the form of *umgangela* was a means by which districts could cope with the tensions unleashed by the fragmentation of traditional power and the tendency towards balkanization of the territory, generated by the increasing absence of the unifying effect of the age regiment system'.[21] Between the 1930s and 50s these engagements turned increasingly violent.[22]

Stick fighting's cultural power was probably strengthened by its structured organisation and elaborate vernacular code of conduct. 'Individuals [in Pondoland] might get carried away in the heat of battle, but hitting an opponent when he was down was deeply deplored. Thus, even though stick-fighting was rough play, it was play nonetheless, with its own rules.'[23] Oral evidence collected by the Zulu-speaking colonial official James Stuart (1868–1942) further highlighted how 'no one was allowed to use an assegai [short spear] when fighting against their tribesmen, i.e. in faction fighting or fighting between individuals. This was a regulation observed in Tshaka's as well as Dingana's and Mpande's reigns. It was thoroughly well-known and never infringed.'[24] The existence of a 'strict set of rules that, among other things, prohibited stabbing and other potentially lethal war techniques' was designed to ensure fairness and avert severe injuries.[25] We know that the '"rules of the game" apparently provided an ethos which kept the game within bounds' because these rules were occasionally disregarded.[26] There is evidence of a tendency that arose in the final period of Zulu independence of 'sharpening one end of the *umtshiza* (fighting stick) and jab the opponent in the eye or face therewith, King Cetshwayo passed a law prohibiting this practice, as a piece of cowardice and unfair fighting, under the death penalty, or heavy fine, according to the seriousness of the hurt inflicted, and eventually the practice ceased'.[27]

This royal intervention and reinterpretation of the local sporting code suggests how the fluid and negotiable oral code of agrarian sport – typical of traditional African legal practices – shared some common features with modern sport's fixed, rigid written rules.[28] It seems that the idea of sporting laws and, to a large extent, the codification of rules was not introduced by modernising British colonisers.

With age, gender identities, norms, and expectations changed. The martial masculinity of youth, emphasising physical prowess and stick-fighting skills, gave way, in ideal terms, to a mature masculinity defined by restraint, negotiation, and oratorical ability, leadership qualities, and knowledge of customary law.[29] The sport and leisure practices of young men differed significantly from those of boys.

MEN'S SPORT: CATTLE RAIDING, RACING, AND HUNTING

Among the mixed-farming communities of pre-colonial southern Africa 'cattle-raiding was a manly sport and a way of increasing one's wealth'.[30] These aggressive forms of playful leisure gave men, especially those between the ages of eighteen and forty, a chance to assert their manhood, contribute to homestead wealth by quickly expanding the family herd, and possibly raise their social status. If carried out with excessive zeal (or success), cattle raids could lead to turmoil, even violent conflict. Raiding and warfare became more frequent in the eighteenth century, intensifying further during the nineteenth century as a result of social, economic, and political transformations caused by white settlement of the interior, land loss, environmental stress, changing demographics, and Mfecane upheavals and migrations.[31] Zulu and Swazi *amabutho* (age-regiments), for instance, gained a fearsome reputation for pre-datory incursions because raiding cattle was a primary function of their service to local aristocracies.[32]

Cattle's significance to indigenous sport was reflected in the popularity of racing. In Lesotho, 'racing [was] an old sport. Formerly special oxen were raced over arduous courses of many miles.'[33] Among the Xhosa, racing provided both ritual and competitive entertainment. The Xhosa historian John Henderson Soga (1859–1941), outlined the importance of cattle racing (*uleqo*) by stating, 'this sport occupied, in the estimation of the people, much the same position as horse racing does in England'.[34] In his early anthropological study of the Bomvana Xhosa, Peter Cook claimed that racing was linked to ancestral worship, initiations, and weddings, adding that an 'ox race is highly thought of, and natives will rarely miss one'.[35] Xhosa men, like their Basotho counterparts, raced specialised oxen, although it is unclear whether this early specialisation included training outside of competitions. In any event, races began when the 'oxen are driven off very early in the morning to some point about ten miles or so from the kraal. They are then turned homewards the men running or riding horses not behind the cattle but on either side. They do not ride the oxen. The *izibongo* [praises] of the oxen are yelled out, of ancestors and many weird shouts urge on the beasts.'[36]

Great excitement surrounded the races: 'the road or track which the oxen follow is lined with onlookers and the men join in here and there running a distance before they fall out. Everybody shouts at the top of his voice to urge the oxen on.' The first ox to reach the designated homestead won the race: 'the owner praises his triumphant ox, loudly and at some length. The oxen are driven off while the race is eagerly discussed.'[37]

Hunting complemented raiding and racing cattle in pre-colonial sporting traditions. Nineteenth-century European missionaries and travellers described hunting for both subsistence and leisurely purposes among Xhosa, Sotho, and Zulu communities.[38] An organised collective recreational enterprise carried out by chiefs and (male) commoners alike, Zulu game hunting, for example, was a skilled discipline with the kinds of elaborate strategy and tactics and propitiatory rituals associated with Zulu military campaigns. Typically, men from different areas grouped into companies (*amaviyo*) assembled at the host homestead. Participants called for ancestral protection, danced, and recited praise songs so as to build a sense of common purpose and unity ahead of the chase.[39] A.T. Bryant described the tactics of organised hunting in terms of the pincer movements of Zulu *impi*: the hunt was 'a systematically and scientifically arranged "battle" with the beasts, with its central "chest" (*isifuba*) and its two encircling wings or "horns" (*upondo*) like an army on the field'.[40] The link between hunting and warfare was even more explicit if the men were setting out to hunt dangerous animals such as lion, leopard, hippopotamus, rhinoceros, and elephant. On such occasions, it was reported, a doctor (*inyanga*) would sprinkle medicine (*umuthi*) on the hunters' limbs, a practice borrowed from Zulu forces' preparations for war.[41]

This overview of men's sport and leisure gives some indication of the vibrant vernacular gaming traditions found in nineteenth-century South Africa. The South African case corroborates the conclusions of scholars John Bale and Joe Sang, who argued in a recent book about Kenyan athletics that while 'pre-modern Kenyan body culture has little to do with modern athletics . . . improved performance and competition – two basic ideologies of modern sport – were part of the consciousness of traditional Kenyan societies'.[42] To shed further light on how agrarian sports and African understandings of fitness, physical competition, and improved performance facilitated the diffusion of the British export of football in South Africa, dance must be incorporated into South African traditional athleticism.

RITUAL AND COMPETITIVE DANCING

A creative, communicative cultural form involving skilful handling of the body, dance could combine art, entertainment, ritual, and competition.[43] Some Sotho, Xhosa, Venda, Zulu and Swazi dancers worked long and hard to improve their performances. Competitions featuring disciplined team dancing took place at both sacred and secular rituals, including initiations, religious ceremonies, weddings, harvest festivals, beer parties, and preparations for war.[44]

Basotho dances such as the dynamic *mohobelo* style required extensive practice, physical prowess, and collective co-ordination.[45] Described by one source as a 'vigorous men's dance . . . [that] requires a great deal of energy and endurance to be done well', *mohobelo* was the most athletic of Basotho dances.[46] It was performed during rain ceremonies before industrialisation, but after the rise of migrancy to the mines, *mohobelo* changed into a secular recreation.

Dancing was a regular feature of Xhosa social life. The principal characteristics of Xhosa dance movements were the 'rapid undulation or shaking of the thorax so that the whole of the spine appears to be rippling'.[47] Men and women enjoyed the *tyuluba*, moving in ring formation, singing and clapping, with the main action being 'to stand on the toes and bend the knees slightly, then all in time quickly bring the weight down on the heels, one heel coming down slightly before the other, straightening the knees vigorously and causing the muscles of the body to quiver in a wonderful way. The greater the quivering the greater the dancer.'[48]

Dancing ability could affect a person's status and prestige in the community. Young male initiates performed *umtshilo* and other dances, while female initiates and young women took part in a set of dances known as *umdudo*; and the *ngqungqa* was for both boys and girls.[49] Senior men presiding over initiation rites ranked young Bomvana dancers according to skill, physical prowess, and stamina. Drawing from traditional dances such as various initiation dances and *tyuluba*, migrant Xhosa mineworkers performed *umteyo* and *xhensa* dances on the Rand. These competitive dance forms allowed miners to escape temporarily the persistent fear of death, injury, and disease that came from working long shifts in dangerous underground conditions and living in grossly overcrowded dormitory rooms. Team dances were also an arena for the display of masculine toughness, the expression of collective identities, and the material and spiritual identification with the rural livelihoods many longed to return to.[50]

The relationship between dance and warfare was especially close in the militarised Zulu kingdom that dominated northern Nguni territories in the nineteenth century. The new martial ideal of Zulu manhood defined by bravery, loyalty, and endurance was enacted in spectacular public dances during rituals and combat situations. A style called variously *umzansi*, *indlamu*, and *isiZulu* was a team dance whose main action was 'the muffled thud of bare feet'.[51] This stamping dance was 'distantly related to the regimental dances of the old tribal fighting days',[52] and probably among those performed during the first-fruits ceremony (*umkhosi*), an annual ritual spectacle that promoted and legitimated Zulu authority.[53] In twentieth-century competitive dance events in Durban and on the Rand, *indlamu* was 'permeated with the tensions between dancers from different regions . . . [because it] afforded an opportunity to assert ties of solidarity based on common regional and ethnic origin'.[54] In addition to facilitating identity formation, the co-ordinated, highly disciplined choreographies of *indlamu* and more recent styles like *isishameni* upheld and perpetuated the idea that 'dancers consider themselves as soldiers (*amasoja*), and a great deal of the ethos of a performance is couched in military forms'.[55]

The martial roots of Zulu dance were most obviously found in *ukugiya* (or *ukugida*), an individual style often referred to as a 'war dance'. This style emphasised kicking and leaping, and was accompanied by loud praising. Soldiers performed *ukugiya* immediately preceding and following military campaigns. In nineteenth-century preparations for war, *amabutho* approached the royal homestead singing regimental chants (*amahubo*), and then 'warriors harangued one another about their fighting prowess (xoxa'd impi)' once inside the cattle enclosure.[56] At the exhortation of the king, *amabutho* challenged one another, giyaing and praising until sunset.

There are some analogies to be drawn between Zulu dance and sport. The first shared characteristic was that regimental dancing executed tactical plans handed down by the *induna* (commander) in public displays of virile masculinity. These spectacles emerged from highly specialised training, co-ordination, and discipline – key properties some specialists have used to define 'sport'.[57] Body movements also linked dance and sport: 'dancing in preparation for a physical conflict has a scientific foundation as do "warm-up" exercises for athletes prior to a game'.[58]

Zulu martial dancing, while culturally specific, also shared some common features with warrior dancing and military drills found in other African societies. This similarity is most transparent in *ukugiya*'s functional purpose of 'affective readying' – that is, mobilising team spirit and emotionally gearing up the armed forces before a campaign, another key component of modern sport.[59] The manly grace, competition, and constant striving for improved performance that distinguished *ukugiya*, like some of the Sotho and Xhosa styles observed earlier in sacred and secular, ritual and non-ritual settings, illustrate the ways in which African '[d]ances could therefore be play, games, sport, and/or physical and moral education, depending on context, use, and user'.[60]

The prominence of competitive dancing, stick fighting, cattle raiding and racing, and hunting in pre-colonial African societies in southern Africa formed a vital part of a local vernacular athletic worldview. Indigenous sporting traditions were elaborate public spectacles of fitness and physical prowess, technical expertise, strategy, and tactics. Skilful performances were remembered through praise naming and rewarded with greater status and prestige. Accomplished male youths could assert their masculine power. Theatrical confrontations often delineated or strengthened territorial identities, stressing the utilitarian and social value of martial skills and the need to 'play by the rules' of vernacular gaming codes. In many ways, then, 'indigenous movement cultures provide[d] the athletic soil into which the seeds of British sports would be later planted'.[61]

CHAPTER 2

The Origins of Colonial Football

Soldiers, sailors, traders, and missionaries brought football to South Africa during Britain's commercial and imperial expansion in the second half of the nineteenth century.[1] On 23 August 1862 soldiers and employees of the colonial administration played what is perhaps the earliest documented football match in Africa in Cape Town. The contest was advertised in the *Cape Argus* newspaper on 21 August under the headline 'Foot-Ball', and the article read: 'We are happy to find this fine old English school-game has been introduced among us. On Saturday next sides consisting of fifteen officers of the army and a like number of gentlemen in the civil service will open the Ball with a game on the race-course at Green Point.' The civilians' squad included the 21-year-old John X. Merriman, later prime minister of the Cape (1908–10), who worked as a clerk for the colonial government.[2]

These early contests featured elements of both rugby and association football, which was not unusual because different sets of football rules – among these the Cambridge (1848), Sheffield (1857), and Uppingham School rules (1862) – existed at the time. According to one source, the Winchester School rules were used in the Cape in the 1860s, lending themselves to a game of 'accurate kicking and dashing play'.[3] Another Capetonian participant in these early contests described rugby-like teams of fifteen men and scrums using a round (rather than oval) ball and playing under rules which imposed severe restrictions on the use of hands. Most importantly, a 'goal was scored whenever the ball passed between the posts and over a line drawn between them . . . [and] the finesse of the game lay in dribbling'.[4]

Football matches of various kinds between South African whites were not restricted to cosmopolitan Cape Town. Informal, robust matches between 'City and Garrison' squads were staged in the Market Square in Pietermaritzburg, the capital of Natal colony. According to an observer of a rough contest that took place on 26 September 1866: 'We can hardly call it football . . . as almost every player used every part of his body more than his feet.'[5] In 1869, fifteen civil servants of the Port Elizabeth Colonial Board Football Club posed for a photographic portrait clad in long white trousers and jerseys; one of the men standing in the back row cradled a round ball in his hands.[6] Very little other information is known about this Eastern Cape club.

The success of the game in some places was dependent on the efforts of individuals. For example, in 1881 an unnamed Scottish ex-player for London's Queen's Park Rangers reorganised soccer in Port Elizabeth until his death put an end to this revival.[7] Overall, the earliest forms of the game in South Africa resembled both the chaotic, rowdy football of nineteenth-century English public schools and universities and the organised pre-industrial 'folk' game of artisans, apprentices, and rural workers.[8] This ambiguity is not surprising given that public school and university alumni gathered at the Freemason's Tavern in London to codify the laws of 'Association Football' on 26 October 1863.[9] After the codification of Rugby Union rules in 1871, the practitioners of association football became known as 'soccers' (an abbreviation of 'assoc'), while followers of the rugby code called themselves 'ruggers'.

The Anglo-Zulu War of 1879 and the subsequent war with the South African Republic (Transvaal) in 1880–81 brought a large influx of working-class British soldiers who popularised football further. In this period, whites in Natal founded the first stable, formal football organisations: the Pietermaritzburg County Football Club in 1879 and the Natal Football Association in 1882. Then, in 1892, a group of mostly English-speaking civilians and military officers formed the South African Football Association, which excluded blacks. Team names such as Middlesex Regiment, Royal Artillery, Loyal North Lancashire Regiment, Old Natalians, Civil Service Club, and Victoria Athletic reflected the military, educational, and colonial roots of the imperial game.[10]

A visit by the leading British amateur team, the Corinthians, invigorated the local football scene in 1897. In their first foreign tour, the Corinthians, who 'probably thought of their trips as part holiday and part football missionary work',[11] dominated all-white local, provincial, and national teams. Large crowds gathered to watch the English gentlemen amateurs in action at Cape Town, King William's Town, Queenstown, Grahamstown, East London, Port Elizabeth, Durban, Johannesburg, Bloemfontein, and Kimberley. The Corinthians overcame the challenges posed by an intense travelling schedule and the hard, barren, uneven South African pitches (with the exception of Cape Town and Durban). Playing 23 matches in two months, the English visitors won 21 matches and drew 2, and scored 113 goals while allowing just 15.[12] Subsequent visits by the Corinthians in 1903 and 1907, as well as a South African tour of Argentina and Brazil in 1906, suggest that soccer was quite popular among whites on the eve of the formation of the Union of South Africa in 1910.[13]

THE DECLINE OF SOCCER AND RISE OF RUGBY AMONG WHITES

Among whites, however, the popularity of soccer proved to be temporary, and rugby soon gained ascendancy. The strong influence of indigenous sporting traditions on black South Africans' acceptance of British football fostered a perception of soccer as plebeian and black and rugby as patrician and white. Rugby lent itself more readily to the construction of exclusionary social boundaries based on race, class, culture, and gender.[14] Internal dynamics such as these highlight the importance of understanding the process of sport diffusion to colonial South Africa as more than simply the result of successful British cultural imperialism.[15] As Morrell noted, 'For a gentry attempting to seal itself off from blacks, soccer became emblematic of threatening, socially integrative forces within society. As it forged its class identity, so it took to itself the rugby code as an additional, racially exclusive, identifying feature.'[16]

The cult of rugby in South Africa initially developed in the English-speaking public (boarding) schools, which sought to inculcate a sense of fair play, manliness, and Britishness among students.[17] The imperial games ethic was etched in the memorable words of Harrow headmaster the Revered J.E.C. Welldon: 'The pluck, the perseverance, the good temper, the self-control, the discipline, the co-operation, the *esprit de corps*, which merit success in cricket or football, are the very qualities which win the day in peace or war. [. . .] England has owed her sovereignty to her sports.'[18] In a speech to the Natal Rugby Union in 1893, the governor of Natal echoed Welldon: 'the taste for sport, for athletic sport and exercise, which distinguishes our race has been one of the main factors in the success which has attended the exertions – whether in improvement at home or in colonisation abroad – of the Anglo-Saxon race'.[19]

The impressive victories of the touring South African Springboks over England in 1906–07 and 1912 escalated the level of rugby's popularity among whites.[20] By the time Afrikaner students formed the Stellenbosch University rugby club in 1919, this sport was increasingly seen as the domain of white gentlemen, while 'soccer was stigmatized as the corrupt persuasion of the lower classes and blacks'.[21]

THE RISE OF SOCCER'S POPULARITY AMONG BLACKS

The competitive ethos and creative performance that characterised spectacular public displays of physical prowess in agrarian movement cultures – discussed in Chapter 1 – demonstrates the ways in which agrarian African societies were animated by what historian Stephen Hardy calls the *sportgeist* – or the spirit of sport.[22] Furthermore, as other historians have shown, the black (male) elite's enthusiastic adoption of cricket, rugby, and, to a lesser extent, football, in the second half of the nineteenth century signified a determined willingness on the part of these *kholwa* Africans to absorb British civilisation.[23] African sporting achievements seemed to project the idea of equality with whites, and *kholwa* men's participation in sport stemmed 'from a desire to emphasize their social advantages, class position and consciousness, as for the joy of the game itself'.[24]

The discovery of diamonds in Kimberley in 1867 and gold on the Witwatersrand in 1886 transformed South Africa from an agrarian society into an industrial capitalist state in the lifespan of a single generation and had tremendous repercussions for the history of sport. In the last quarter of the nineteenth century Kimberley became a hotbed of black sport.[25] Alongside the church, sport was the most important social activity in the mining town's growing black community.

Mission-educated Africans organised most of the first teams and competitions. The South African nationalist Sol Plaatje, for example, was the secretary of Eccentrics Cricket Club, one of two African sides in Kimberley in 1896.[26] The summation of all this sporting activity was the establishment in 1897 of the first black national sports body – the South African Coloured Rugby Football Board.[27] The following year, a Bloemfontein-based Orange Free State Bantu Football Club toured England. Virtually nothing is known about this group that earned the distinction of being 'the first SA team to play in Europe'.[28]

In this formative period for local sport a wide range of black wage-earners took up football.[29] Indian service workers 'who would have spoken English and closely observed the mores of English working-class men, and with the small community of Indian Christians', took up the sport. There were four Indian football clubs in Durban in 1886.[30] On the Rand, it appears that three Scottish émigrés, Messrs. MacSweeney, Smith, and Maclachlan, helped in organising the early Indian teams, with MacSweeney forming his side in 1875 – eleven years before the founding of Johannesburg.[31] These early clubs featured names that expressed proud group identity ('Prides of India'), or belied their British connections ('Blue Bells'). In 1896 the Indian clubs came together to form the Transvaal Indian Football Association.

The influx of nearly half a million British soldiers during the South African War (1899–1902) accelerated the spread of soccer in a dramatic fashion. 'Without doubt football's popularity throughout the entire Army was unsurpassed,' argued historian J.D. Campbell recently; 'the amount of time and energy spent by soldiers on football . . . was far more than one would normally expect for a mere "leisure pastime".'[32] African, Coloured and Indian men watched and, most likely, played the game with British soldiers in besieged towns such as Kimberley, Ladysmith, and Mafeking.[33]

Sol Plaatje recounted in his diary written during the siege in Mafeking how the Boers' observance of the Sabbath allowed the British to organise Sunday sport in the town square.[34] Soon after the cessation of hostilities, the South African Indian Football Association (SAIFA) was founded in Kimberley on 18 September 1903, becoming the first black national soccer association.[35] Sam China (1855–1931), the founding president of the SAIFA, had emigrated from India in 1863 and made a small fortune as a shopkeeper in Kimberley.[36] He donated a silver and gold trophy for an inter-provincial competition. The inaugural Sam China Cup competition in 1903 did not feature Natal Indians because the authorities denied them the required travel permits.[37] This competition saw Transvaal defeat Griqualand West.[38]

Between the Peace of Vereeniging in 1902 and the outbreak of the First World War in 1914, black football matches in major cities and smaller towns gradually increased in popularity but remained informal affairs. 'People playing football' (probably African *togt* [daily] labourers since the docks were the main employer of African labour in Durban) shattered street lights in the Durban harbour in 1899, thereby provoking angry protests from exasperated municipal employees tired of

National Library of South Africa

Group of British soldiers with ball marked 'Northampton Regt.', (c.1900).

replacing the electric bulbs.[39] In Johannesburg, slumyard residents formed their own 'Yard Clubs' and gambled by 'challeng[ing] one of the other yards to a game in the streets. Each team would collect a small amount of money (a pound or two) and hand this to the referee. The winning team would take the jackpot.'[40] Coloured footballers in Cape Town travelled (with municipal permission) to the city's periphery for football matches, only to clash with local white residents and dairy farmers. The latter protested the 'frequently riotous' games, noting how 'the behavior of these Coloured players is simply disgraceful, and our cattle chased about, as this is a milking area'.[41]

Although material poverty and a lack of facilities meant that blacks struggled to find suitable playing space in urban areas,[42] football nevertheless grew in popularity. With the onset of industrialisation and tighter white rule in South Africa in the late nineteenth century, rural cultural and athletic idioms were integrated into colonial leisure activities such as football and influenced new social formations in the towns.[43] The players in this transformation, both the literate *kholwa* elites and rural youth commoners who migrated to the Witwatersrand gold mines and the port cities of Durban and Cape Town, adopted British soccer to cope with the dislocations of urbanisation and build vital alternative networks.

The way in which indigenous athletic traditions stoked South Africans' in-candescent passion for football is similar to the spread of *beni* and *kalela* dance groups in eastern and central Africa during the colonial period.[44]As Terence Ranger has demonstrated, these voluntary associations of African workers borrowed from an older competitive leisure tradition while creating a mutual aid society through sociability and mimicry.[45] Inexpensive and relatively easy to play, soccer was transformed into a sphere of action where expressions of African modernity could be forged, tested, and negotiated. With the emergence of the Durban and District African Football Association in 1916, black football began its transformation into a social sphere for leisure, cultural expression, and the playing out of power relations during South Africa's segregation era.

—— CHAPTER 3 ——

'For the Love of the Game'

Durban Football, *c.*1910–30s

The Durban and District Native Football Association (DDNFA) – founded in 1916 – became the first major urban African football organisation in the country in a period when the South African game transformed itself from a local leisure practice for the relatively privileged classes into an urban pastime for the overwhelmingly male black working class. Indeed, football's 'remarkable ability to penetrate among the poorest, most exploited group in the society' led to the conclusion that by the 1930s '[f]or the African working-class soccer *was* sport'.[1]

The corresponding institutionalisation of African soccer took place during the enormous social transformations of the 1920s and 30s brought about by increasing urbanisation, industrial expansion, and intensifying racial segregation. The massive growth of cities, the most important social development between the wars, was evident in the rise of South Africa's official urban population from 1 478 000 in 1911 to 4 300 000 in 1946.[2] Africans were pushed out of rural labour reserves created by the Native Land Act of 1913 and from slowly mechanising white farms and into Johannesburg, Durban, and Cape Town.[3] Migrants were also pulled to town by a need for cash to pay taxes and a desire – especially among the youth – for adventure, new commodities, and greater freedom from patriarchal control.

In cosmopolitan Johannesburg, the Witwatersrand gold mines attracted Africans from all over the Union and indeed southern Africa. As a result, Johannesburg's African population sky-rocketed from 118 353 in 1921 to 387 175 in 1946.[4] In Durban, where the local economy was based on the harbour – a key outlet for Witwatersrand production – and a large and diversified industrial sector, the Indian and African (overwhelmingly Zulu) populations rose dramatically during the same period.[5] The port city's African population rose from 17 925 in 1918 to 108 866 in 1946, by which time it was roughly equal to the total Indian population of 113 440.[6] In Cape Town, where Coloureds made up the largest black group (44,7 per cent of the total population in 1946), the number of Africans (overwhelmingly Xhosa from the Eastern Cape) saw a sharp jump, from 1 581 in 1911 to 31 258 in 1946 (8,1 per cent).[7]

By the end of the Second World War there were more Africans than whites living in urban areas, many of them having moved there permanently. In response to African urbanisation, the Union government and local authorities tightened pass laws to restrict the movement of Africans to and within towns. Discriminatory labour legislation entrenched a two-tiered system that reserved higher-paid skilled and semi-skilled jobs for whites and low-paid, unskilled work for Africans.[8]

KHOLWA BEGINNINGS

The *kholwa* roots of African football in Natal were clearly evident: mission school students, workers, and people living on or near mission stations made up a significant portion of the membership of most clubs. African students and teachers saw football as an attractive aspect of Western culture, embracing and enjoying the game for their own reasons and on their own terms.

As they had been on the Kimberley diamondfields, the *kholwa* were critically important to the development of African football in Natal after the South African War. Representing about 2 per cent of the Zulu-speaking African population in the province, this class contained subtle internal divisions, most notably between wealthy landowners and mission-school graduates in the lower ranks of white-collar professions.[9] Most of African football's first organisers came from these modestly privileged backgrounds. They were people with access to leisure time and space, and in search of a sphere of social action in which their increasing marginalisation in the South African political economy could be addressed. At a time when an emerging nationalist movement represented by the Natal Native Congress (established in 1900) was coming to the fore, sport presented an opportunity to build African unity and, at the same time, to advance the individual ambitions and class interests of the *kholwa* elite. Football was in the process of transforming itself into an arena of play for power relations.

The sons of one of the most prominent *kholwa* families in Natal, William and Charles Dube, played an important role in the early history of the game in this region. Their brother, John Langalibalele Dube (1871–1946), was considered '*the* spokesman of the *kholwa* community'.[10] He founded the Ohlange Institute in 1900, modelled after Booker T. Washington's Tuskegee Institute, launched the first major African newspaper, *Ilanga Lase Natal*, in 1903, and went on to become the first president of the South African Native National Congress (later African National Congress, ANC) in 1912.

The Dube family's interest and understanding of the game's growing popularity among their *kholwa* audience is likely to have inspired *Ilanga*'s coverage of football competitions from the very first year of publication. Much like the contemporary Xhosa newspaper *Imvo Zabantsundu*, the Zulu/English newspaper became an important medium of information for the emerging African football community in Natal.[11] A typical example of early football reporting was an anonymous column in the fourth issue of *Ilanga* under the headline 'ETekwini Eze Bola' ('Football in Durban').[12] A brief play-by-play account written by a knowledgeable practitioner (or observer) documented an exciting match between rival African clubs founded in 1902: Vultures and Unity.

The American Board Mission (ABM) also played a powerful role in the initial organisation of football in Durban.[13] American Board clergymen in South Africa employed sport as an evangelising tool. The American missionaries endorsed the *mens sana in corpore sano* (healthy mind in healthy body) ideals of 'muscular Christianity', which were at the heart of the rational recreation movement popular in Victorian England and the United States.[14] Soccer also offered the American missionaries a safer alternative to more violent forms of the game; namely, the gridiron football of North American colleges and universities, and the dominant white sport in South Africa: rugby.[15] British-run mission schools for Africans in the Eastern Cape were the exception to this rule because they emphasised rugby over soccer. This historical peculiarity seems to explain rugby's continuing popularity among Xhosa-speaking Africans in that region to the present day.

An Irish ABM missionary, the Reverend Onslow Carleton, founded the famous Bush Bucks Football Club at Ifafa mission station near Durban in 1902.[16] Carleton was known by Africans as a 'fanatical footballer and a strong coach', a person who worked tirelessly to provide sporting opportunities for African youths.[17] He invited boys from Ifafa, Amahlongwa, and Mtwalumi missions on camping trips highlighted by serious football training. Among the original group of players was the father of Jackson Ngidi, a long-time player and coach of Bush Bucks in the mid-1940s to the late 1950s (see Chapter 7). Parents and relatives, usually the men, recruited generations of teenage players for the family club. Family loyalty to specific clubs was much easier (and more common) in the mission stations since the rest of Durban's young African male migrants left older members of their families in the countryside. Ngidi recalled how Carleton 'trained the boys and to encourage them in their efforts, he bought two trophies which were to be competed for'. With the exception of Ohlange Wild Zebras (formed in 1901), Bush Bucks's opponents came from other American Board missions around Durban. These clubs included Ocean Swallows of Umbumbulu and Victorians, established in the 1880s and probably Durban's oldest African teams, as well as Adams College Shooting Stars and Natal Cannons of Inanda, which competed against outside teams beginning in the 1890s.[18]

The best documented of the first mission-based football sides is the Shooting Stars Football Club of Adams College. Known as Amanzimtoti Training Institute before 1914, Adams was founded by the ABM in 1849 and became one of the best schools in southern and central Africa.[19] Borrowing from the model of the British public schools, sport was a mainstay of the academic curriculum and the student experience at Adams.[20] As was the case elsewhere in Africa, India, and the West Indies, and indeed throughout the colonial world, sport provided an important meeting ground for Western and indigenous cultures.[21] Football quickly established itself as the most popular sport at Adams. Young Africans' deep passion for football inspired missionaries and school officials to rely on the game to recruit students.[22]

In a broader social and economic context shaped by Africans' marginalisation and poverty, Adams occupied a privileged position in Durban's sporting landscape. Ownership of playing grounds, for example, meant that Shooting Stars did not have to depend on the largesse of Durban's white municipal authorities for access to sporting space. This unusual degree of independence from white control allowed students to train more assiduously, a key to competitive success. Between 1908 and 1913 the team reached the semifinals and finals in several local competitions.[23] Control of sporting space also enabled Adams to host entertaining weekend matches against clubs from Durban and surrounding areas. The availability of only one football field (and one tennis court) for about 200 potential student-athletes delineated the contours of Adams's range of autonomy.[24] Even so, Shooting Stars coped admirably well, at least until the creation of second and third teams in the early 1930s placed added pressure on existing facilities. Ultimately, football boosted the visibility, status, and influence of Adams, its students, and staff in the changing social life of the bustling port city.

BUILDING A CITY FOOTBALL ASSOCIATION

With at least seven African clubs active by around 1910, Durban was gradually developing into a major football centre. Joining the *kholwa* clubs were teams of workers from the higher ranks of blue-collar employment, usually formed along regional and occupational lines. A club called Wanderers was one of Durban's earliest workers' sides. Known today in the professional ranks as African Wanderers, the club was founded in 1906 by a Mr Scotts from Nyasaland (modern Malawi) and clerical employees of the colonial government including T.H.D. Ngcobo, A.J. Ndlovu, and Ntombela Kanys.[25] The name was probably borrowed from the English side Wolverhampton Wanderers, but it seemed intriguingly appropriate for a local club because Durban was a major destination for African travellers in search of wage-earning jobs.[26] In other words, the British name may have expressed an acute consciousness of their status and identity as African migrant workers in white-dominated South Africa.

Male migrants in Johannesburg and Cape Town, as well as Durban, established and maintained soccer clubs that enabled them to identify individually and collectively with their rural hometowns and districts. (For further insight on migrant culture and football in Johannesburg and Cape Town see elsewhere in this chapter as well as Chapters 4 and 5.) According to John Khambule, president of Wanderers from 1942–58, his club was initially made up of workers from Pietermaritzburg but then, after quickly earning a reputation as a formidable football side, Wanderers began accepting people from the northern Natal towns of Ladysmith and Newcastle.[27] A broader support base and increased membership caused internal divisions due to the greater competition for a fixed number of playing and administrative positions in the club. Wanderers was typical of a broader trend observed in African football over time – when club membership reached

(Durban) Wanderers Football Club (1945).

about twenty, a group of people would leave and form a new club.[28] Beginning in the 1930s, Wanderers suffered a series of splits – at least fifteen by the late 1950s[29] – that led to the formation of new teams based on regional identities and loyalties, such as Ladysmith Home Boys and Newcastle Home Lads.[30] In 1939 a major split in the club resulted in the formation of the Zulu Royals, nicknamed *Usutho* after the name of a famous royal Zulu regiment under Cetshwayo.[31]

By the First World War African soccer in Durban was too popular to remain a loosely organised affair. The flourishing football activities in the coastal city, powered by men who, in the absence of financial rewards, played 'for the love of the game', had generated an organic need for the structured formalisation of sporting relations and competitions.[32] Beginning in 1907, African players and white missionaries had been meeting at the ABM hall on Beatrice Street to discuss the formation of a formal football association.[33] Then, in 1916, a group of African officials (T. Ngcobo included), Onslow Carleton and Mr Berry of the ABM, as well as Douglas Evans, superintendent of the municipal Depot (Somtseu) Road Men's Hostel, founded the Durban and District Native Football Association (DDNFA).[34]

The rise of a football organisation can be interpreted as part of Africans' broader struggle for leisure space in Durban. The white authorities' growing encroachment on the lives of Africans in the city threatened the limited time and space for football that Africans had carved out for themselves.[35] In the years leading up to 1916, the municipality had developed the 'Durban System' to segregate and control the urban

African population. It had legislated residential segregation (Native Location Act of 1904) and established a municipal beer monopoly (Native Beer Act of 1908) to finance Native Administration.[36] The Durban town council also enacted stricter controls on African labour and mobility, which included a night curfew. The DDNFA's founding coincided with the Durban town council's creation of South Africa's first municipal Native Affairs Department (NAD),[37] although I have found no evidence of a clear connection between the establishment of the two. The local government did not control the football association, but it viewed African football's formalisation favourably, seeing it perhaps as an opportunity to impose order on unruly soccer crowds. Gambling and drunkenness associated with an autonomous urban popular culture elicited special fears among the whites. Informal 'football was one field in which people could gamble their money', said Ngidi, and like Johannesburg's 'Yard Clubs', Durban 'clubs would challenge each other and both sides would lay a bet of £5 saying that it would win. The result was many faction fights between the clubs.'[38] A white man employed by the newly established NAD took the helm of African football in Durban: his name was Douglas Evans.

Evans oversaw the initial 'ordered growth and development' of city football when the game was 'run by a small coterie of individuals'.[39] He was president of the DDNFA from 1916–23. Evans combined an avid passion for the game – he had played in England and South Africa – with his NAD duties for what he believed was the benefit of African football. Opportunistically, the local NAD endorsed Evans's initiatives. He perceived football to be a fun, healthy, social form of leisure that had the added benefit of functioning as an escapist ritual of social control for low-paid, politically voiceless black workers. In his words, 'football did one good thing, it kept the boys who stayed in the hostel off the roads and away from the shebeens [speakeasies]. Everyday after work they would talk about the past matches and the forthcoming matches, and at the weekends they would go and spend the whole day in the playing fields.'[40] He trained 'very good referees, men we could rely upon', and he officiated matches, coached, and occasionally even played on the association's representative team. Evans was pleased that the DDNFA's committee structure followed the British parliamentary model and that Africans had adopted the rules of the International Board – the official guardian of football's laws. 'There were no differences in the way African soccer was run and the way European football is run,' according to Evans. 'From the very word go we followed European rules, the Africans did not introduce anything. We took all the English rules and introduced them into our constitution as they were.'[41] While African organisers in Durban seemed willing to co-operate with Evans, others were vehemently opposed to him.

Racial nationalism created divisions within African football in Natal. For example, African sportsmen in Pietermaritzburg, a hotbed of political radicalism at the time, refused to join the new Natal Native Football Association (which Evans had proposed) because Durban had a white president.[42] Officials representing

Durban, Pietermaritzburg, Ladysmith, Dundee, and Newcastle held several meetings in 1919 to negotiate a solution. Durban adamantly opposed Pietermaritzburg's request for Evans's dismissal, arguing that 'we had a European President who had the interest of the Native at heart'.[43] No compromise was reached. In 1920, Durban, Ladysmith, and Dundee went ahead without the dissidents and founded the Natal association – the first regional African soccer organisation. The first officials were Evans, B.M. Ngcobo (president), S.D. Mashaba, A.E. Smith, A.M. Molepe, and T.A. Nene.[44]

The racial sentiments expressed by men like E.O. Msimang in Pietermaritzburg reflected a wider African resentment of white stewardship in the 1920s.[45] This enduring proto-nationalist opposition eventually persuaded Evans to resign from his leadership posts in both the Durban and Natal bodies in 1923.[46] Upon receiving his letter of resignation, shocked Durban officials presented Evans with an 'Illuminated Address', which expressed 'profound regret' for the decision and praised his 'strenuous work' for 'Native football'. The African executive honoured Evans for his 'untiring and self-sacrificing efforts to improve the status of Native football in Durban and District [and] the efficient manner in which [he] piloted the Association from its infancy to its present stage through all sorts of difficulties'.[47] Satisfied that Evans's departure had resulted in full black control, Pietermaritzburg joined Natal in 1925.[48] It is interesting to note that, according to the minutes of the meetings of the Durban association, Evans continued his involvement with African football following his resignation. He participated in several planning committees and commissions of inquiry after 1923, acting in his capacity as an 'Elder of the Association' and 'Honorary Life President'. Evans also began to lobby the Durban town council in an attempt to secure municipal funding for the construction of an enclosed Native Recreation Ground. The examples of co-operation and confrontation in Africans' relationship with Evans show how racial and interracial nationalism, in football as in politics, appealed to broad segments of the black population and co-existed in uneasy tension.[49]

In sporting terms, the formation of the Natal association initiated regular inter-town competitions that popularised the game in the province. The maturation of important clubs outside of Durban, most notably the Ladysmith Rainbows Football Club, which began to play in 1902, ensured novel and exciting entertainment for the fans. Matches between town teams representing Durban, Ladysmith, Newcastle, and (after 1925) Pietermaritzburg spawned rivalries. Events on the pitch crystallised emerging urban identities and territorial loyalties, as players and spectators publicly expressed belonging and allegiance to their respective towns. Overall, the launching of a provincial association and inter-town competitions allowed African football in Natal to expand its audience, popularity, and operations, even though Durban's organisational power and sporting success tended to overshadow the smaller towns. There was a vertiginous increase in the number of African football clubs in Durban: from 7 in 1917 to 26 with more than 1 000 players in 1931, and then 47 with 1 500 registered players in 1935.[50]

FROM GROSS NEGLECT TO BENEVOLENT PATERNALISM

The provision, access, and control of sporting space became a crucial site of struggle between Africans and the local political authorities. Between 1910 and 1930, the Durban town council, unwilling (or reluctant) to accept massive black urbanisation, refused to provide recreational facilities for Africans. This pattern of gross neglect – a national trend – resulted in only three football fields being available for African use until the mid-1930s.

Despite the shortage of grounds, the Durban association ran an official playing season from April to October. With demand for football space always outpacing supply, the season frequently extended play into November. Without enclosed fields admission charges were virtually impossible. 'People never paid to watch our games,' remembered Moses Molelekoa, who played in the 1930s and 40s; crowds were large 'because it's free! Anybody can come in and just line up [on the sidelines].'[51] The exceptions to this rule were marquee matches, when temporary barriers and gate attendants permitted the collection of admission fees. A typical football season in the first years of the Durban association featured two rounds of round-robin league play based on the point system.[52] The winners of the first and second rounds of competition received trophies, such as the Bush Bucks Challenge Cup (originally donated by the missionary Onslow Carleton). The two sides then met in a climactic season-ending match with the city championship at stake. These contests were played before crowds of at least 5 000 spectators on a bumpy dirt pitch that made qualitative football very challenging, but no less exciting. On special occasions, African sides were invited to play in front of white audiences. For example, Wanderers and Railway Tigers, two leading black working-class teams, were selected to play a match at Kingsmead – a stadium normally reserved for whites – during the Durban leg of the South African visit by the British heir apparent, Edward, Prince of Wales, in 1925.[53]

Denied access to adequate facilities, Africans resorted to organising matches in informal spaces. Using voluntary labour and extremely scarce material resources, the DDNFA cleared and marked uneven, abrasive, gravel playing areas like the one near the disused Alice Street tramway sheds known as *Ematramini*.[54] These leisure spaces were more difficult for the authorities to patrol, so they offered temporary escape from police harassment, pass laws, liquor restrictions, and curfews. Compared to tightly regulated leisure spaces like the municipal beer halls, *Ematramini* was a relatively free zone where dock workers, washermen, rickshaw-pullers, domestic workers, traders, and others carved out an autonomous leisure experience.[55] But African football's grip on urban space was always tenuous. As an official of the Native Recruiting Corporation – the labour recruiting organisation of the Chamber of Mines in South Africa – pointed out in an address to the DDNFA in 1930: 'The Native footballers have been booted out by the Durban Corporation from one football ground to another – from Western Vlei to Lords Grounds, and from there to Eastern Vlei, and each time this happened the Europeans or Indians followed to occupy the grounds.'[56]

Operating under extraordinary structural constraints and in an increasingly segregationist political economy, the organisers of African football worked with Douglas Evans to defend DDNFA's feeble hold on recreational space in the heart of the city.[57] Footballers had learnt to exploit white support to their advantage. 'Thus [Durban's African] workers, in shaping their leisure time, were never simply the victims of the "system"; some at least also understood how to work the system to defend their interests.'[58] Evans helped the association to cope creatively with the hard-line segregationist stance of the manager of the local Native Affairs Department, C.F. Layman, and his allies on the Durban town council.[59] Endorsing the opinion of the Stallard Commission's report of 1922, which stated that Africans should only be allowed into 'white' towns to work, these white officials opposed the provision of permanent recreational facilities for people considered 'temporary sojourners' in the city.[60]

Ematramini and other uncontrolled places of African entertainment were still in use when a municipal strategy to defuse rising black militancy led to tighter regulation of leisure space. In mid-1929, militant dockworkers, the ICU *yase* Natal and the Women's Auxiliary, and *amalaita* street gangs banded together in a widely supported boycott of municipal beerhalls – the largest source of revenue for Native Administration and the key to the 'Durban system'.[61] This high-point of popular African resistance in 1929–30 culminated in a ruthless campaign of police and para-military repression that turned Durban into a combat zone. According to official sources, two white members of the police forces and four black workers were killed.[62] As a result of the recommendations of the De Waal Commission (1929–30) that investigated the causes of the riots, the town council violently clamped down on militants; it curbed the influx of Africans, especially women, tightened the pass system, and created a purely consultative Native Advisory Board.[63] The municipality also made a partial concession to permanent black urbanisation. It launched a programme of social amelioration for Africans that funded housing construction and sport and leisure activities. Over the next decade or so, the Durban town council established several segregated African Locations, including Lamontville (1934) and Chesterville (1943), and the new migrant workers' hostels at Dalton Road (1934), Somtseu Road (1938), and Jacobs (1939).[64] Some of these new residential ghettos and migrant workers' compounds included a playing field or plans to add one in the foreseeable future.

The provision of leisure was part of the town council's 'extensive program to depoliticise African popular cultural expression'.[65] Towards this end, the municipality appointed a Native Welfare Officer in 1930 to run sport programmes. J. Rawlins, the first Native Welfare Officer (1930–34), stated the town council's social control objectives in unambiguous terms: 'Under the guidance of officials of the Municipality, and the provision of suitable ground accommodation, it would be possible to set up sporting attractions which would be a powerful factor in directing native activities to a more congenial atmosphere.'[66] Rawlins explained what he meant by congenial: 'the native community of Durban could be molded into a law abiding and contented section of the community of the Borough'.[67] He went on to say that 'contented workmen would mean more efficient labour', so that sport programmes for Africans would provide 'better and more healthy distribution of energy . . . resulting in a diminution of vice, the elimination of discontent, and a healthier native community both from a physical standpoint and a better mental outlook.'[68]

The following year the town council moved to extend its supervision of black sport.[69] It established the Bantu Recreational Grounds Association to manage African playing facilities in the city.[70] According to its constitution this body was comprised of four whites – the chairman of the Native Affairs Committee, the Native Welfare Officer and two others 'interested in African sports' – and African representatives from the Native Advisory Boards, sports associations, and clubs. One of the main duties of the Grounds Association was the collection of a 15 per cent share of any gate receipts. This money went into the Native Revenue Account (separate from the general municipal fund) – the main source of funding for African sport. This way, white taxpayers and officials did not have to pay for African amenities.[71]

As the most popular sport, football generated the lion's share of the revenue so the town council was keen on making football a centre-piece of social reform. Municipal funds ranging between £1 000 and £1 500 were budgeted annually for African sport and recreation.[72] This level of funding, as others have noted, 'was significant more for its minimal size than anything else'.[73] Minute as they were, such expenditures posed an additional problem: they threatened the ability of the DDNFA to maintain its independence from government control. The association's concerns about white encroachment intensified after the Native Welfare Officer, whose salary consumed a large portion of funds earmarked for black sport, intervened in an authoritarian manner in local football affairs. In an attempt to prevent their partial autonomy from being further circumscribed, representatives of the DDNFA met with the town council's Native Affairs Committee and Native Affairs Department in November 1930. The African delegation selected Albert John Luthuli, later ANC president (1952–67) and Nobel Peace Prize recipient, as its spokesperson for this highly sensitive encounter with white authorities.[74]

This meeting suggests the ways in which Luthuli's diplomatic aplomb, management skills, and firm leadership assisted the development of local football.[75] A leading *kholwa*, Luthuli joined the DDNFA executive as vice-president in 1929, after serving for many years as secretary of the Adams College Shooting Stars Football Club, one of contemporary Durban's highly successful sides. The most important issue discussed that morning was whether the Native Welfare Officer, J. Rawlins, had the authority to require that the association obtain his permission to charge admission at the gate. Luthuli and his colleagues politely but resolutely criticised Rawlins's position. During the discussion, it became known that the association charged only for marquee matches and that the average gate-takings were between £9 and £10. These funds were used for maintenance of the grounds and for meeting travelling expenses of DDNFA teams playing in inter-town contests in Ladysmith and Pietermaritzburg.[76]

The African spokesmen defended their right to charge admission by pointing out how the municipality had funded, in years past, the erection of a barbed-wire fence around most of the main ground in central Durban. 'The Council had expressed the view that the Natives should do something to assist themselves and it was by means of these admission charges,' said DDNFA president T.H.D. Ngcobo, 'that [Africans] were able to support and maintain the grounds without having to approach the Council for assistance on every occasion.'[77] By highlighting the municipality's earlier endorsement of the association's self-help approach, the DDNFA delegation effectively worked the system to its advantage and, in doing so, moderated the pernicious effects of white interference. H.E. Arbuckle, chairman of the Native Affairs Committee, eager to prevent an escalation of tension in Durban's volatile political climate, ordered that any future conflicts over sport between Africans and whites needed to be solved not by the Native Welfare Officer's unilateral decisions but through consultation.[78]

White intrusion into African leisure stimulated African political consciousness. Perhaps the most powerful example of this development lay in the name change of the Durban association. In 1932 the term 'Native' was dropped as the organisation adopted the new name of Durban and District *African* Football Association.[79] This expression of rising African nationalist consciousness could be traced back at least to 1923, when the South African Native National Congress adopted the title of African National Congress.[80] Radical and progressive Africans increasingly used the term 'African' in the 1920s and 30s.[81] The direct involvement of Luthuli, trade unionists, ANC members, and others in sanctioning the DDAFA name change suggests how football was part and parcel of a process in which 'race-conscious populism provided the African elite with a viable ideological approach to the problem of class division in the black community'.[82] As Chapter 4 shows, similar title changes occurred simultaneously around the country.[83]

Growing pressure from ordinary workers and African officials compelled the city to address the leisure needs of Africans for the first time.[84] Walking a tightrope between autonomy and accommodation, the DDAFA leadership used its working relationship with sympathetic whites to gain municipal funding for a fully enclosed sports ground.[85] The extensive renovation and upgrading of the Native Recreation Ground at the Somtseu Road Location, completed in 1936–37, produced two grass football fields, a large dressing room for the teams, and public lavatories for spectators. The new Somtseu Ground improved the quality of soccer and enabled the association to attract larger crowds, which strengthened the financial prospects of the African game. Indeed, the DDAFA raised enough revenue to contribute funds to fledgling sports such as tennis, cricket, boxing, and cycling.[86] The black popular press observed how in Durban 'soccer is the most powerful [sport] . . . . Football is a magnet . . . The [people are] so interested in this game that the other sister games are simply dwarfed.'[87] The *Bantu World* newspaper put it in unequivocal terms: 'Bantu Sportsmen in Natal Know Only One Game – Soccer.'[88]

The profound popular passions associated with urban African sport did not escape the attention of the Union government. Through its central NAD office, Pretoria proposed to DDAFA in 1928 that it help create a South African Non-European Athletic Union.[89] The proposal emerged in response to an invitation to participate in the first Pan-African Games in Alexandra, Egypt, in 1929, extended to the DDAFA by the Egyptian Olympic Committee.[90] The Non-European Athletic Union was probably designed to facilitate state oversight of black sport. The plan envisioned a pyramidal institutional structure with local associations representing individual sports at the bottom, provincial Central Boards at the intermediate level, and a national executive at the apex.[91] The South African government may have been embarrassed by the successful and popular black-run sporting organisations in cities and towns. After all, these activities flew in the face of the government's Stallardist policy towards African urbanisation encapsulated in the Native Urban Areas Act of 1923. The authorities may also have perceived football clubs and competitions as subversive because they challenged the local notion that blacks lacked the ability to manage their lives without white supervision. In any case, plans for the South African Non-European Athletic Union fell through due to the cancellation of the Pan-African Games and the onset of the Great Depression. Pretoria retreated from black sport for two decades.

CLASS DYNAMICS AND TRANSFORMATIONS IN MASCULINITY

During the steady expansion of African football in Durban in the 1920s and 30s, the urban proletariat joined the *kholwa* elite as the game's main social constituency. About one-third of employed Africans in Durban in the mid-1930s were young male domestics between ten and twenty years of age; about half were older *togt* labourers, washermen, rickshaw-pullers, and lumpen elements; one-tenth were factory workers; and one-tenth were traders.[92] The majority of African footballers and fans were young single men, migrant workers performing menial jobs for an average monthly pay of £2.8s. Most workers had little or no formal education (though some reached a level of self-instruction), spoke Zulu rather than English or Afrikaans, and often belonged to independent African churches and/or practised indigenous religions. The depth of male working-class passion for football is brought out by the fact that many Africans earning meagre wages and working long hours were willing to make time-consuming and expensive journeys across greater Durban to play and watch football on weekends.

Older educated African men turned to football administration for self-advancement and for what some perceived as the charitable upliftment of their community. The enlightened self-interest of the leadership could be sensitive to the practical concerns of working-class players and fans. For example, in 1923–24 a major reorganisation divided Durban's clubs into three geographical sections: six in the North Coast, nine in the South Coast, and eight in Durban Central.[93] The realignment offered tangible benefits to the *kholwa* elite, who saw the number of previously scarce and highly prestigious executive positions triple. But players and clubs also supported the restructuring, hoping to cut transport costs and travel times. Sub-sections became responsible for running their own sectional leagues. Section winners qualified for a final round-robin tournament beginning in August or September with the city championship at stake. A series of short, but extremely popular, knock-out competitions (single elimination tournaments modelled after the English Football Association Cup) were also added to the expanding African sport calendar.[94]

While the support base for football widened considerably during the segregation era, management of the association remained in the hands of a *kholwa* clique. These men were variously known as '*amarespectables*, "Black Englishmen", *izemtiti* (those who had gained exemption [from pass laws]), *izifundiswa* (the educated in general) and even *amabhuka* (traitors)'.[95] Magubane's sociological profile of DDAFA officials during the 1924–60 period highlighted their privileged background.[96] Of the 103 men included in Magubane's survey, two-thirds were professionals and clerks; the majority were Christian; 80 per cent had at least ten years of formal education; and most enjoyed an average tenure of ten years in office.[97]

Formal Western education was a key weapon in the Durban leadership's ability to obtain white-collar employment and maintain power and control in football management. Only men in middle-class occupations could afford to take on unpaid administrative positions which required, among other things, regular attendance at weeknight meetings.[98] These exacting demands discouraged working-class men from active involvement in managing the association's affairs. After all, young men in manual labour occupations or domestic service could ill afford to miss work after attending candle-lit meetings that could (and did) open at 8 p.m. and close at 6 a.m. the following day.[99]

Knowledge and use of English complicated rank-and-file attempts to join the executive committee. The indigenous elite had a long-standing tradition of using English rather than African languages in public life. This practice was partly an endorsement of Pan-Africanist arguments that 'if Zulu were to be used other nationalities would suffer'.[100] However, since Zulu was the first language of nearly every African in Durban, English was more than just a linguistic glue. For urban powerbrokers it was a powerful marker of modernity, 'respectability', and differentiation from lower-class men with minimal or no formal Western education. The association went to the extent of passing a constitutional amendment in 1932 making English the official language of the association; delegates wishing to address meetings in Zulu were required to receive the chairman's permission.[101] In Durban, as in the rest of South Africa, African languages and English were commonly used in club and association meetings, but the minutes were almost always recorded in English.[102]

Emboldened by a virtual monopoly of skills and income necessary to carry out the duties and responsibilities of football administration, incumbent committee members held a tenacious grip on power. This trend was captured in the extraordinarily long management career of NAD clerk T.H.D. 'Telephone' Ngcobo. He served as founding vice-president from 1916–23, then as president from 1924–31, and again in 1935 and 1939. The executive committee for the 1927 season featured many white-collar members of the leadership of the 1920s.[103] William Luvuno's participation calls attention to the elite character of this group. A former mine clerk, Luvuno was a businessman who owned nine acres of land, served as spokesman of the interracial Joint Council in Durban, and was the secretary of the African Co-operative Trading Society.[104] The presence of A.R. Ntuli, a member of the Industrial and Commercial Workers' Union (ICU) and the Native Advisory Board, provides further evidence to show that the African elite actively participated in football organisations as part of a general involvement with a wide range of voluntary associations.[105]

A focal aspect of everyday life, football strengthened the connections between *kholwa* and working poor. In fact, the game's capacity to bring together various strata of mission-educated elites and migrant- and non-migrant African workers had a special appeal for Albert Luthuli. He explained in his autobiography how 'what has attracted me as much as the game has been the opportunity to meet all sorts of people, from the loftiest to the most disreputable'.[106] Cross-class interaction could be challenging. Gideon Sivetye, a member of Shooting Stars and a teacher at Adams College in the period under consideration, recounted the difficulties of bringing elite student-athletes into regular contact with proletarian players and fans. 'As teachers we were criticized for going to Durban to play with the wild boys who were working in Durban,' Sivetye said. 'We had to answer questions of ministers, etc. I am glad to say our principals joined us; they thought it was a way of attracting them, to co-operate with us . . . . It did a lot of good, this playing with those people in town. We got to know each other.'[107]

Local conditions tended to foster solidarity in sport. One-third of association officials came from the interstitial class of wage earners in between the manual labourers and the *kholwa*. Pass raids, price increases, and declining real wages encouraged these small-scale traders, artisans, policemen, and shopkeepers to identify closely with poorer, less-educated Africans who comprised the majority of players and fans.[108] Of course, the African bourgeoisie shared not only the affront of racial discrimination, but also lived perilously close to desperate poverty.[109] Finally, the city's spatial dynamics also shaped social relations because 'dock workers in Durban's harbour area, the Point, lived within walking distance of the city-centre where dance halls, churches, and soccer fields provided a fertile ground for the fusion of élite culture and working-class dance and music'.[110]

The ICU in Natal seems to have understood better than any other contemporary African political organisation the value of sport to the creation of a politically conscious popular culture. Certainly, it viewed sport more constructively than the Communist Party of South Africa (CPSA). Eddie Roux, a leading organiser of the white-dominated CPSA in the late 1920s to early 30s, remarked how 'sports and games absorb a lot of the thinking of the people ... [making] it very difficult organizing them for serious effort to oppose their oppressors ... Sunday sports attract so many people that we cannot get a hearing on Sunday'.[111] But as a black trade union with a cross-class membership, the ICU used boxing and soccer as conduits for cultural communication between the leadership and the rank and file. *The Workers' Herald*, the official organ of the ICU, featured articles on sports (mostly on boxing). At times it expressed political satire through the ecumenical language of football. An amusing front-page cartoon on 15 November 1926 portrayed ICU founder and president Clements Kadalie, clad in an ICU playing kit, blasting a shot into the net past a helpless, obese, balding, white goalkeeper! Like ICU ballroom dances, *isicathamiya* choirs, and brass bands, football was an idiom of popular culture that strengthened black political cohesion.[112]

The connections between the ICU and football may be responsible for the first documented example of trade unionism in black South African sport. Angered by a spate of violent attacks against them, Durban referees in the early 1930s formed the Referees' Association.[113] This sporting trade union was strong enough to negotiate a collective bargaining agreement with the association. It secured the right to hold the DDAFA liable for any damages and injuries suffered by referees for lack of security at the grounds. The Referees' Association also earned the privilege of receiving match allowances for its members. This remuneration ranged from 2s.6d. for first-class match officials down to 6d. for unqualified ones. The money was used for routine expenses, such as travel and washing uniforms. A former referee in Durban in the 1930s, Edward Jali, spoke about the need to reward individuals doing a potentially dangerous job: 'referees are people who should be paid because for them it is a great risk to referee some of the matches .... There are times when you just wonder how you will get out.'[114] Aggressive, occasionally violent, challenges to the referee's authority on the field of play can be understood within broader transformations in African gender and generational dynamics.

Football functioned as a vehicle for asserting changing urban black masculine identities. In a modern industrial workplace that reserved manual labour for Africans, sport played a vital role as an arena for black men's self-expression and affirmation. In Durban the influence of denigrating labour conditions was especially pronounced given that more than 16 000 of the city's African male migrants, one-third of the total African population, worked as domestic servants for whites in the late 1920s.[115]

Like *amalaita* youth gangs and traditional *ingoma* groups, football teams and competitions created a social space that enabled a martial masculinity undermined by colonial capitalism to be reconstructed and articulated in new forms.[116] The rise of a dominant working-class athletic masculinity reflected continuities, as well as changes, with the pre-colonial past. 'African men newly in the city,' argued Robert Morrell, 'fought to maintain their masculine identity and utilised forms of organisation familiar to them to do so. Zulu men experiencing the harsh new urban conditions of Durban, for example, banded together and reaffirmed their rural roots and "established ethics and codes of masculine conduct".'[117] In Durban the ties between town and countryside were particularly strong and evident because many African migrants retained family and cultural links to the rural hinterland.

Indigenous sporting traditions that valued physical force, tenacity, skill, bravery, and territorial identities dictated soccer sensibilities and styles. Images from the natural world found in the names of urban football clubs suggest the enduring influence of rural culture on emerging forms of African masculinity. Established teams like Bush Bucks, Shooting Stars, Wild Zebras, Cannons, Ocean Swallows, Vultures, Wanderers, and Victorians were joined by more recent sides such as Wild Savages, Come Agains, Rebellions, Willows, Assegais, Lions, Jumpers, Springboks, Rainbows, Flying Wings, Candidates, Antelopes, Fight for Evers, and Natal Government Railway Tigers.[118] The abundance of animal metaphors evoking 'viciousness, fury, and savagery' can be linked to the Zulu tradition of *izibongo* (praise poetry) – a resilient form of oral literature emphasising natural imagery, war, and masculine virility.[119] Footballers self-consciously looked down upon upper-class sports like tennis, describing them as 'effeminate'.[120] The participation of women in tennis and the 'tenderness and beauty' reflected in the names of tennis clubs such as the Daffodils and Winter Roses further revealed the gendered labels associated with certain sports.[121] For young men and adolescent boys, football's competitive rituals provided a space for the public display of manly grace. Like stick-fights in the countryside, soccer matches were the domain of vigorous (but immature) youth, but administration of law and discipline was seen as the customary domain of senior men.[122] Football and pre-colonial physical competitions shared the capacity to act out both athletic and patriarchal masculinities.

The endurance of age-defined norms and expectations indicate how generational divisions influenced male identities and the exercise of power and authority in modern sport. To begin with, DDAFA officials were referred to as 'elders'. In ways reminiscent of homestead heads, football's patriarchs oversaw the everyday business of the DDAFA 'family', organised leisure festivals, settled disputes, and assigned (playing) fields. An intensely legalistic approach characterised the executive's handling of match protests and disciplinary cases (most of which dealt with cases of alleged player ineligibility and accusations of biased refereeing).[123] This obsession with 'procedural virtuosity', some have posited, reflected African officials' concern with asserting a modern urbane identity, as well as the resilience of rural African jurisprudence founded on seniority, negotiation, and compromise.[124]

Referees represented another form of patriarchal authority with rural roots since homestead heads were known to referee stick-fights.[125] In the modern city, however, poorly trained soccer referees struggled to earn the respect of the competitors. Because clubs provided the referees themselves, a practice that carried on at least until the late 1940s, charges of favouritism were common, and sometimes referees were assaulted on the field of play.[126] The DDAFA sought to curb the violence by imposing stiff fines of up to £1 for such improper conduct – almost half of the average monthly wage for Africans in Durban.[127] Despite the elders' efforts to enforce discipline and obedience, crowd hooliganism persisted, though at a relatively low level in the 1920s. The minutes of the association indicate that fights took place on the fields and that referees and players submitted formal protests after being attacked by opponents and fans during and immediately following matches.[128] These incidents suggest the limited power of older men in exercising authority over younger, independent men eager to assert their manhood in spectacular public displays. The changes in indigenous masculinities observed in urban football illustrate quite clearly the creative force of African men in negotiating identities and adapting, rather than capitulating, to economic hardship and racial oppression.

THE DDAFA SUFFERS A SETBACK

The DDAFA's balance sheets demonstrate the transformation of football from an elite pastime to a popular urban practice. Between 1924 and 1931 the association's annual net income increased nearly fivefold, from £52 to £252.[129] This financial turnover was a tremendous achievement for the African association, especially given the lack of enclosed grounds, which made it extraordinarily difficult to get spectators to pay admission charges. Moreover, the growth in revenue suggests that, despite restrictive labour and pass laws and very low wages, some Africans in Durban were accumulating small amounts of disposable income which they chose to spend on football matches.[130] The extent of the DDAFA's success was clarified further when compared to the income of £395 2s.3d. reported by the white Natal Football Association at the end of the 1931 season.[131]

Just when the DDAFA seemed to be on sound footing it suffered a temporary setback. Between May and August 1932, the president, treasurer, secretary, and vice-secretary were all charged with financial mismanagement and suspended. Affiliation fees and income from fines and gate-takings had disappeared in the hands of unscrupulous treasurers before, but never had so many members of the executive been charged.[132] A commission of inquiry was appointed 'to report on the various complaints, laid by certain clubs, against your association'.[133] The commission held twelve meetings between 17 December 1932 and 22 February 1933. Citing copious and persuasive evidence, its final report blasted the accused officials for exercising power arbitrarily, prejudiced decision-making, financial improprieties, disregarding correspondence, keeping unintelligible and partial minutes, and failing to train and protect referees. The commission recommended, among other things, that a fin-ancial audit be undertaken on a regular basis to ensure greater accountability and transparency. It also called for a full-time paid secretary to improve the day-to-day running of the association – a change enacted the following season. But the crisis was not over. Conflicts between factions and individuals jostling for power and influence led to disaffected officials breaking away in 1933 to form the Durban Bantu Football Association. The secessionist organisation collapsed within a year because the Grounds Association, supported by the local authorities, denied it municipal playing grounds in order to keep African soccer centralised under a single body. The ten breakaway clubs returned reluctantly to the DDAFA which, by 1935, had expanded to forty-five clubs and boasted a membership of 1 500 players.[134]

Gradually, football became bound up with black popular culture and political consciousness; black players, fans, and officials began to see with greater clarity the inextricable links between sport and politics.[135] Having built itself up into a powerful organisation in less than two decades, the DDAFA initiated contacts in late 1930 with the Transvaal African Football Association, a new group founded by clerks and mine managers on the Witwatersrand gold mines, to discuss the possibility of establishing a national football organisation.[136]

CHAPTER 4

'A Morale and Production Booster'

Football on the Witwatersrand

Football in the Johannesburg/Witwatersrand area only became formally organised after the First World War. Prior to this, however, much activity took place on an informal basis. Richard Msimang, one of the founders of the South African Native National Congress (later ANC), 'told of the period between 1907 to 1918 when, thanks to keen interest of the Military stationed on the Rand, the game received a strong impetus and made great strides'.[1] According to his nephew Dan Twala, a leading organiser of black football, Msimang 'spoke enthusiastically of the Old Natalians, the Crocodiles, the Olympics, and the Ocean Swallows – teams that had to cycle from one end of the reef to the other for a fixture to be played on roughly shuffled grounds, where one could not follow the game for dust'.[2]

In 1917 mine clubs established the first African soccer body in the Johannesburg area – the Witwatersrand and District Native Football Association (WDNFA).[3] The WDNFA formalised football competitions with the approval of white mine compound managers, who hoped to curb militancy, increase discipline and production, and improve health.[4] In the rest of the metropolis football was still loosely organised: children, teenagers, and young men played informally – in the streets, on top of mine dumps, and on open wasteland where fiercely competitive, scrappy matches took place. Teams and their vociferous supporters often gambled for money, a practice that occasionally led to violence and police intervention.[5]

LEAGUES AND COMPETITIONS ON THE GOLD MINES

Workers' teams, rather than company teams, were the heart and soul of soccer on the mines. Many of the first clubs comprised surface workers drawn from the ranks of the better-paid *mabalane* – mission-educated, Zulu-speaking African clerks.[6] The modestly privileged world of these secretarial workers dressed in jackets and trousers saw them living with their families rent-free in the married quarters, rather than eking out a living in the overcrowded compounds of single men. Unlike migrant miners, clerks were also unofficially recognised as permanent employees. Even though a 1946 Chamber of Mines report concluded that both migrant and 'permanent' workers played football on the Rand mines, the more sedentary clerks had more time and energy to devote themselves to athletic activities than underground miners doing long shifts of tough manual labour in appalling conditions.[7]

The Old Natalians Football Club of Simmer and Jack Mine (Goldfields) was, by all accounts, the most successful and respected WDNFA side. Founded in 1906 by clerks from northern Natal, the Old Natalians were instrumental in setting up the mine association in 1917. They dominated football on the mines for the next two decades, winning numerous trophies, including the prestigious Transvaal Challenge Cup in 1938.[8] Area-based clubs such as Old Natalians and All Blacks at City Deep Mine provided workers with an opportunity to (re)construct their regional and school ties through physical exercise and competition. Old Natalians was not just a football club: like other mine clubs it became a cultural and social organisation that expressed a distinct group consciousness and identity based on status and respectability, geographical origin, and physical prowess.

After the 1920 African mineworkers' strike, football influenced industrial relations on the gold mines. Companies encouraged labour stratification by implementing a divisive sport strategy. The mines promoted competitive 'tribal dancing' for underground miners who made up about 90 per cent of the African workforce, but sponsored football and cricket for clerks, policemen, and other surface employees.[9] Recognising that the *mabalane* occupied a key role between management and underground miners, mining companies built leisure facilities and encouraged them to dedicate themselves to sport.

> The educated elite of mine clerks were always seen as a potential threat to industrial order because of their key role as intermediaries between the mine managers and the mass of the African workforce in the compounds. This was a powerful reason for mine companies to develop special recreational activities for them which not only occupied their leisure time and emphasised their elite status but also promoted an ethos of loyalty to the mine.[10]

Captains of mining also viewed sport as a production booster – for worker morale seemed to rise after soccer matches – and as a safety valve for restive labourers perceived as faction fighters, alcoholics, dagga (cannabis) smokers, and sexual predators. Mine management tried to use sport to keep migrant miners from travelling to the townships on weekends and public holidays, where they socialised and often built relationships with permanent residents of the city, particularly single women and politically minded men.[11] As early as 1923 the Chamber of Mines newspaper *Umteteli Wa Bantu* reported that 'all kinds of sports are organised and in various other ways provision is made to keep the Natives wholesomely amused'.[12]

The inexpensive costs of football had an irresistible appeal for a mining industry bent on maximising profit by keeping its production costs as low as possible. The nature of the ore deposits in the Witwatersrand strongly influenced mining companies' desire for a cheap labour force. The thin gold-bearing reef outside Johannesburg slants downward into the earth for several hundred kilometres, so that deep-level mining operations became necessary after an initial decade (1886–96) of relatively inexpensive outcrop mining. The low quality of the ore required the extraction of unusually large amounts of ore to produce small quantities of precious gold. Until 1933 the international gold standard fixed maximum prices for gold, further heightening the need for mining magnates to keep production costs low.[13]

Mine management supported the formation of workers' teams and competitions. Some mine managers in the 1920s elaborated their views on sport provision for African mineworkers in these terms:

> The native is intensely imitative, often vain, and always clannish, and all these are qualities which would further 'sport' – a parochial spirit of sport if you like – but one which would forge ties of interest and *esprit de corps* between the laborer and his work-place. A patch of ground, a set of goal-posts and a football would not figure largely in the expenditure of a big mine.[14]

Some African workers quickly took advantage of companies' support of sport. For example, Philip Q. Vundla, a leading figure in the Western Native Township Native Advisory Board and the ANC in the 1950s, 'always claimed that he only got it [a job as a mine clerk at Crown Mines in the 1920s] because he was a good cricketer. The mining communities take their sports very seriously and he was expected to play cricket for the mine that engaged him.'[15]

The idea of company sport attracted the interest of manufacturers, and not only on the Rand. For example, the development of industrial football in Pietermaritzburg goes back to at least the 1930s. African workers at Sutherlands Tannery founded Tannery Sweepers and black railway employees set up Railroad Tigers, both of which competed in the Pietermaritzburg and District African Football Association.[16] North of the Limpopo, sport for African labourers also appeared on the copper mines of Katanga (Shaba) province, Belgian Congo. The mining giant Union Minière du Haute Katanga (UMHK), the colonial government, and the Catholic church established the Union des Fédérations et Associations Sportives Indigènes (UFASI) in 1925, in order to create a disciplined, efficient, 'moral', and healthy African working class.[17] Overall, it is unclear whether (and to what extent) football contributed to the 'relatively quiet years' of labour relations on South African gold mines from 1921 to 1937.[18] Certainly, by the 1920s, missionaries, white liberals, and the municipal Native Affairs Department shared the mining companies' enthusiasm for football. Sport was seen primarily as a force with which to counteract growing black protest and resistance, as seen in ICU and Communist Party activity, as well as the stinging effects of crime, alcohol abuse, and gambling on urban African communities.[19]

THE POLITICS OF RACE AND LEISURE

As elsewhere in colonial Africa, the dramatic expansion of indigenous sport in the 1930s was partly the result of social welfare programmes supported by liberal and missionary philanthropic organisations, in co-operation with private (mining) companies and municipal authorities.[20]

These diverse white interest groups sought to harness football's popularity to defuse growing political unrest, win converts, and moderate the effects of severe economic deprivation. The quest for autonomous sport in black communities was a critical aspect of the broader struggle for survival waged by urban Africans in South Africa and in colonial territories north of the Limpopo. As Frederick Cooper reminds us: 'Colonial officials, mining companies, and railway administrators built their cities, mines, and workshops, but not as they would have liked. [. . .] As workers sought to shape their lives as individuals and as members of collectivities, they too shaped the life of the city.'[21]

Whites shared similar goals but had different reasons for organising African soccer in Johannesburg. The central government followed the lead of the municipal authorities. When the Native Economic Commission (1930–32) recommended that provisions be made for African sport in cities and towns it was endorsing the Johannesburg NAD manager's suggestion. The commission stated that 'the experience gained from providing recreation for Natives shows clearly that money spent on it has been effective in reducing by a far greater amount the expenditure or loss through crime and drunkenness'. As a result, the commission declared, '[I]t is very desirable that local authorities and large employers of Native Labor should make provision for recreation for Natives under the guidance of Native sports organizers.'[22] Among the white officials who took notice was George Cook, the Superintendent of Native Locations for Cape Town's Native Affairs Department. In an official report compiled in 1932, Cook stated that he 'fully endorse[d] in every way the views of the Native Economic Commission on native recreation', and he began to address, albeit belatedly, the lack of suitable sporting facilities available to African athletes in Langa and Ndabeni townships.[23]

American Board missionaries, most notably Ray Phillips,[24] did the grassroots work of 'moralizing the leisure time of natives' in the ghettos of Johannesburg.[25] Meanwhile, the Joint Council and the South African Institute of Race Relations, organisations whose aim was to promote interracial co-operation and African social welfare, conducted research and pressured white authorities to provide facilities for African sport.[26] The major achievements of Phillips and the white liberals included the construction of the Bantu Men's Social Centre (BMSC) in 1924 and the opening of the Bantu Sports Club in 1931.[27] The BMSC, located on Eloff Street Extension near the Wemmer Hostel in central Johannesburg, was conceived as a private, socially and gender-exclusive indoor cultural centre where educated, 'respectable' Africans could read and play under white supervision.[28] The Bantu Sports Club was built on twelve acres of land donated by two prominent white liberals, J. Howard Pim and John L. Hardy, who were active in both the Joint

Council and the Institute for Race Relations.[29] The *Umteteli Wa Bantu* of 11 April 1931 reported that an overflowing crowd of 10 000 spectators attended the Bantu Sports Club's inaugural festivities which featured, in a symbolic articulation of the existing ties between white liberals and middle-class Africans, a rare cricket match between an African and a white team. The opening of the Bantu Sports Club in 1931 created a private urban space for African football in the heart of the city, which was beyond the control of the Johannesburg City Council. The extraordinary significance of the Bantu Sports Club as an autonomous leisure space crystallised after the temporary disappearance, for unknown reasons, of the mine-based WDNFA in 1928–29.

The closure of the mine-based league prompted the philanthropic whites and educated Africans of the Bantu Men's Social Centre to fill the vacuum: they formed the Johannesburg Bantu Football Association (JBFA) on 18 April 1929. About twenty teams joined the JBFA out of the forty-five clubs active in the greater Johannesburg area previously under the aegis of the WDNFA.[30] The remaining teams continued playing informal matches or disbanded, some temporarily, others permanently. The JBFA's first executive exposed the tight control of its affairs by white authorities; while Richard W. Msimang was elected president, the NAD manager Ballenden was a patron and adviser, his Native Sports Organiser Sol Senaoane was secretary, and Ray Phillips was first vice-president and, shortly thereafter, treasurer.[31]

Disgruntled racial nationalists opposed to white oversight moved to form an African-controlled organisation. Resentment of white leadership was clearly articulated in the black press, where the JBFA was derided as a 'municipalised' sporting body.[32] The problems between the African nationalists and their pragmatic opponents continued. Cleopas Xaba, an executive member of the dormant WDNFA, invited the East Rand and District Native Football Association (founded in 1923)[33] and the JBFA to discuss the formation of a provincial body at the Bantu Men's Social Centre in May 1930. H.L. Msimang presided over the drafting and ratification of the constitution of what became the Transvaal African Football Association (TAFA).[34] However, due to personal conflicts and a fear of losing power, privilege, and status, the JBFA delegates refused to join the new organisation. Unperturbed, TAFA went ahead without the dissidents. In 1931 it launched the inter-district Henochsberg Cup. In that year Zulu clerks resurrected the old mine association, eliminating ethnic sections and renaming it the Witwatersrand and District *African* Football Association.[35] This name change reflects race-conscious nationalism and suggests a more assertive opposition to white stewardship. The *mabalans* persuaded the Chamber of Mines and several small private companies to sponsor knock-out and round-robin competitions such as the Native Recruiting Corporation Cup and the Hadley's Cup. Co-operation with management developed alongside a vigorous thrust to defend autonomous African leisure.

Conflicts over decision-making powers and control of gate-takings at the Bantu Sports Club led to the JBFA's transfer to the football ground located at the municipal Wemmer Hostel (for migrant workers).[36] The municipal compound at Wemmer was home to the only other enclosed sporting facility for Africans in Johannesburg. Wemmer also housed the headquarters of the municipal NAD, an indication of the involvement of white authorities in the administration of the JBFA. In reaction, officials at Bantu Sports founded the rival Johannesburg African Football Association (JAFA) in 1933 and immediately affiliated with TAFA.[37] Dan Twala, the young general secretary of the Bantu Sports Club, soon joined the JAFA executive, first as secretary and later as president until the early 1960s.

The established JBFA and its allies railed against this breakaway faction while struggling to gain popular approval. In the Chamber of Mines' newspaper *Umteteli Wa Bantu*, Phillips wrote an angry column, bemoaning secessionist tendencies in football and Christian institutions; he said that, '[t]his split in Bantu football is to be roundly condemned. It is an action of the same divisive nature which has resulted in the formation of 294 Separatist Churches in the Bantu ranks.'[38] Phillips and the NAD manager, Graham Ballenden, set up parallel 'Bantu' associations in 1933 with assistance from some African officials. JBFA stalwarts I.H. Rathebe and Sol Senaoane, respectively president and secretary, assumed the mantle of leadership, but Ballenden and NAD managers from affiliated areas influenced the organisation from behind the scenes.[39] JBFA administrators sought to protect their spheres of influence and authority over local football by strengthening ties with the municipality. Phillips and the NEAD supported this strategy in the hope of marginalising the JAFA and extending white stewardship. In the mid-1930s the 'Bantu' group attempted – unsuccessfully – to invigorate popular interest in its games by organising a national tournament (the Suzman Cup), and the Godfrey South African Challenge Cup, which pitted Transvaal 'Bantu', Indian, and Coloured teams against each other in official inter-racial matches for the first time.[40]

During this time of tremendous turmoil and transformation, the Transvaal African Football Association entered into negotiations with Natal to discuss the formation of a national football association for Africans. Since Durban dominated Natal and the Rand controlled TAFA, the discussions were, essentially, a Durban-Johannesburg affair.[41] The idea for a national body seems to have originated in Durban. In 1931 the DDAFA executive had approached A.F. Baumann of Bakers Limited for the donation of a trophy for a national competition.[42] DDAFA president T. Ngcobo and Natal vice-president Albert Luthuli led the Durban contingent that formalised the union of Transvaal and Natal in founding the South Africa African Football Association (SAAFA) in 1932.

The Orange Free State African Football Association and the Cape Soccer Board joined in 1934 and 1936 respectively, giving SAAFA a truly national character. The introduction of the Orange Free State forced the tournament to adopt a round-robin format it would retain (in expanded form) for a quarter century.

The Cape Soccer Board, which began a biennial Lord Clarendon Governor-General Shield tournament in the 1930s, did not field a representative team in the Bakers Cup due to geographical distance and prohibitive transport costs – obstacles

Ndabeni soccer field (n.d.)

that would resurface many years later with the advent of professionalism. The Cape Peninsula Bantu Football Association, established in 1927 at Ndabeni, Cape Town, and later headquartered in Langa township, was an important force in the regional game.[43] This association changed its name to Western Province African Football Association in the mid-1930s and included these clubs: Zebras, Pirates, Rainbows, Hungry Lions, Blues, All Blacks, Shooting Stars, Dangerous Points, and Antelopes.[44]

The other force in Cape football was the Transkeian Territory Football Association founded in Umtata in the mid-1930s. Its teams, listed in the *Bantu World* of 18 November 1939, included St John's College, Umtata Home Defenders, Mqanduli, Teko, Blyswood, Idutywa, Engcobo, and Tsomo. Eastern Cape boarding schools such as Lovedale, Fort Hare, Healdtown, St Matthews, and Clarkesbury did not join any formal organisation. However, in the 1930s and 40s, Fort Hare embarked on several successful football tours during the academic winter break to Natal, Transvaal, and the Orange Free State.[45]

SAAFA's inter-provincial Bakers Cup immediately became domestic football's premier event.[46] The first Bakers Cup took place in a single afternoon, featuring an eighty-minute contest staged at the Native Recreation Ground in Somtseu Road, Durban, on 1 August 1932, a public holiday. Thousands of home fans spurred the predominantly Durban-based Natal side to a 4-2 triumph over the visitors from Transvaal.[47] The 'Bantu' camp responded on 31 December 1933 by establishing the South African Bantu Football Association (SABFA), which never seriously challenged the hegemony of the larger, better organised, and more visible 'African' association.[48] By the mid-1930s football in South Africa had become a sharply divided national institution. The deep racial balkanisation of local football reflected the segregated

Langa Zebras 'B' division (1946).

Western Province African Football Association pick team (1941).

George Thabe, *It's a Goal!* (Skotaville, 1983)

George Thabe, *It's a Goal!* (Skotaville, 1983)

nature of South African society. Five national associations had emerged: the (white) South African Football Association, the South African Indian Football Association (launched in 1903), the rival SAAFA and SABFA, and the South African Coloured Football Association (1933).

Beyond the existence of organisational fault-lines and ongoing conflicts with whites, the most important process unfolding on and off the field of play was the indigenisation of the game and the forging of a specifically African subaltern football culture. While white organisers of black sport mistakenly believed that 'from the very word go we followed European rules, the Africans did not introduce anything', the Africanisation of the colonial game was central to its growing significance in urban everyday life.[49]

CHAPTER 5

'Shaping Common Social Bonds'

The Africanisation of Football

The inter-war years signalled the dawn of a new era in South African football. The Bakers Cup (established in 1932), the Suzman Cup (1935), and the Godfrey South African Challenge Cup (1936) were new national competitions that electrified crowds of 5 000 to 10 000 people in Johannesburg and Durban. Tours by professional clubs from Britain added to the enormous excitement, an atmosphere sustained by popular discourse and improving sports coverage in the black press. Matches between Indians, Africans, and Coloureds also became more frequent and popular.[1] During this time, the inherited institution of British football was increasingly transformed to suit local customs and traditions, a process of Africanisation that embraced religious specialists and magic, various rituals of spectatorship as well as indigenous playing styles.

RELIGIOUS SPECIALISTS AND MAGIC

In Johannesburg, as well as Durban and Cape Town, the transformation of football involved the active participation of diviners and healers, the widespread use of magical propitiatory medicines, and elaborate ritual preparations for important contests. The solicitation of an *isangoma* (diviner) or an *inyanga* (healer) aimed to secure a strong performance on the field and protection from the polluting magic of rival religious specialists.

Rolfes (R.R.R.) Dhlomo, assistant editor of *Bantu World* from 1933–43 and one of only fifteen African editors of the white-owned Bantu Press, focused on football at least twice during his decade-long 'R. Roamer Esq.' (also 'R. Roamer') column first published in the *Bantu World* in March 1933.[2] In his writings, Dhlomo described African clubs in Johannesburg employing healers, diviners, and sorcerers to prepare their squads ritually before a match. Ritual preparations included pre-game consultations with a diviner who threw the bones to predict the outcome of the match. Healers also strengthened athletes by rubbing players' legs with *umuthi* (propitiatory medicine) or making them inhale 'some smoke from herbs so that they bring fear and weakness on the opponents'.[3] Such practices were also common in Durban in an earlier period. For example, the discovery of a small bottle filled

49

with *umuthi* in one of the goals during a championship game in the early 1920s led to accusations of witchcraft, which exploded into a major controversy. After several weeks of lengthy, heated meetings between the teams, match officials, and the Durban association, the white president of the DDNFA, Douglas Evans, tried to end the dispute in paternalistic fashion, 'tell[ing] the two clubs that football was a European game played according to European rules and that no "muthi" can work'.[4] Evans and some *kholwa* Africans criticised the use of magic in football as 'uncivilised' but were unable to stop this powerful and creative indigenous adaptation.

This practice became so widespread that, for example, by the 1950s, nearly every football team in Durban relied on the professional services of a religious specialist.[5] An *inyanga* could be hired for sums of up to £200 per season in order to imbue players with courage and determination and to protect them from the spells of rival magicians.[6] Earnest competition for the best doctors developed. As one informant put it: 'the biggest club gets the biggest muthi men – that's right. The richest get the best, the muthi men had to get paid after all.'[7] But if the team underperformed or lost, then the *inyanga* was usually held responsible and dismissed. This twentieth-century practice was consistent with traditional martial norms, whereby 'an unsuccessful doctor is ignored and another employed . . . if the impi is unsuccessful'.[8]

The linguistic and cultural homogeneity of Durban's predominantly migrant Zulu-speaking African population facilitated the percolation of Zulu pre-colonial rituals into metropolitan soccer. For example, traditional Zulu martial practices diffused into the urban game. African teams in Durban participated in 'camping' rituals.[9] Before an important contest, teams were known to go on a retreat to a secret place to re-enact purificatory rituals performed by nineteenth-century Zulu *amabutho* (age regiments) before major military encounters.[10] 'The night before a match they [players, club officials, and selected supporters] must "camp" together around a fire. They all sleep together, they must stay naked and they are given umuthi and other medicines by the inyanga. Incisions are made on their knees, elbows, and joints.'[11] The following morning the players drank a powerful emetic and vomited, emulating the *ukuhlanza* (vomiting) cleansing ritual of Zulu soldiers before going into battle. The sprinkling of *umuthi* on the football and on players' boots also recalled the 'doctoring' of warriors' weapons, as did the burning of special roots.[12]

The symbolic recreation of past African military prowess aided in the construction of team spirit and fostered camaraderie. In a variation of the regimental column march to the battlefield, participants in the camping ritual were expected to 'go together on the same bus to the match . . . . Even when the group has to take a bus from one part of town to another where the football field is, they still make every effort to maintain . . . a very tight formation with every man touching the man in front of, behind and beside him.'[13] Once inside the stadium, teams drew on *ukugiya* (war dancing) traditions. One observer noted that teams were '[m]oving out onto the actual playing field with their stylised trotting step, the group acts very hostile to outsiders for fear that intruders will attempt to bewitch the players in some way to weaken the *umuthi* or the medicine of the *inyanga*'.[14]

The use of magic was not an exclusive practice of Zulu footballers. An elderly Cape Town-born Xhosa player remembered in an interview that before important matches in the 1940s, 'a witchdoctor or whatever will come and smear some Vaseline on our shoes and whatever it was. When I ask him what it is all about he says: "this is going to make you run faster, kick great" and so on. [Laughs].'[15] Informants were generally reluctant to discuss magic. Most times, individuals gave deliberately vague descriptions of such practices, probably because they had taken an oath of secrecy or because they suspected disapproval from a foreign interviewer.[16] A representative comment on the use of *umuthi* was the following: 'I didn't believe in that stuff. It was mostly people who come from the rural areas who believed in witchcraft. People born here [in the city] don't believe in those things.'[17] Even so, the overwhelming majority of players, whether educated, urban, and Christian or not, seemed to accept – whether by choice or peer pressure – the ritual use of magic because of its positive psychological and team-building qualities. The infusion of agrarian beliefs and rituals reveals a way young African men de-colonised football through cultural practice and, in so doing, influenced the institutional growth of black soccer in the 1930s.

RITUALS OF SPECTATORSHIP

As the popularity of soccer grew, weekend and holiday crowds of men, women, and youths – ranging from domestic and factory workers, miners, lumpen elements, and the unemployed, to traders, clerks, messengers, teachers, and students – made their way to football grounds across the country to participate in sporting rituals of urban popular culture.

Bantu Sports and Wemmer in Johannesburg and Somtseu in Durban became major entertainment centres and community meeting grounds. A woman writing in the *Bantu World* opened a window on the social relevance of football as a black cultural space in the city: 'such a common meeting ground provides the only possible condition of a real community life, and of wholesome relationships between parents and children and classes in the community. At the Bantu Sports Club grounds thousands and thousands of footballers have met for the first time to make up those ties and relationships that are serving them well today.'[18] It was not coincidental that a woman was writing about the importance of sport in black popular culture. To discover a woman writing about sport is evidence of the fact that young urban African women at mission schools had begun to play tennis, field hockey, netball, and basketball with great interest.[19] While much more research needs to be done in this area, it seems clear that sport was not the exclusive leisure domain of men.

The Africanisation of the game also transpired through rituals of spectatorship. As the *Bantu World* of 19 August 1933 reported, fans cheered and chanted in support of their team, jeered the opposition, sang, danced, and strummed ukuleles and guitars. The most interesting appropriation of the game was giving players nicknames, a practice borrowed from the rural tradition of *izibongo* (Zulu) or *lithoko* (Sotho), or praise names.[20] According to Liz Gunner and Mafika Gwala, *izibongo* 'identify a person, embody his personality'; they mark the subject 'so that it is in a way outside the power of the individual to remove it or contest it . . . it becomes part of their identity'.[21] Commenting on football nicknames, Sam Shabangu, a founding member of Orlando Pirates, said: 'It is the same with the Zulu warrior . . . a recitation: I know your story, you did this, you killed like this . . . that's exactly what these names are for. It's through your actions, your bravery, that you get your name. The fans are saying these players are their great warriors.'[22] Not only did *izibongo zebhola* (football praises) express agrarian cultures' continuity and change in the urban milieu, they also symbolised the meritocratic possibilities of sport in the sinister context of intensifying racial discrimination. Nicknames helped to strengthen the identification of fans with their sporting heroes.

A footballer's physical attributes or technical abilities often inspired fans' nicknames for him. Players could also be compelled to deliver a particular style of play in accordance with their nicknames. Praise names revealed interesting aspects of the contemporary urban experiences of working-class Africans. In an interview, for example, Peter Sitsila, a leading footballer in the Western Cape in the 1930s who later coached and served as an association official into the early 1960s, recalled that his trademark dribbling move – the half-moon – earned him the name 'Jikeletshobeni' ('he who controls the reins' in Xhosa).[23] He played with his older brother Shadrack for Zebras Football Club, then a dominant club in Cape Town's Langa township. A prolific inside-forward and respected team captain, Shadrack Sitsila was known as 'British Empire' after working on the Kimberley diamond mines.[24] On the Rand, teams fielded men nicknamed 'Cape to Cairo', 'Prince of Wales', 'Junior Certificate', 'Waqafa Waqafa' ('heavy drinker, delinquent' in Zulu), 'Buick', and 'Scotch Whiskey' because his play 'drives the sorrows away and brings enjoyment' to the crowd.[25] Players' nicknames demonstrate how spectators shaped the collective experience at the arena in affirmative ways.

Football grounds were also the site of fights and riots that, occasionally, caused serious, sometimes fatal, injuries. Organised ethnic gangs of migrant youth employed as domestic servants, known as the *amalaita*, were accused of igniting clashes. At Bantu Sports in 1933, 'in the presence of a crowd of about 3 000 the Amalaita suddenly attacked those who were playing football and a dangerous situation arose. Women and children fled before a shower of stones. Many people were injured including the referee.'[26] Alcohol consumption often acted as a catalyst for disorder. Players were seen drinking skokiaan (a strong homebrewed concoction) and even smoking 'something wrapped in dirty brown paper bags', ostensibly to render themselves 'brave and fearless'.[27] Fans bought beer and alcoholic concoctions from illegal brewers, often Basotho women, and shebeen owners active at, or in close proximity to, the grounds. Municipal beer halls erected near the main football grounds in Johannesburg and Durban further exacerbated the problem of intoxicated crowds.[28] *The Star* of 23 May 1938 reported that hundreds of Africans pelted policemen raiding for beer near Bantu Sports with missiles and stones.

The first documented killing of a South African referee by an angry mob occurred in Johannesburg in 1940. This tragedy shows, among other things, the way football hooliganism reflected sport's vulnerability to the forces of an increasingly violent and miserably poor urban society.[29] In the grave words of Rolfes Dhlomo: 'our soccer fields at times are just fields of battle where savages are given a chance to murder each other . . . because of the hardships under which they live in this country'.[30]

Despite the occasional violence, the staggering increase in the number of teams demonstrates the widening appeal and popularity of the game. JBFA membership grew steadily from 39 in 1930 to 103 teams in 1935; JAFA expanded from 50 in 1933 to 84 teams in 1935.[31] As has been shown already, in Durban the number of teams rose to an all-time high of 47 in 1935. In the Western Cape, the Cape Peninsula Bantu Football Association, which served a significantly smaller African population, recorded more modest growth: from 7 to 9 affiliated clubs from 1932 to 1936.[32] New competitions such as the Transvaal Henochsberg Cup and the Governor-General's Shield in Natal sparked excitement, adding to the attraction of local leagues. Players used the platforms of city and district matches to prove their mettle to the provincial selection committees, which were made up of three to five executive officials with playing experience. Until the 1950s provincial selection for the prestigious Bakers Cup was the highest honour a black player could achieve; it could lead to greater respectability and status in the neighbourhood or location, as well as provide travelling experiences and foster camaraderie.

COMPETITION AND CAMARADERIE

The sporting spectacles staged for the national Bakers Cup comprised a key feature in the autonomous leisure world that Africans sought to shape through football. These competitions also illustrate the prominence of football festivals in the panoply of contemporary urban leisure and entertainment. The Durban biscuit manufacturer Bakers Ltd. donated the trophy, one of the earliest attempts by white business to capitalise on the commercial potential of soccer in black communities.[33] Matches were regularly staged on holidays when businesses closed and black workers enjoyed some free time. Natal won the inaugural 1932 Bakers Cup in Durban and travelled to the Rand to defend its national title in 1933. Travelling costs were paid by the national association, which also arranged for all the necessary permits from the government. The SAAFA staged the 1933 championship on a public holiday, thus ensuring a large crowd and teams at full strength. A crowd of 4 500 paying spectators and many more non-paying fans crammed into the Bantu Sports Club. A thunderous roar welcomed the teams' entrance onto the pitch: a 'band of miners with their lanterns, leading their Transvaal team into the field as mascots', and SAAFA vice-president Albert Luthuli escorting the Natal side.[34]

Newspaper accounts reveal that the home crowd enjoyed 'excellent and thrilling soccer', although most people left disappointed after Richard 'Wireless' Khumalo, star forward of the Ladysmith Rainbows, scored the winning goal late in the game to give Natal a 2-1 victory and a second consecutive national title.[35]

A typical Bakers Cup festival took place on 4–6 August 1934 at Bantu Sports in Johannesburg. Tickets for Saturday's matches cost 6d. for adults and 3d. for children, slightly more than the 4d. bus fare from the suburbs to city centre when the average monthly wage of an unskilled worker in Johannesburg was about £5.[36] For this reasonable admission price spectators were first treated to a Henochsberg Cup contest between representative teams of the Witwatersrand and District African Football Association and the Johannesburg African Football Association at 2:15 p.m.; then to a Bakers Cup match between the Transvaal and the Orange Free State at 3:45 p.m. The weekend programme resumed before even larger crowds on Monday, another public holiday. The festivities began with a youth match at 10:30 a.m., followed by a Henochsberg Cup game, and then the mid-afternoon Bakers Cup contest between the Orange Free State and Natal. The holiday entertainment ended with a spectacular evening gala at the Bantu Men's Social Centre.[37]

The Natal team's travelling experience, recounted by their manager in the pages of the *Bantu World*, demonstrates how football sustained and gave meaning to people's social lives. Like generations of Zulu migrant workers, the Natal team journeyed by train to the Rand. 'We went to Johannesburg to play soccer,' recalled a Natal player, 'we played it all right but we had so much besides, that our tour was not far different from a cook's pleasure trip.'[38] The Natal team was housed and fed at the Witwatersrand Native Labour Association compound, an arrangement that revealed the ongoing ties between mining companies and black football on the Rand.[39] The athletes from Natal visited the offices of the *Bantu World* and the new segregated African municipal township of Orlando. Other players and officials were taken by car on a sightseeing tour of the city, Western Native Township, and the freehold townships of Sophiatown and Alexandra. One man observed that in Alexandra 'the African has proved his great love of ownership and ability to use what has been laid at his disposal. To think that these residents had to purchase stands at an exorbitant price of £200, and be able in the bargain to erect what cottages there are gives one enough courage to face the seemingly dark future.'[40] The weekend's highlight was the closing concert and dance at the Bantu Men's Social Centre.

This concert-and-dance party highlights the profound connections between sport, music, dance, and liquor in South African popular culture.[41] One guest reported that the evening party had featured a 'fine show with the beautiful lighting and decorations . . . fine speeches . . . interspersed with melodious musical items . . . and delicious refreshments further supported by Randites who were in cheerful spirits and quietly made us feel at home that one felt like a little lord with a rosette that gave him so much respect and brought so many a function made in his honour'.[42] Women such as Dora Twala, often wives of prominent soccer officials, helped to plan and cater for these social events. The most visible and highly respected of the contemporary African jazz dance bands, the Merry Blackbirds Dance Orchestra, played at this BMSC soccer gathering as it did for many clubs and associations throughout the 1930s and early 40s.[43] Like many soccer players and most officials dancing before them, the Merry Blackbirds were teachers, clerks, and social workers involved in the social institutions of comparatively privileged Africans. The band modelled itself after the Glenn Miller Orchestra and 'played for the full-range of social and organisational functions of middle-class African society', of which soccer events were among the most popular.[44] Some musicians not only performed at football socials but also played the game themselves. For example, in the 1930s, the iconoclastic Dan Twala was a drummer for the popular Rhythm Kings while a member of Highlanders Football Club; he was also the general secretary of the Bantu Sports Club and a high-ranking official of the Johannesburg African Football Association.[45] Despite losing the match, the exciting experience in Johannesburg left an indelible mark on the youngest Natal athlete. Riding the train back to Durban he said: 'I wish we were still on our way to the Rand and not on our way back home for the fine times we had in Johannesburg will always remain fresh in my memory.'[46]

Football's sociability fostered camaraderie and created new personal and social bonds. The manager of the same Natal team noted that he was 'still receiving letters from the members of the team' weeks after the trip to the Rand in 1934, adding that 'they all speak of the Johannesburg they are still sorry to have left behind them . . . . For some days yet our objective will be to play soccer so well that we can once more visit the City of dreams and unimaginable realities "Kwa Ndongaziyaduma" (the place where thunder emanates from the [mining] scars in the land).'[47] These individual and collective experiences suggest how football in urban South Africa created an arena of cultural autonomy and opportunity that relieved the lives of people deeply affected by the drudgery of underemployment and the painful constraints of institutional racism. But, in order to understand the game's integration into popular culture in the segregation era more fully, it is necessary to explore soccer's changing techniques, tactics, and aesthetics. The emergence of the *marabi* and *Motherwell* vernacular modes of play indicate that fans and players valued the specific ways in which the game was played; the ethic of performance was a critical factor in crowning football the king of black sport.

CHANGING TACTICS AND INDIGENOUS PLAYING STYLES

The organically competitive nature of football led to technical improvements and tactical innovations that have been documented in the black press and reconstructed in oral history narratives. Most contemporary South African teams, black or white, employed the direct British kick-and-rush style, featuring long passes to the forwards and aggressive, physical play on defence. Environmental factors produced regional variations. The dry climate, high altitude, and rock-hard, dusty pitches of the Rand led to a faster, end-to-end game featuring flesh-ripping tackles and the ball often in the air. Down on the coastal belt, the preferred approach was instead a slower version of kick-and-rush, mostly due to the demanding conditions found on the wind-swept, soggy pitches of sub-tropical Durban (in summer) and temperate Cape Town (in winter).[48] Thus, the historical trend of South African teams encountering significant challenges when travelling outside their ecological zones was established early on.

The dominant tactical formation during the inter-war period was the 2-3-5 scheme.[49] Also known as the 'pyramid', this system dominated Latin American and Eastern and Central European football until about 1950. Both Uruguay and Argentina used the 2-3-5 in the first World Cup final in Montevideo in 1930. It should be noted that, at the time, players had more 'poetic licence' to create and improvise in the ebb and flow of the match than they do today. As an Argentine member of the 1930 World Cup final squad recalled: 'We didn't talk about tactics – we just went out and played and each of us knew what it was that we had to do.'[50] In the same vein, a column in the sport section of the *Bantu World* on 24 August 1940 argued that while 'individual abilities must be all subordinated to one end – the team', it was equally important that 'we should fit the *plan of play to our players* and *not* our players to the plan' (emphasis added). Be that as it may, the pyramid emphasised offensive play, with the three midfielders expected to support the attack and anticipate on defence. The central midfielder was the 'brain of the team, the instigator of attacking moves, the decision-maker, the leader. He was an all-rounder.'[51]

Enoch 'Joko Tea' Samaniso, so nicknamed after a brand of tea popular among Africans, was one of the outstanding exponents of this position in South Africa in the 1930s. Widely respected for his silky dribbling skills and legendary toughness, Joko Tea won many titles at club and district levels playing for Old Natalians of Simmer and Jack Mine, where he was employed as a clerk, and the Witwatersrand and District African Football Association representative side. He also led the Transvaal to national titles in 1934, 1935, 1937 and 1938. His 1937 Bakers Cup performance was typically strong: displaying his 'wizardry with the ball'; Samaniso 'was in his element and played ducks and drakes with the Natal left half, who could not stop him'.[52] Samaniso died playing a match in May 1941. His achieved status and fame were such that, despite a last-minute scheduling change, hundreds of people attended the funeral in Benoni on the East Rand. The executive directors of the Transvaal African Football Association gave Samaniso's widow a £10 contribution, while the white mine staff and compound manager sent wreaths; his team-mates and colleagues from Simmer and Jack Mine acted as pallbearers and guards of honour at the burial.[53]

Samaniso's combination of artisanry and artistry made him an unusual player in the 1930s, when a high number of goals were scored from corner kicks, goalmouth scrambles, and long-distance shots. Former players and journalists attributed these trends to weak goalkeeping skills.[54] Goalkeeping, a despised position in street soccer, was made even less attractive by the tolerance of physical charges on goalkeepers in control of the ball.[55] As the quality of football improved many teams recognised that experience and physical force alone could not guarantee success. Some players began practising once a week, either playing on their own or organising a late afternoon intra-squad scrimmage on an open ground.[56] The lack of formal coaching, regular fitness training, and the abrasive or waterlogged pitches severely stunted the organic development of the game. The impact of material conditions on the way black South Africans played the game can be inferred from the scarcity of goals that developed from crosses from the flanks, combination passing, corners, and free kicks – plays that thrive only with extensive practice time, formal instruction, and decent playing surfaces.

MARABI FOOTBALL

The increasing popularity of football in the inter-war period was not met by a corresponding growth in the provision of sporting facilities. As a result, African, Coloured, and Indian players developed their skills as youths in the narrow confines of township streets and school playgrounds. In these spaces, ball control, individualism, toughness, and improvisation outweighed the importance of moving without the ball, creating and using space, passing, and field vision. 'Like we were kids, we had nothing to do, we played with the tennis balls,' remembered Conrad Stuurman, a former professional player in the 1960s who learnt to play football in the early 1940s in the streets of Windermere, a large black working-class area in Cape Town destroyed by apartheid-era removals.[57] Stuurman said that 'when we played in the streets we maybe played three or four or five 'cause in the streets it's very narrow you can't take a big team . . . . Then, when I've got the ball and I wanted to beat somebody, I played the ball against the pavement, on the other side I'd get the ball back again. That's how we came to know the wall pass. I didn't even know there was a name like wall pass! [laughs].'[58] Oral testimony captures the remarkable resilience and creativity of black athletes; it also highlights how specific structural constraints influenced the development of different aesthetic tastes and a variety of vernacular styles of play.

The social context of grim locations, labour camps, factories, and mines shaped black sport and leisure in concrete ways. On weekends, football grounds were packed with the same miners, day labourers, factory and municipal workers, domestic servants, and other African men and women who created a working-class *marabi* culture between the wars. *Marabi* was a form of syncretic (traditional and modern) music that dominated lower-class urban black leisure between the wars.[59] The famous saxophonist Wilson 'King Force' Silgee recalled the inebriating atmosphere of *marabi* parties:

> Marabi: that was the environment! It was either organ but mostly piano. You get there, you pay your ten cents. You get your scale [drinking cup] of

whatever concoction there is, then you dance. It used to start from Friday night right through Sunday evening. You get tired, you go home, go and sleep, come back again: bob a time, each time you get in. The piano and with the audience making a lot of noise. Trying to make some theme out of what is playing.[60]

Footballers and *marabi* musicians alike were self-taught urban artists who shared a common experience with their audiences. Sports grounds, like the rowdy shebeens (speakeasies), beerhalls, and other drinking establishments where many Africans spent their leisure time and limited disposable income, provided spaces for entrepreneurship, social interaction, and entertainment.[61] Stylistically, the improvisational, flexible nature of street soccer – a game with neither referees nor time limits and enjoyed by as many participants as space allowed – produced ways of playing that resembled the 'rhythmically propulsive' piano-based *marabi* music.[62] An enduring legacy of the *marabi* football aesthetic in South African soccer has been the 'spectacular display of individual talent . . . often more memorable, more enjoyable, and ultimately, even more desirable than the final score'.[63] On the Rand, Orlando Pirates, African Morning Stars of Sophiatown, and Eastern Leopards of Eastern Native Township (George Goch) earned a reputation among soccer enthusiasts as performers of the unorthodox, giddy, thrilling *marabi* football style (see Chapter 6). A range of approaches to the game were developing alongside *marabi*. In the 1930s, for example, a genre called Motherwell acquired special relevance.

MOTHERWELL AS A TAYLORIST GENRE
In their lucrative tours of South Africa in the early 1930s, the Scottish Motherwell Football Club systematically defeated all-white provincial and national teams and, in so doing, radically changed how black South Africans thought about and practised the game. The sophisticated network of ground passes and disciplined positioning of the Scots dazzled thousands of white and black South Africans in attendance at segregated stadiums across the country.[64] The new tactical and technical approaches of the professional teams from overseas captured the imaginations of black fans, officials, and players who, in the tradition of black South African sporting culture in the protest era, cheered the visitors' victories over local white sides.[65] In 1937 the *Bantu World* recorded that five hundred 'jubilant' Africans paid a half-crown (2s.6d.) to sit in the 'non-European' section of the Wanderers Ground in Johannesburg to watch another Scottish side, Aberdeen Football Club, defeat South Africa 5-1.[66]

The considerable popular interest generated by the Scottish professionals' triumphant displays was in part owed to their extensive coverage in the black press. A black reporter, most likely an African player or official given his highly specialised knowledge of the game, provided a snapshot of football culture between the wars in his account of the 'test match' between Motherwell and (white) South Africa in

Johannesburg in 1934.[67] The *Bantu World* journalist praised the order, punctuality, conformity, and sportsmanship that reigned at the Wanderers Ground.[68] He applauded the visitors' rigorous discipline as they tackled the ball rather than the man and refrained from charging the opposing goalkeeper. Highlighting the security benefits of a fence separating players and spectators, the reporter noted that the teams, referee, and linesmen 'were not seen "hanging" around the ground until 2 or 3 minutes to the [kickoff] time'. The effective interplay of the match officials limited dissent on the pitch, a frequent occurrence in black amateur football where accusations of bias plagued referees and linesmen usually selected by the competing teams. Also, time was not 'wasted', the columnist added, with announcements of players' names and backgrounds – a common feature of the spectacle of black football matches at Bantu Sports and Wemmer.[69] At these grounds Dan Twala (later a Bantu Radio commentator) and Sol Senaoane habitually 'called each name, the player would respond and take the field, amid tumultuous applause from the crowd'.[70] Finally, the white players were 'properly dressed . . . unlike many of our popular ones', who, as Sam Shabangu pointed out, often 'had no money, we had to beg our parents for equipment . . . we used to play our matches – [in] shirts of various colors and it was the same with the shorts – khaki shorts, all kinds of shorts we could lay our hands on'.[71]

The altruism and teamwork – 'they have no "I's" but "we's"' – of the touring professionals deeply struck black enthusiasts. The Scots favoured a collectivist, Taylorist approach.[72] The mechanics of the Motherwell style were simple and, at the same time, revolutionary: 'it is the ball that does most of the running. Once a Motherwell player gets the ball he knows without hesitating where to pass it to for he knows the player he's thinking of passing to is there waiting to receive it.'[73] As a result of the tours, some African teams began experimenting with Motherwell's coordinated short-passing attack and more guarded defensive play, moving away from the spectacular individual dribbling moves and improvisation that gave *marabi* soccer its colourful character and meaning.

'Playing a fine Motherwell' became a distinguishing philosophy, a symbol of urban sophistication and success.[74] This was especially true of teams dominated by members of the mission-educated elite. 'Highlanders Football Club Copies Motherwell Style of Play' declared the *Bantu World* on 14 May 1932, in reference to one of Johannesburg's most successful and entertaining teams. Based at the Bantu Men's Social Centre, Highlanders applied the rapid ground passes, specialised positional play, and collectivist ideals of 'Motherwell' to gain wide acclaim.[75] Thanks to teams like the Highlanders, the Johannesburg African Football Association (JAFA) earned a reputation for staging 'Motherwell-ised football exhibitions'. These competitions attracted knowledgeable fans who appreciated a genre distinct from both the 'traditional English virtues of speed, strength, stamina and directness' found in colonial kick-and-rush and the improvised showmanship and rowdiness of *marabi* soccer.[76]

(Johannesburg) Highlanders Football Club.

Teams with a reputation for 'play[ing] with true Motherwell skill and precision' became major attractions.[77] JAFA used the self-conscious Motherwell style as a successful marketing tool, increasing attendance and strengthening the group's financial autonomy from white authorities.[78] 'The Public is assured a good game,' stated a JAFA match preview in the black press in 1935, 'as both parties are modeling their football on the Motherwell-All India lines.'[79] The reference to 'All-India' illustrates the admiration of some black fans for India's national team, which lost only one out of sixteen matches against South African Indian sides during a 47-day tour of the country in 1934.[80]

The absence of racially integrated football in South Africa meant that visiting professionals were often the standard by which fans and managers judged amateur black players. When JAFA defeated the South African Native College (Fort Hare) 1-0 at Bantu Sports in 1934, the black press described the deft ball control of JAFA's Joe Chiloane and Herbert Makhothe as 'excellent to watch and would have caught the eye of Motherwell's [coach] Hunter for international honors'.[81]

The influence of the Scots further demonstrated itself in the spread of the Motherwell name among black clubs on the Rand. The Rhodesian Motherwells, for example, were founded in the mid-1930s by Jonah Masaiwana from Bulawayo, Southern Rhodesia (Zimbabwe).[82] Competing in the JBFA Championship division, the Rhodesian Motherwells were a team composed predominantly of domestic workers from Matabeleland who had been migrating to Johannesburg in great numbers since the 1920s, along with men from other areas of Southern Rhodesia as well as Nyasaland (Malawi). These single men had occasionally received some formal mission education in Southern Rhodesia, and many more became self-educated on the Rand, where they were contemptuously called *makirimane* ('clean men') by Zulu-speaking Africans.[83] Motivated by a desire for visibility, urban integration, companionship, and escape from working in 'stringent isolation, in a culturally alien environment and under conditions of considerable tension',[84] the well-dressed *makirimane*s actively participated not only in football but also in other competitive forms of Western leisure culture, such as ballroom dancing.[85] The case of the Rhodesian Motherwells illustrates the important role of football in the crafting of social identities among lower-class Africans.

The urbanisation process evident in the adoption of the Motherwell name did not transform amateur soccer players into professionals, or cause the migrants from north of the Limpopo to shy away from enjoying football on their own terms. Benedict A. Mambwe, a disheartened supporter of Rhodesian Motherwells, criticised Rhodesian Motherwells for what he termed 'the habit of making style and tricks at the center of the ground . . . before you have scored', rather than aiming for victory.[86] This passionate fan's public rebuke of his team's 'playing to the gallery' rather than focusing on winning indicates that Motherwell's machine-like progressive style did not suffocate indigenous interpretations of the game.

A possible explanation for this outcome was that football's dominant position in the world of black leisure was linked to the idea that it was *not* work. The prevailing aesthetic among players and spectators alike reflected a desire to escape, albeit temporarily, those values which the Motherwell model represented, that is, the Taylorist philosophy of the industrial workplace – discipline, teamwork, constant motion, positional play, and specialisation.[87] Other imported modes of play that emphasised overly structured, planned, synchronised movements also encountered criticism from the sports-loving black public. The WM system, a defensive mode of play popularised in England by Arsenal manager Herbert Chapman after the offside rule changed in 1925, was described as the 'much-abhorred third back game' after Transvaal applied it in the 1938 national tournament.[88] To sum up, by the end of the 1930s, fans could appreciate an unprecedented variety of football genres, techniques, and tactics. Technical styles rejecting colonial mimicry survived the radical technical and tactical transformations. For example, when the Durban champions Union Jacks visited Johannesburg in 1939, an expert observer noted the resilience of the *marabi* way: 'Too much dribbling may arouse much cheering from the pavilion, but it is not, in my opinion, good football.'[89] The contemporary black working-class South African aesthetic continued to place more value on the cleverness and beauty of feinting and dribbling. These stylish moves elated audiences and, at the same time, symbolised the cultural importance of knowing how to get around difficulties and dangerous opponents in an oppressive society with creativity, deception, and skill.[90]

SOCCER, BLACK POLITICS, AND SOCIAL CHANGE

As the irrepressible expansion of football continued in the 1940s, the game's powerful ability to shape common social bonds in a society deeply divided along racial, class, linguistic, gender, and regional lines caught the attention of some black politicians. In 1938, together with Dr James Moroka (ANC president, 1949–52), Alexandra businessman, ANC executive member, and SAAFA treasurer Richard G. Baloyi donated a glittering new Moroka-Baloyi Cup to replace the Bakers Cup.[91] A few years later, acting on an idea put forward by ANC president A.B. Xuma, Baloyi organised a historic match between the rival Transvaal Bantu and African teams to raise funds for the ANC.[92] On 6 August 1944 – the ANC's thirty-second anniversary – the Africans won 5-3 in a widely reported 'great game' at Bantu Sports.[93] Described by the politically judicious *Bantu World* as 'a welcome sign of the awakening which is taking place among the people throughout the length and breadth of southern Africa', this match appears to be the first documented example of an overt connection between black liberation movements and football before apartheid.[94]

The national growth of SAAFA may have influenced the formation of the ANC branch structure in 1943 after the adoption of a new ANC constitution.[95] Through its four provincial associations, SAAFA developed branches in Durban, Ladysmith, and Pietermaritzburg in Natal; West Rand, East Rand, and Johannesburg in the Transvaal; Bloemfontein, Bethlehem, and Kroonstad in the Free State; and Cape Town and Umtata in the Cape. In so doing, football could bring together disparate locations, towns, and cities and forge an 'imagined community' of black South Africans united by a shared sporting experience.[96] As has been noted elsewhere, one of the ecumenical attributes of sport is that 'diverse cities and regions can be united through sport networks and leagues, and sport successes are clear factors in engendering national pride and thus helping to integrate often diverse groups of citizens'.[97]

Certainly, the inter-war years saw the beginnings of the diffusion of soccer to more remote small towns and rural villages. The African workforce on the Witwatersrand gold mines rose from 200 634 in 1930 to 363 908 in 1941.[98] Migrant workers returning from the mines brought the sport back to the countryside where youth appropriated the game, a process aided by the resonance of modern sport with vibrant indigenous traditions of physical prowess and competition (see Chapter 1). In Lesotho by the 1940s, 'the game was universal', according to a Sotho-speaking informant; 'herd-boys spent any spare moments kicking a tennis-ball around', learning how to juggle, pass, and trap by 'kicking a tennis-ball up against the wall of one of the typical round-huts. This was excellent practice since it demanded absolute accuracy.'[99] The spread of the game to rural areas led to the founding of the Transkeian Territory Football Association in Umtata in the mid-1930s.[100] In 1942 in Natal, white farmers and sugar planters interested in creating football leagues for labourers on sugar estates expressed surprise upon discovering that 'the Natives of Empangeni and District already have a properly organised

Football Association with eight affiliated clubs which play regularly for three trophies'.[101] For the Chief Native Commissioner of Natal the existence of football was 'a new development, as far as I am aware of, outside of urban areas'.[102]

By the end of the Second World War soccer was the leviathan of black sport. The emergence of football as a popular leisure practice for black South Africans was inextricably connected to broader social, political, economic, and cultural changes brought about by massive urbanisation and an expanding manufacturing economy. The formation of new national associations and competitions, the improvement of sports coverage in the black popular press, and the articulation of vernacular modes of play like Motherwell and *marabi* demonstrated football's growing integration into black popular culture during the segregation period. Out of the deeply passionate football culture bursting from the entertainment-starved municipal location of Orlando on the southwestern periphery of Johannesburg emerged the Orlando Pirates, the People's Club, to whose early history we now turn.

—— CHAPTER 6 ——

The World the Pirates Made

Football and Society in Orlando, Soweto

In an interview, Skumbuzo Mthembu recalled, 'In those days [Pirates] players used to weep if they lost. They had the commitment of a soldier fighting for his country. This patriotism was because he is from Orlando and his family and friends are watching.' 'When Pirates won something,' added Sidwell Mokgosinyane, 'old ladies would run into the streets banging big pots and singing. That night, you knew, you would be able to buy beer for 10 cents in Orlando. The players would be right there with you, celebrating.'[1] Such descriptions suggest how Pirates Football Club infused meaning and granted some relief to the people of Orlando, a black township opened in 1931 by the Johannesburg city council in the area that would later be known as Soweto (the name derived from its official title of 'South Western Townships').

Orlando was planned as a 'model location' for families evicted in slum clearance programmes. However, its regulated uniformity and distance from the city centre made it unappealing to most Africans because of the extra transport costs and the lack of community ties. Orlando lacked basic amenities such as electricity, shops, banks, parks, and sports grounds, and the housing was poor quality. Two- and three-roomed houses were cheaply built and close together on a grid pattern of streets that were not tarred and had no names.[2] Ultimately, the municipality resorted to coercive measures to move people from central Johannesburg to Orlando, which led to a significant increase in the township's population – from around 12 000 to 35 200 – between 1936 and 1938.[3]

In this context, football in Orlando was an exciting diversion from the dreariness of working life as well as a mobilising force. Through soccer, people created a social institution that instilled civic pride and forged community bonds. Between the founding of the team in 1937 and the first years of the apartheid era, the Orlando Pirates climbed out of the anonymity of the lowest Witwatersrand amateur leagues. While Pirates became synonymous with Orlando because of the residents' love for soccer, the links between football team and township generated parochial loyalties, self-identification, and pride. Gradually, Orlando Pirates evolved into one of the country's most popular and successful soccer clubs. This early history of Pirates opens a window through which to observe the changes taking place in South African soccer and the game's impact on African urban life just prior to and during the early years of apartheid.

FROM ORLANDO BOYS' CLUB TO PIRATES

A group of schoolboys founded Pirates Football Club in 1937 at the Leake Hall Boys' Club in Orlando.[4] The Orlando Boys' Club was part of a large network of Boys' and Girls' Clubs that white liberals and missionaries established on the Reef in the late 1930s to serve unemployed and out-of-school black youths.[5] The team's founders were mostly students of relatively privileged working-class African families who had migrated to Johannesburg after the South African War, leaving white farms in the Transvaal, Natal, and Orange Free State, and had subsequently been moved to Orlando.[6]

The boys participated in indoor sports such as draughts, table tennis, weightlifting, and boxing. Among the first teenagers to use the Leake Hall facility were Sam Shabangu, Isaac Mothei, and Reggie Nkosi. 'We had everything there, except football,' said Sam Shabangu in an interview with Richard Maguire, 'so we thought to ourselves, why don't we have a football team of our own? We came to an agreement and formed a team, it was 1937 . . . it wasn't called Orlando Pirates then. It was called Orlando Boys' Club.' Many members of the Boys' Club team met during inter-school soccer competitions or during lunch-break matches played with a tennis ball on the dirt playgrounds of mission schools such as St Mary's, Methodist, and Dutch Reformed.[7]

The young footballers left the Boys' Club in 1938 as a result of a dispute with Philip Mashego, a social worker whom the students suspected of stealing funds intended for the purchase of the team's first uniforms. In the words of surviving founders, 'he ate the club's money'.[8] So, in 1939 the team held a meeting at the home of player-coach Andries 'Pelepele' ('hot like peppers') Mkwanazi to settle on a new name. Goalkeeper Reggie 'Hasie' Nkosi suggested renaming the club 'Pirates', perhaps after having watched the film *Sea Hawk* (starring Errol Flynn).[9] After a lengthy discussion, members unanimously decided to call the team Orlando Pirates Football Club.[10]

The club competed in the JBFA Wednesday League, a competition for secondary schools that had started in 1936 and had grown to 88 teams by 1939.[11] After winning the school league, the club moved up to the JBFA Saturday League and earned promotion to the JBFA's division sponsored by Stewarts Lloyds – a local, white-owned business – in 1940. This division often played its fixtures on Sundays, the only day off for thousands of black workers, so Pirates occasionally performed before bigger crowds. The rising attendance at black soccer matches in Johannesburg, Durban, and Cape Town during this period stemmed primarily from the dramatic increase in the number of Africans migrating to cities to find work in the war-driven manufacturing expansion of the 1940s.[12]

The Orlando youngsters' collective will and sense of purpose enabled them to overcome material hardships, enjoy their soccer, and 'succeed' against all odds. The team had problems reaching the grounds in time for matches scheduled far away from the southwestern township. Depending on their financial situation, Pirates travelled by train, tram, four-to-one bicycle, even on foot, from Orlando to the Waterval Ground near Sophiatown, a round-trip of some 40 kilometres. In addition to the extra time and cost of transportation, many of the first Pirates played barefoot because they could not afford appropriate soccer shoes.[13] Unperturbed, they turned this apparent disadvantage into an asset. 'We knew what the disadvantage [was] if we played barefooted and how to avoid somebody with boots,' recalled Shabangu, the team's goal-scoring centre-forward, in his interview with Maguire: 'you don't have to collide with him. Let him chase the ball, before he gets close . . . I dish my ball off. That's what taught us good football!' This resilience illustrates how the material conditions of their lives directly affected the way in which these Africans played soccer and how, in turn, these structural constraints influenced the development of a particular style of play. Despite such difficult circumstances Pirates won the 1940 title in the Stewarts Lloyds division.[14] The following year they were promoted to the Union College division where they placed a respectable fourth.[15]

The indefatigable Mkwanazi guided Pirates' ascent through the ranks of the Rand amateur leagues. A successful boxing instructor and former boxer linked to prize fighters such as Jake Ntuli (British Empire flyweight champion in 1951), Mkwanazi toured Orlando's schools to discover young talent. He recruited Jimmy 'Hitler' Sobi for the first Pirates reserve side of 1940. Sobi said: 'We were all from school in Orlando – I was from Dutch Reformed. Mkwanazi was working night shift, but on his way to work in the afternoon he would watch the schools play and choose [players] for the second division. We were determined to be in the first team but we never got frustrated. Football was so nice – it was exciting.'[16] Shabangu elaborated: thanks to Mkwanazi's commitment and thorough understanding of the game '[t]he schools were raided and there we uncovered the nucleus of what I still think was the best football combination. We got fellows like Elliott "Buick" Buthelezi, Alex "Motto" Tshabalala, James "Hitler" Sobi, and Israel "Dingaan" Ramela.'[17] Rankus Maphisa, a supporter since the founding of Pirates, summed up the general consensus that 'Mkwanazi is the man who made us to be what we are'.[18]

Friends and families of Pirates complemented Mkwanazi's relentless work with their own efforts and exemplified the indissolubly intertwined destinies of Pirates and the Orlando community. The club's requirement that members or their parents be from Orlando, a constitutional policy by the 1940s, fostered township chauvinism. Parents encouraged their sons to join Pirates. They paid for their equipment and yearly fees of 1s.6d. out of meagre family monthly wages that, on the Reef in 1950, averaged £12.6s.6d., according to the South African Institute of Race Relations.[19] When opposing soccer clubs tried to lure a player away from Pirates, fathers dissuaded their sons from betraying the township club.[20] Many residents of Orlando supported Pirates because they believed that football was a means to develop self-respect and civic-mindedness among the youth – a healthy alternative to joining the *tsotsis* (urban toughs, street criminals) in township streets.[21]

Civic involvement with the soccer team seemed to have kept the young players out of trouble. In the words of Rankus Maphisa in his interview with Maguire: 'We Pirates were not very wild. We were never arrested or anything like that.'

Willard 'Ndoda' Msomi, whose nickname was based on that of an axe-wielding killer of the time, illustrated how links between Pirates and the Orlando community translated into an asset for the recruitment of new members. Msomi said: 'When I was recruited into Orlando Pirates it was because of the influence of his [Elliott Buthelezi's] brother, Ace, who was my friend, and Motto [Tshabalala] was my cousin.' Msomi went on to say that:

> Pelepele was always there, always there . . . just to come and see us playing in primary schools. So at one time he wanted to know where I lived. I said, 'in Orlando.' Then he wanted the address; Ace came to me and got the address and handed it over to Pelepele. The next thing I saw Pelepele walking in at home. They knew each other, with my father that is. Now, during that time, parents knew each other in Orlando so you couldn't do monkey business, really you couldn't! So the next day my old man called me and said: 'As from today, this man [Pelepele] is going to be in charge.' I didn't just understand; then he said I must join the other boys [at Pirates].[22]

Pirates's patriarch Andries 'Pelepele' Mkwanazi was a key figure in promoting and strengthening family and community ties through the ambitious team, but it was Bethuel Mokgosinyane who transformed Pirates into a symbol of Orlando.[23]

BONDS OF BROTHERHOOD AND THE 'PRAY-AND-PLAY' ETHOS
Bethuel Mokgosinyane believed that Pirates should not only play superb soccer, but should also serve the community.[24] A carpenter by trade, Mokgosinyane lived in Orlando and worked as an *induna* (foreman or supervisor) at a furniture factory in the Johannesburg area. He was a firm supporter of Mkwanazi's policy of restricting membership of the club to Orlando residents and their sons. Neither wealthy nor educated, Mokgosinyane had grown up in Brits, a town about 48 kilometres north of Johannesburg. When he migrated to Johannesburg in search of work he became an enthusiastic footballer and joined the Puur Vuur (Afrikaans for 'Pure Fire') team. According to Elliott Buthelezi, Shabangu, and Jimmy Sobi, Mokgosinyane became Pirates's most dedicated supporter during their first season in the Stewarts Lloyds division. After seeing the scrappy Orlando youngsters holding their own against more experienced sides on the hard, dusty fields of Western Native Township, Sophiatown, and Wemmer, Mokgosinyane took the Pirates under his wing, becoming the club's first patron manager in 1940.[25]

The players named Mokgosinyane president of the club, and he began a life-long mission to link club and township into one indissoluble entity. His first major change was his donation of his former team's black jerseys and white shorts to Pirates. Black and white thus became the official team colours. Conveniently, the first set of uniforms came emblazoned with a 'P' (from Puur Vuur) for Pirates on the chest![26]

Mokgosinyane imbued Orlando Pirates with a 'pray-and-play' ethos. A devout Christian and self-styled social worker, the president once quipped that 'were it not for football, I would have been a priest'.[27] His former protégés thought back to when '[Mokgosinyane] used to say to people: "Pray and play: football is the sport . . . if you let your child play, you will save him from trouble." He encouraged good habits . . . [we] who played under his supervision know what is right or wrong.'[28] Described by people who knew him as 'naturally clever', 'ambitious', with 'that goodwill to help people', the president envisioned Pirates as a sports club to keep Orlando youth out of trouble – a bridge to healthy community relations.[29] Soccer was Mokgosinyane's religion. Team meetings at his Orlando East home opened and closed with a prayer – a ritual that symbolised the centrality of the pray-and-play ethos and helped to entrench it into the day-to-day affairs of the club.[30]

Mokgosinyane fostered Pirates's image as a benevolent institution by making the club into a burial society. Evidence of this fascinating aspect of Pirates history survived in the pages of club minute books filled with records of 'death collections'. These monetary contributions helped to cover funeral costs incurred by members and their extended families. Inquiries about relatives' deaths were a standard item on the agenda of club meetings. When such cases occurred, the person(s) in question revealed when and where the funeral would take place, when the money was needed, and to whom it could be delivered. Contributions varied according to the class background and age of individuals, but averaged a half-crown (2s.6d.) during the period under examination. The customary practice was to send a letter of condolence to the family of the deceased along with the cash collected. A draft copy of a mournful missive survived in the minutes:

From the Committee of Pirates Football Club
To the Parents of Alex Tshabalala
Orlando Township, 16 June '45

Dear Parents,

We have regret in having heard that our fellow player has lost one of his relatives. So the committee decided to finance him with a few shillings which we have raised and thought of it, to be of great help to the family.

Your children in regret and in sorrow.
Secretary Bennett Mpshe
Captain Isaac Senoa
Vice Captain Isaac Mothei
In Anticipation for Pirates Football Club,
President B. Mokgosinyane.[31]

In the case of a member's death the club undertook an extraordinary financial responsibility by paying for the entire funeral. According to Pirates's minute books, when a member named Eddie Madlala passed away in 1947 'money was taken out of our subscription to aid this funeral. He [Mokgosinyane] bought all the necessities including food and other things . . . then the President told us that he had borrowed £10 from his employer to meet the occasion. Later it was cancelled to £5 to be paid by the President to the employer. The President asked the club to nominate a delegation that would go with him to the home of our late loyal member.'[32] The carefully recorded entries indicate that 30 individual donations from playing and non-playing members contributed £7.19s.6d. to Madlala's burial costs. To this money Mokgosinyane added the £5 loaned to him by his employer so that Pirates raised virtually all of the £13.2s. needed to cover the costs of their comrade's funeral.[33]

The burial society was the foremost example of Pirates's social awareness and civic responsibility. It cemented the community of interests of sporting club and township society.[34] It is important to note that while the fundamental importance of Bethuel Mokgosinyane to the history of Orlando Pirates cannot be overstated, there can be little doubt that his civil religion of sport would have produced few results without the full commitment and agreement of the players themselves.

The establishment of a players' fund highlighted the centrality of solidarity and reciprocity to the club's existence. The 'insurance scheme', as the minutes referred to it, functioned as a workers' compensation fund 'so that when one is in trouble he can quickly be helped'.[35] Members paid 1s. monthly so that fellow athletes could recover lost wages that resulted from work missed due to injuries suffered on the football pitch.[36] This internal co-operation coupled with the organisation of, and participation in, township social events such as weddings and goat slaughters rekindled relationships and fostered community spirit.

The values of friendship, trust, and mutuality served as resources for conflict resolution. In one particular meeting, a heated discussion arose over the partial failure of a recent 'death collection'. The vice-chairman resolved the argument by appealing to 'brotherhood and quoted instances and explained the meaning of brotherhood'.[37] The following week the missing gifts were paid. This kind of mutual understanding stemmed from having founded the club together, and having shared experiences as neighbourhood friends (and relatives) in a new black working-class quarter speaking the same languages – mostly Zulu and Sotho.

This common background facilitated the creation of a sense of unity and purpose that, among other things, made them a more effective and durable soccer team. 'We had love for each other . . . [it was] more than just football,' Shabangu said in his interview with Maguire. Such romanticised memories emerged as a constant theme in oral history interviews with former players. The elderly men enjoyed remembering their youthful days of athletic prowess, vigour, and popularity. Despite segregation and apartheid there was a nostalgic longing for the 'good old days'. As oral historian Sean Field has pointed out, these interpretations of the past are not trivial and should not be dismissed cynically because such reconstructed memories help 'people live their lives in difficult times . . . and serve the vital function of enhancing and defending an ageing self'.[38]

Moreover, the club minutes documented how solidarity and reciprocity, both in ritual and everyday forms, governed the early Pirates's *modus operandi*. A ritual process of initiation soldered the bonds of brotherhood. The team developed an informal rite of passage that inculcated the 'proper way of doing things'. The initiation process began with an applicant writing a letter asking for admission. The person might then be invited to the mid-week club meeting at Mokgosinyane's home. At this time, the prospective member was introduced to the assembly and asked to explain first his ties to Orlando and then his worker or student status to determine the appropriate joining fees and annual dues. Finally, an executive official read the laws of the club to the neophyte, a practice that resembled the taking of an oath of loyalty or, perhaps, religious vows.[39]

Access to wage employment fortified loyalty to the club. Theo Mthembu, a leading sport reporter in the contemporary black press, said that playing for Pirates 'really helped a lot to get a job'.[40] Rankus Maphisa agreed with Mthembu's assessment, adding that: 'Mokgosinyane and Pelepele used to find a player a job and if he didn't have to work they would pay out of their pockets. Our unity came like that . . . we used to share everything accordingly.'[41] A combination of material, ritual, and social factors contributed to individuals' self-esteem and camaraderie, and to the team's overall success. Orlando Pirates Football Club provided a 'means of integration and fellowship' in the township – a social and economic safety net at a time of great political uncertainty and material insecurity.[42]

The bonds of brotherhood and the pray-and-play ethos distinguished Pirates from their Soweto rivals: Orlando Bush Rangers, Orlando Brothers, Kliptown Rangers, and Pimville Champions. These local clubs, unlike Pirates, faded away when the founding generation aged, married, or moved to new jobs and places.[43] This fundamental difference led Richard Maguire to make the insightful conclusion that the historical significance of the Pirates 'is that they – among hundreds of clubs that sprouted in the rapidly industrialising Witwatersrand of the late 1930s and 40s – were one of the few clubs to . . . become an institution and a symbol, not just for a street or a patch of territory but for an entire community – and thousands more'.[44] According to Maguire, 'while many clubs were "people's clubs" in their beginnings and in their rootedness, none of them developed along these lines to the extent that Pirates did'.[45]

Mokgosinyane's vision of a community soccer club had contributed to the development of a popular social phenomenon in Orlando. As Pirates ascended the JBFA ranks during the early 1940s, most players abandoned their schooling because their parents could not afford the costs of education.[46] According to sociologist Ellen Hellmann, one-third of African youth in the Johannesburg area left school due to financial hardship during this period.[47] In other words, the relatively privileged working-class members of Orlando Pirates shared similar concrete constraints as their poorer neighbours. Be that as it may, in 1944 Pirates won the First division league title and finally qualified for the Championship division. Later that year, Pirates defeated traditional powerhouses Mighty Greens and Naughty Boys to advance to the final of the 1944–45 senior knock-out Cup, a tournament that featured the Rand's top amateur sides.[48] A dramatic final encounter against Sophiatown's African Morning Stars at Wemmer Sports Ground early in 1945 became the most critical match in the history of Pirates: 'that was the match that brought us in a larger light' declared Sam Shabangu.[49]

PIRATES'S PLAYING STYLE

Both interviews and written documents agree that 'the match that "made" Pirates was the 1945 game at Wemmer sports ground against their arch-rivals for years to come, African Morning Stars'.[50] Pirates appeared set to take their game and fame to unprecedented heights when they clashed with African Morning Stars in the JBFA knock-out Cup final that summer. There was extra anticipation among soccer fans on the Reef for this match because the two teams had claimed titles in the JBFA's top two divisions at the end of the 1944 season. The winner would earn the unofficial title of Witwatersrand and, by extension, Transvaal champion. A large Sunday crowd travelled to the Wemmer Sports Ground, and witnessed a hard-fought, goalless draw. As a result, Pirates and Morning Stars faced each other in a replay the following Sunday. Pirates won the dramatic replay by two goals to one – heralding the club's entrance into the Rand's footballing elite.

There was no time for celebration on the pitch, however, because as soon as the final whistle blew the Sophiatown team assaulted the winners. At the time, African Morning Stars included several members of the Americans, one of the most famous gangs in Sophiatown. Led by a man known as 'Booitjie American', the gang's main activity was robbing freight trains. 'The Americans were flashy: they were smart dressers, they were reputed to go out with the prettiest girls, and some of them even drove round in large expensive, imported cars.'[51] Morning Stars players and fans saw the Orlando lads as 'unsophisticated', calling them *kalkoens* (Afrikaans for 'turkeys') because of the fast Zulu slang spoken in Orlando.[52] At Wemmer that afternoon, Mkwanazi and Lucas Buthelezi – a centre-forward who had just been called up from the second team – suffered severe beatings while Shabangu and the rest of the Orlando players ran for their lives. 'I remember them chasing us around Park Station,' said Elliott Buthelezi, Lucas's brother; Shabangu laughed as he recalled running 'the fastest race of my life' to the train station, where he hid in the whites-only toilets.[53] After the Morning Stars brawl, Mkwanazi – who retired from active football that year – helped the young Pirates to avoid future physical abuse by training them in boxing and weightlifting at Mokgosinyane's place.

This new emphasis on fitness training became part of an innovative way of playing. Pirates's style differed sharply from the colonial 'kick-and-rush' approach still dominant in South Africa in the 1940s, which featured unimaginative direct play mainly through long aerial passes to the forwards. Instead, Pirates adopted a heterogeneous system that borrowed from both the short-passing, positional 'Motherwell' style and the crowd-pleasing, individual ball control of *marabi* examined in Chapter 5 in the context of Johannesburg in the 1930s. In addition, a relatively unchanging first team during the 1937–53 period encouraged the articulation of a more systematic approach to playing.[54]

Pirates's mode of play was forged at every club meeting at Mokgosinyane's home in Orlando East. A salient feature of these Wednesday-night gatherings was a collective analysis and discussion of the previous match followed by tactical preparation for the forthcoming game. Buthelezi appreciated Mokgosinyane's technical expertise: 'At his house we used to sit in there and have this thing like team talks . . . he would advise us, and he would tell us "why did you take this ball and go that way instead of cutting?" . . . he was a real good man.'[55] The president introduced chalkboards for tactical explanations. The minutes of a typical meeting during the period under examination reported that:

> [d]uring the general discussion the systems boards were taken out for explanation and the vice-manager also revealed mistakes he noticed from players in the last Sunday match. His facts on this point were aided by players and the president. This was found to be very interesting and the chairman requested that we attend the meeting on time on Sunday to allow this to be discussed furthermore.'[56]

In other words, Pirates's playing style was a product of extensive practice and collective introspection – a delicate balance of athletic craftsmanship, physical toughness, and analytical skill.

During the 1940s and into the early 50s very few South African teams spent as much time as Pirates discussing tactics and ways of playing. In their role as 'organic intellectuals' of the game, Mokgosinyane and Mkwanazi encouraged players to think about their individual movements on the pitch and inculcated discipline and purpose into their play. Shabangu gave a specific example:

> he [Mokgosinyane] could study the game and he could study the player . . . if you're taking the wrong direction, even if that ball worked with your direction, he would still ask you 'why? what was the purpose of you taking the ball in this direction?' You got to tell him why; if you can't, then he'd tell you . . . 'you should've taken this ball in this direction to attract somebody to follow you and then send it back to the direction [where] there's somebody waiting.'[57]

Opponents learnt from Pirates, thus causing a 'boomerang effect' that stiffened competition for the Orlando team.[58]

Pirates's style was as exciting as it was methodical. In the words of a former member: 'we played to a system but we could switch play and use various formations.'[59] Pirates were the only African team of the period reported to shift formations during a match.[60] Contemporary observers noted how Jimmy Sobi, the team's tall, burly centre-half who earned the nickname 'Hitler' for his aggressive play, retreated from midfield into defence to assume the third back or 'stopper' position (the trademark of the man-to-man marking WM system) while the two fullbacks moved out wide to cover the opposing wings.[61] Tactical diagrams found in the minute books provide corroborating evidence of the team's adoption of both the WM and the 2-3-5 pyramid. Players described their system as 'trap and push, trap and push, that was our way'.[62] What separated Pirates's play from all other African sides at the time was an effective combination of tactical acumen, technical flair, and resolute defence. What Pirates shared with their opponents was the performance of pre-game rituals – an established practice in African soccer's cultural landscape.

The night before a game the Pirates slept at Mokgosinyane's home in Orlando East.[63] According to participants, a secret ritual with rural origins took place in the backyard shack. Mokgosinyane

> would take a glowing coal and put it on the ground . . . and he would put a ball of some fatty substance on the coal. It made smoke so that you couldn't see the person next to you, only by feeling his shoulder would you know he was there. But as soon as he strikes a match and puts it on the coal – by the wink of an eye the smoke would vanish. We had to jump that flame on the way out and all the way to the match we wouldn't speak to anyone. We would sit on one part of the train . . . a few supporters traveled with us but we would just nod our heads in acknowledgment if someone greets us.[64]

At the grounds the Orlando Pirates did not just entertain, they performed for the crowds. Mike Tseka watched them as a youngster in the 1940s and joined the club in 1952.[65] He described the style of Pirates as 'unique . . . . They advanced as a team in a V and when they retreated into defense, it was rhythmical, a musical kind of thing. So it was most exciting for people watching.'[66] Spectators like Peter Mngomezulu found Pirates's imaginative style irresistible and became devoted fans: 'With Pirates it was a different machinery altogether; they could change anytime, accelerate anytime, kill the ball anytime.'[67] 'Back then,' Shabangu pointed out with evident satisfaction, 'we were not getting paid through football, it was just a pleasure. With us it was not winning that was important, but how the goals were scored. We would play to win by all means, but win with style, with pleasure.'[68]

A QUEST FOR AUTONOMY AND SPACE
Pirates became black football's trailblazers. The club's sporting achievements and rising popular fame stimulated the formation of an independent association based in the southwestern townships. In 1946 Pirates abandoned the JBFA, a dramatic move caused by the city association's indifference to Mokgosinyane's formal protests against the aggressive conduct of African Morning Stars towards Pirates. This

official passivity reinforced Pirates' perception of JBFA favouritism towards Morning Stars. This charge had some validity. Many JBFA directors lived in Sophiatown – the home of Morning Stars – a crucial fact given the centrality of parochial networks to African football during this period. The presence of Anglican minister Father Trevor Huddleston as 'patron' of the JBFA corroborated the existence of profound connections between Sophiatown and the JBFA.[69]

The exodus from the JBFA had two major consequences for Pirates. Firstly, the team turned to a series of barnstorming ('freelancing') matches, which provided competition and revenue – usually a 50 per cent share of the gate-takings went to the club's treasury. These enterprising games had a contradictory effect: they enhanced Pirates's reputation throughout the Transvaal and in major urban centres such as Bloemfontein and Kimberley, but they also hindered the team's technical progress owing to the lack of regular league engagements.

The second, more important, consequence of leaving the JBFA was that Pirates, emboldened by their sporting triumphs and rising status, assumed a vanguard role in trying to wrestle control of local soccer in the southwestern townships away from the city-based JBFA. With this goal in mind, Pirates formed an Orlando association and an Orlando Sports Board of Control.

Pirates and its Orlando supporters asserted local residents' right to autonomous leisure. After a short-lived return to the JBFA, the Pirates executive and E.P. Ngoqo (a dissident JBFA official who lived in Orlando) founded the Orlando Divisional Bantu Football Association in September 1947. In January 1948 the association applied for official recognition to the Non-European Affairs Department (NEAD). The organisers cited civic pride and financial and transport difficulties as their principal motivating factors for secession from the JBFA. The Orlando group argued that the community's sporting interests would be better served by local administrators rather than by JBFA elites based in the distant western areas of Johannesburg. To support their plea, the Orlando men highlighted the decrease in affiliations to the JBFA by football clubs from the peripheral townships, attributing the cause to the cost of weekly transport – £1.5s., or £27.10s. for a 22-week regular season – a prohibitive amount for African athletes and fans earning meagre wages.[70]

The formation of the independent association enjoyed popular support in Orlando. In his official correspondence with the NEAD manager, L.I. Venables, Recreation Officer J. Graham Young observed that 'the ODBFA has persuaded some of the Orlando teams to break away and join a new league' and added that 'I foresee nothing but trouble if this is permitted.'[71] The NEAD found a compromise solution that denied the Orlando association official recognition but granted it temporary use of the open ground behind Leake Hall at the Donaldson Orlando Community Centre (DOCC).[72] Having scored a partial victory by working the cracks of an oppressive system to their advantage, Pirates returned as well-known champions to the bumpy pitch where they had first played as young barefooted footballers a decade earlier.

During these difficult times, divisions surfaced within the club. Unsurprisingly, the players, many of whom had risen to heroic status in Rand townships, were not supportive of the club's departure from the JBFA, criticising the poor quality of the opposition in Orlando. But the executive downplayed these grievances arguing that 'we should not worry about that state of affairs because this association we build for our children and younger brothers. We should keep courage and spirit . . . fight like soldiers . . . as the formation of this association is not for us but for the younger ones to follow.'[73] In the struggle to assert local control over soccer and to obtain playing fields, Mokgosinyane enlisted the help of squatter leader James Mpanza.

Mpanza's link with Pirates was extremely significant because he was known as the 'King of Orlando'. In 1944–46 he had taken over responsibility from the city council for more than 4 000 people and built a shantytown of hessian sacks in Orlando West – Masakeng (the place of sacks) – for homeless families and discontented traders.[74]

The identification of Mpanza with Pirates is an early illustration of a broader change in the post-war relationship between black sport and society. Local powerbrokers, often men with past playing experience, frequently found township football clubs an ideal vehicle through which to accumulate personal prestige and social visibility. As the game became increasingly central to African popular entertainment in the 1940s, some educated and modestly priviliged African men who had dominated the administrative ranks of urban associations in the segregation era transformed themselves into patrons of clubs. In this way, patron-managers ingratiated themselves with neighbourhood people, attracted customers to their businesses (usually shebeens and general stores), and forged local networks that boosted their power and influence in township communities.[75] Football teams benefited from having patrons like Mpanza and vice versa. As Mike Tseka, a former member of Pirates explained: 'when Sofasonke got involved a lot of people followed. This is one reason for the pride in the club.'[76]

A former footballer at Adams College in Durban, Mpanza combined a passion for the game with populist objectives in an attempt to link himself with Pirates. He attended matches in the township and occasionally gave speeches at Pirates' social events.[77] Mpanza's defiant occupation of municipal land in Orlando West paralleled Pirates's establishment of the Orlando association against the will of the NEAD. When the association put hessian sacks around the DOCC field to charge admission for its matches, the symbolic connection between Pirates and Mpanza was unmistakable.[78] As a result of his relationship with Pirates, the squatter leader and Orlando's revered soccer team came to share the same *izibongo* (praises): *Izinyama ngenkani ezikaMagebula ezagebula umhlaba kaMaspala*, which means 'the forceful black ones of Mpanza who usurped part of the Johannesburg municipal ground'.[79]

Encouraged by growing popular support, the Orlando association launched a bid to become the controlling body in the southwestern townships.[80] It changed its name to Johannesburg Municipal Townships Football Association (JMTFA).

Pirates men were highly influential in the JMTFA: Mokgosinyane was its chairman and Bennett Mpshe filled one of the three remaining executive positions. Mpanza bolstered Orlando's vanguard role by serving as the JMTFA's 'honorable patron'.[81] After a full season of competition in 1948 on the lone DOCC field, the JMTFA requested that the municipality 'release all grounds in Orlando' for the use of its twenty affiliated teams. But the local authorities, unwilling to relinquish white oversight of African football in the area, refused.[82] Despite this setback, the resilient directors of Pirates and Mpanza continued their activities on behalf of the Soweto association. They attended several meetings with the NEAD and African sport officials that discussed proposals for a Johannesburg Sports Board of Control, as well as a possible merger of the JBFA and the JAFA.[83]

In these and other discussions with local government officials, Mpanza had brought his experience and determination in dealing with the white authorities to bear on the struggle for autonomous leisure in the southwestern townships. Mpanza demanded football pitches for 'his children and his people' and made stinging references to the JBFA strongholds of Sophiatown, Newclare, Martindale, and Western Native Township, claiming that: 'I've never gone to Western to take those children's grounds.'[84] Such statements influenced the city council's flawed view of Mpanza's actual role in township football: 'Mpanza seems to have widened his claims which were originally on behalf of the people of Orlando, for more fields under the control of local residents . . . includ[ing] Moroka, Jabavu, and Pimville.'[85] The populist leader did not challenge the authorities' overestimation of his position, probably because he found this convenient in that it enhanced his elevated status and self-presentation as a community leader. Be that as it may, the shocking structural deficiencies affecting African soccer, and sport in general, defied easy solution. As the apartheid era began, the structural deficiency affecting African sport continued to shape the struggle for autonomy and leisure space in fundamental ways.

A survey of African football grounds in Johannesburg in 1946 concluded that a total of 30 'insufficiently equipped' fields for an official population of 370 972 was vastly inadequate.[86] The two main football associations were forced to play as many as 324 matches per ground during the season. One of the immediate effects was the shortening of matches to 60 minutes.[87] Acutely aware of the extreme pressure on African facilities and the potential disorder that might result from it, the white authorities opposed the formation of the Orlando Sports Board of Control (OSBC) in 1949. The township's white superintendent warned that the issue of playing space was 'so serious that bloodshed can be expected in Orlando any weekend if the question is not amicably settled very soon'.[88] But there was no violence.

Instead, the ambitious Board of Control, under the guidance of Eban Gwambe, a Mozambican immigrant, NEAD clerk, and a prominent official of Pirates, planned to build a stadium for Pirates in Orlando.[89] According to one informed view, Gwambe 'was an early example of a man of some substance or prominence who attached himself to the club more with an eye on personal benefits than with the intention to improve the club'.[90] Even so, Gwambe and the Board of Control went to sympathetic white individuals and organisations to garner support for the Orlando Stadium.[91] Unfortunately, the potential loss of control trumped any concerns about the dire need for sporting infrastructure in African communities, and so the NEAD blocked the project – officially owing to a shortage of funds.[92] The archival evidence shows that the NEAD had consistently opposed the Board of Control from its inception, intepreting it as a threat to the *status quo* and a challenge to the entrenched authority of the more malleable JBFA.[93] The municipality's obdurate opposition notwithstanding, the House of Pirates persevered in building the association and fighting for sport space and local control.

THE MOVE TO JAFA'S BANTU SPORTS CLUB

The difficult circumstances in which Pirates found themselves required a solution if the club was to continue as a powerful force in Johannesburg football. Most important, frustration and discontent spread among the first team players. While these young men understood fully the executive's motivations for striving to secure autonomous control over the game (and supported their stadium plans), the ethos of brotherhood and social concern seemed to have had limited appeal for footballers at the peak of their athletic careers. A gloomy air filled Mokgosinyane's home at a Pirates meeting held in April 1949:

> our members as a whole have lost the interest and the spirit of the club. The reckage [*sic*] is brought about by the newly formed association . . . the play of the club has deteriorated on account of one thing and that is they do not get good practice and there is no club to play hard against. The result of this is that our club will die.[94]

The players' general feeling was that it was 'heartbreaking to see the club having lost its standard of play' and that 'they should better go and join other clubs to play in another association where they will play proper soccer'. The directors and older supporters disagreed: 'Pirates members who claim that they want to join other clubs in other Associations to have better play are ignorant of what name they have got and fame is in them . . . . We are not aware of the fact that we are sitting on top of gold.'[95] On the contrary, players were all too aware of the wealth of opportunities they were missing. A week later, two leading Pirates accepted money from an opposing club to play a match.[96] This episode provides rare documentation of the well-known infiltration of illegal money into the black amateur game. The willingness of some players to abscond to play 'proper soccer' highlighted the different priorities of athletes *vis-à-vis* non-playing members and the limited appeal of Mokgosinyane's moral economy of football.[97]

The staging of a series of attractive challenge matches temporarily pacified these acerbic conflicts. In the process, Mokgosinyane hatched an unusual public relations plan to revive interest and lift the spirits of the club. He proposed advertising matches in the black press and printing a club sheet with an official team photograph to be sent out to prospective challengers.[98] Throughout these difficult times, the team's thirst for competition was such that 'the house roared with enjoyment' at the announcement of a game against the Orange Free State Coloureds in Bloemfontein.[99] Here it should be noted that Pirates, like many other African teams, often staged unofficial matches against Indian and Coloured teams during the 1940s – a trend that had started with the Inter-Race Board games of the 1930s.

Bailey's African History Archive

Orlando Pirates team (early 1950s).

Where Pirates went, it seemed, African football followed. With the side floundering through another dull JMTFA season, Pirates took a momentous decision and affiliated the glamourous first team with the Johannesburg African Football Association (JAFA). At the directors' insistence, both the second team (later renamed the 'Sea Robbers') and the third team remained in the Orlando association in order 'to prepare the future of our younger ones and pave their way'.[100] The affiliation of Pirates to JAFA had a revealing effect on football in the southwestern townships. By 1951 nineteen clubs from Orlando, including three from Mpanza's squatter camp, and fourteen clubs from Pimville, Moroka, Jabavu, and Kliptown had followed suit and become members of the JAFA.[101]

At JAFA's Bantu Sports Club, Orlando Pirates reached the pinnacle of their success as amateurs. From November 1949 to March 1950 Pirates dominated the JAFA Summer League, winning sixteen matches, drawing two, and losing a single game to Crocodiles, another defector from the JBFA.[102] JAFA's aversion to Pirates's 'touring all the time' kept the squad out of the JAFA regular season until 1951, when the Orlando side curtailed their relatively lucrative challenge match schedule.[103] Player-manager Isaac 'Rocks of London' Mothei was elected to the JAFA's executive committee, thus giving the club a powerful voice among the 122 teams in JAFA.[104] Pirates enjoyed playing at the Bantu Sports Club. It was a superior facility compared to the barren, bumpy Wemmer sports ground, even more so after the city council in 1948 turned this field – one of only two enclosed facilities for African soccer in Johannesburg – into a car park during the work-week.[105] Instead, the Bantu Sports Club, sold by its trustees to the municipality in 1950 on the condition that it remain a facility for African sport, boasted a levelled pitch, a grandstand, and grass embankments for spectators. The entertainment provided by Dan Twala's play-by-play commentary over the public address system added to the ground's mystique and attractiveness. Since Championship division matches always took place on Sundays, when most African men and women had their only day off from work, Pirates performed in front of larger crowds representing a broad range of the Rand's black population that was willing 'to pay their last shillings to see the game'.[106]

The Bantu Sports Club stage elevated Orlando Pirates to new heights of popularity. Between 1950 and 1953, Pirates enjoyed stunning success as they won the JAFA championships, the Robor Shield, the Transvaal Challenge Cup (twice), and four consecutive SA Robertson Cups – including an enthralling 3-2 win in the 1950 final over arch-rivals African Morning Stars before more than 10 000 spectators at the Bantu Sports Club.[107]

Such spellbinding performances earned Pirates the admiration of the black press. In April 1953 *Drum* magazine's sports editor Dan Chocho authored a three-page feature claiming that 'Orlando's Pirates are South Africa's Ace Club'. When *African Sports*, the first (but short-lived) publication aimed at the African public, hit the streets in 1953, Orlando Pirates were commonly described as 'crowd favorites', and their bearded, goal-scoring forward Sam 'Baboon Shepherd' Shabangu described as the 'idol of soccer crowds'.[108] By this time, groups of male migrant workers from Natal housed in municipal hostels located near the Bantu Sports Club also supported Pirates, an acknowledgment of their appreciation for entertaining football – itself a symbolic marker of the urban experience. Hostel-dwellers maintained a dual allegiance to town and countryside as they continued to support teams representing their home districts such as Newcastle Home Lads, Estcourt Try Agains, Ladysmith Cannons, Natal Rainbows, and Natal All Blacks.[109]

Representative matches further popularised Pirates. Shabangu, Mothei, Sobi, and several others appeared regularly for Transvaal province in the Moroka-Baloyi Cup – the highlight of the annual African soccer calendar. A record six Pirates took to the field for national champions Western Transvaal in 1953.[110] Pirates men also represented Johannesburg and South Africa 'Africans' against teams from Basutoland (today Lesotho), Mozambique, Southern Rhodesia (today Zimbabwe), and Northern Rhodesia (today Zambia) in extremely popular inter-colonial competitions.[111] On the Rand, international matches that attracted thousands of southern African migrant workers to the grounds in support of their 'national' teams helped to spread the name of Orlando Pirates throughout southern and central Africa.

There were three major consequences to the upsurge in the visibility, popularity, and influence of Orlando Pirates by the early 1950s. Firstly, Pirates fuelled increased participation in organised soccer. The club's three divisions in 1952 (a fourth side appeared in the mid-to-late 1950s) and the seventeen teams affiliated with the JMTFA in 1949 provided indisputable evidence of the growing demand for soccer in Orlando alone. Secondly, the creation of the Orlando association indicated Africans' determination to assert local control over the game against the will of the JBFA and the NEAD. The third consequence of the team's fame, reputation, and institution-building drive is explored in more depth in the last section of this chapter: the gradual erosion in the House of Pirates of feelings of brotherhood, the pray-and-play mentality, and the social welfare ethos.

THE RISE OF MOROKA SWALLOWS

Absenteeism at mid-week meetings at Mokgosinyane's home was a prescient sign of a fraying founding ethos. From about 1950, poor attendance plagued the House of Pirates despite the president's repeated and emphatic appeals 'to the present men of the first eleven to attend the meetings'.[112] The team's expansion contributed to the gradual decline of the Pirates's moral economy of football. Lackadaisical participation in both the burial society and funerals suggested a diminishing interest in community service. Club minutes in 1951 termed a £1.3s.6d. collection a 'disgrace'.[113] Mokgosinyane pleaded with 'the club again to make that payment for the occasion of misfortune. The President greatly talked on the behaviour of *members of not working hand in hand as brothers and real friends* and should at least appear at such places [the deceased's home] on or before the funeral. He was very angry and brokenhearted when he said this' (emphasis added).[114] Problems also appeared on the field. During one fiery debate about team play, player-manager Isaac 'Rocks of London' Mothei noted how a clash of egos and negative criticism on the field had resulted in men 'playing with fear instead of joy'.[115]

Generational rifts gnawed at the bonds of brotherhood. Younger members, required to prove themselves in the lower divisions to be selected for the first team, questioned the prevailing *modus operandi* and the established ethos. Club minutes registered the youths' complaints at having to compete in the weaker association in Orlando (*vis-à-vis* the JAFA) and of not receiving any coaching, training, or tactical instruction from Mokgosinyane, Mothei, and the senior players.[116] On several occasions the juniors protested their marginality in club affairs though generally they kept a low profile, fearing that open criticism of the first eleven hindered future chances of promotion to the senior side.[117] At the same time, the older generation chided younger members' inability (or unwillingness) to recite prayers at meetings, deploring their 'disrespectful and ungentlemanlike behaviour' (including the use of obscene language) in the House.[118]

These internal tensions delineate how the development of South African football between the late 1930s and early 50s was intertwined with larger structural changes taking place in South African society as a whole. Philip Bonner has pointed out how the pattern of stabilisation that characterised settled Rand townships such as Orlando in the late 1940s and 50s exerted profound social effects on the black population.[119] Most relevant to this history of Pirates was the appearance of a conspicuous gap between first-generation residents who had migrated to Johannesburg from rural areas in their youth and second-generation Africans born and reared in the urban milieu. Among the younger fans of Pirates there were members of the Soweto youth gangs that were emerging at the time and for whom soccer was 'a particularly important point of connection; if there were a nearby soccer field that . . . would become a central gathering point'.[120] As in the more settled townships like Orlando, games between street teams in the shantytowns spawned 'neighborhood networks [that] developed a strong sense of local identity'.[121] In the Johannesburg metropolitan area, where violent crime rose 20 per cent between 1944 and 1949, football became an enjoyable part of the daily lives of youth residing in the burgeoning squatter camps.[122]

The team that challenged Pirates's dominance of Transvaal soccer rose from the sprawling slum of Moroka, where more than 30 000 people set up makeshift shanties on vacant land next to Jabavu township just west of Orlando in 1946–47. Moroka residents lived in cramped corrugated iron and cardboard shacks situated on tiny plots where 'the communal, bucket-system toilets overflowed with excrement, and water outlets were so scarce – and so far away – that fights regularly broke out in the queues'. One resident remembered the crime in stark terms: 'After 8 o'clock you can't go to the toilet because . . . the thugs will get you.'[123] Teenage boys who grew up in Alexandra and had moved with their families to the Moroka squatter camp founded a street club initially called Moroka Sweepers in 1947.[124]

A teenager named Jeremiah 'Ntsimbi' Gumede formed the team that would soon be known as Moroka Swallows out of concern for 'the welfare of his peers'.[125] The enterprising Gumede was the club's first secretary and treasurer while Philip Cele, an older man who lived on Gumede's street, was asked to be the president. Gumede, like his colleagues at Orlando Pirates, viewed the patronage and guidance of an elder as a basic necessity for an ambitious young soccer team. The teenagers from Moroka adopted the name Swallows late in 1947 when competing barefooted in the township league staged at the new Moroka/Jabavu ground.[126]

The squatters of Moroka and the Swallows soccer team shared a dominant, though not exclusive, Basotho ethnic and linguistic background that distinguished them from Pirates, who were not an ethnic side: 'we weren't all Zulu,' said Pirates's Elliott 'Buick' Buthelezi, 'but we grew up together and chose to speak Zulu.'[127] While Swallows expressed a strong ethnically defined identity, 'outsiders' did join the club. For example, Philip Cele was an older Zulu-speaking man, and in the early 1950s the line-up featured two Coloured players: winger Dennis Ford and goalkeeper 'Al Die Hoekies' Meyers. Ultimately, two main factors explain the

Basotho identity of Swallows. Firstly, Basotho immigrants made up a large majority of the squatters movements, including the one that converged at Moroka Emergency Camp.[128] Secondly, Abel Ntoi, leader of the Moroka community and one of the bosses of the MaRashea ('Russians') Basotho gang, was a prominent patron of Swallows.[129] The first match of the now-legendary Soweto soccer rivalry between Pirates and Swallows ended in surprising fashion when Ntoi stole the ball with the youngsters from Moroka trailing seven goals to zero![130] Incidents such as this one explain why elderly Pirates fans believed that 'Russian leaders had a hatred for Pirates from humiliating defeats', and show how a sense of 'Basotho-ness' was imbricated with Swallows from the beginning.[131]

Rank-and-file Russian gangsters viewed football as a metaphor of war. A tangible example of the increasingly violent urban culture of Rand townships, the involvement of organised gangs in football partially explains the rise in fan violence at many grounds during this period.[132] A former Russian, a migrant worker from Lesotho under the pseudonym Johannes Rantoa, linked his love of fighting and passion for football as part of his worldview of 'life as a struggle, as a fight'. Rantoa said:

> A fight is like football. The strength of a football team is at the quarter, at the flanks. Now, in a fight if your flanks are weak and they slack because of the pressure from the other side, those that remain in the fight will be hit from behind and can no longer concentrate on their front because of the people who attack them from both sides. That is where I used to like it. If it was football I would be called Two, at the quarter. Yes, I liked fighting from the sides.[133]

The close relationship between the Russians and Swallows continued into the early 1950s, given that the minutes of Pirates referred to Ntoi as Swallows's 'promoter' in 1952.[134]

As more people moved to Moroka – the population increased to 58 800 in 1955 – support for Swallows grew steadily. In 1948 Moroka entrepreneur Ishmael Lesolang purchased a set of maroon jerseys with a white V-stripe across the chest that became Swallows's trademark. John 'Johnny Walker' Kubheka was arguably the most prominent founding figure in the Moroka club after Gumede.[135] A crowd-pleasing player, an educated man, and a member of the executive boards of the Moroka Summer League and JAFA, Kubheka attended the same meetings with Mpanza, Pirates, and the white authorities.[136] He sat on the eleven-member JAFA Board of Control and on both the Misconduct Committee and the Fixtures Committee, but seems to have been pushed out of Swallows by more ambitious, perhaps wealthier, patrons in the early 1950s.[137]

By that time Swallows were challenging Pirates in the JAFA under the name 'Corrugated Rovers'.[138] The temporary name change enabled the club to compete autonomously while the management of the United Tobacco Company (UTC), for whom captain Difference 'City Council' Mbanya and several team-mates worked as travelling salesmen, pressured Swallows into becoming a 'company team'.[139] Mbanya and the other UTC salesmen travelled by company car from township to township, making deliveries to and networking in general stores and shebeens. This relative freedom allowed the salesmen to socialise and talk about club affairs, weekend matches, and the game in general during their rounds. Moreover, working for UTC gave these black footballers an opportunity to carve out a training schedule more easily than, for example, black workers in the mining and/or manufacturing industries.

Courtesy of Moroka Swallows Football Club

Moroka Swallows team (1950s).

Playing as Corrugated Rovers, an apt name for a team based in a shantytown, Moroka Swallows defeated Orlando Pirates in the 1953 Transvaal Challenge Cup final. After a controversial decision by the referee in the first game had sparked Swallows's official protest, JAFA ordered a replay.[140] A 'big crowd of enthusiastic spectators' at Bantu Sports, most of whom supported the underdogs from Moroka, saw Dennis Ford score the first goal and Joseph Msimanga score two more to give Swallows a 3-2 victory 'amid a tumultuous ovation from the crowd'.[141] The 'Birds' replaced the 'Buccaneers' as the Transvaal's dominant team and opened a new chapter in the history of South African football, while the ageing warriors of Orlando faded away after nearly twenty years of superb competition.

However, instead of disappearing or suffering a split as often happened to township soccer clubs, Pirates entered a rebuilding period. By drawing on strong community ties and organisational experience, the club was able to promote young players from the second and third teams and replenish the depleted ranks of the first-team side. The symbol of this new generation of Pirates was Eric 'Scara' Sono, an eighteen-year-old inside forward who made his debut in the first side against Linare of Lesotho in 1954.[142] Many of Scara's team-mates were recruited through the scouting network nurtured in the schools and streets of Orlando. The team's rootedness in the community ensured its longevity, and Pirates remained a major attraction for football fans on the Reef and beyond.

The influx of Pirates's fans without ties to Orlando became a double-edged sword. On the one hand, larger crowds made the club so famous that players were instantly recognised in the townships and enjoyed privileges unavailable to most Africans – such as being spared police harassment and pass checks.[143] On the other hand, the club's expanded scale weakened Mokgosinyane's moral economy of soccer. Among these outsiders was a small but influential group of reasonably well-educated, older men with some disposable income earned in semi-skilled jobs at a time when more than three-quarters of African industrial workers occupied unskilled positions.[144] Many of these men expressed more interest in contesting elections and gaining a position on the executive committee than in either football or community welfare. So it was no coincidence that these supporters waged a campaign to acquire full membership in the club, earning the right to vote in elections in 1952.[145] That same year, supporters organised their first meeting as a separate, albeit unofficial, organisation.[146] The emergence of a clear-cut division between playing and non-playing members symbolised both a nascent specialisation of roles in club management and the corrosion of egalitarian bonds in the House of Pirates.

In less than two decades Pirates had evolved from an unknown neighbourhood side into a nationally recognised soccer team featured in *Drum* and other magazines. By nourishing local solidarities and articulating a tactically sophisticated and aesthetically pleasing soccer style, Orlando Pirates Football Club achieved prodigious success and popular acclaim. With fame and power in the sporting realm came gradual, yet significant, changes in the club's normative values and social organisation. These transformations were tied not only to performances on the field, but also to the dramatic shifts in the social, economic, and political conditions of post-war South Africa – conditions that contributed to the electoral victory of the National Party on an apartheid platform in 1948. Chapter 7 turns to football's expanding role as popular entertainment, entrepreneurial outlet, and mobilising force against racism in the context of the legislative entrenchment of 'petty apartheid' in the 1950s.

'The Fabulous Decade'?

Entertainment, Entrepreneurship and Nationalism in the 1950s

In his autobiography, Stephen 'Kalamazoo' Mokone – the first black South African to play professionally in Europe – wrote: 'The years 1951 and 1952 were good to me. I was like a poker player with a very hot hand. The [Durban] Bush Bucks Football Club was the best in South Africa. I was honored by their invitation to play for them. Except for the Orlando Pirates and Moroka Swallows in Johannesburg and the [L]inare Football Club from Lesotho, we had virtually no opposition.'[1] Mokone's proud recollections of his fame and success highlight how football's personal and public stories of celebration, triumph, conflict, and defeat inspired and sustained the social lives of black workers and political leaders during the onset of 'petty apartheid' in the 1950s. 'The lives that the blacks were living were pretty appalling,' commented the black journalist and intellectual Lewis Nkosi in Peter Davies's 1996 film *In Darkest Hollywood: Cinema and Apartheid*: 'one could not wait for the revolution to come along and rescue one from this kind of impoverished life. So anything that came along to provide the fantasy was most welcome.'

CHALLENGING APARTHEID

By 1953, when Mokone's Durban Bush Bucks performed in front of thousands of fans across the country, the legislative pillars of apartheid were in place.[2] The growing popular ferment, mass political mobilisation, and mounting government repression of the 1950s occurred at the same time that squatter movements, ethnic and youth gangs, and sporting associations built local networks of power that provided sociability, security, and financial opportunities.[3] In the first decade of apartheid, football was a shared cultural medium through which people involved in formal and informal social groups connected across racial, economic, ethno-linguistic, and political lines. The game evolved in a shifting formal political context. Radicalised by the Congress Youth League's Programme of Action of 1949, the ANC formed a multiracial alliance with Indian and Coloured political organisations, Communists, black trade unions, and women's groups. This broad coalition resisted the implementation of apartheid through direct confrontation. The 1952 Defiance Campaign and numerous bus boycotts invigorated black nationalist politics. In 1954 black and white women founded the Federation of South African Women (FSAW) and, in June 1955, three months after the birth of the South African Congress of Trade Unions (SACTU), the Congress of the People adopted the nonracial, democratic Freedom Charter on an open field used for football matches at Kliptown, near Soweto.[4]

In sport as in wider society, the rise of apartheid provoked an upsurge in popular protest. African, Coloured, and Indian officials founded the South African Soccer Federation (SASF) in Durban in 1951. The Federation strengthened relationships among different segments of black sport. This new organisation formalised ties developed over more than two decades of friendly competitions in many cities and towns, especially in the Transvaal and Natal where Inter-Race Soccer Boards had been established in 1935 and 1946 respectively. This contemporary trend towards integration also manifested itself in black rugby and cricket, reflecting both a shared experience of oppression and the 1950s character as 'a melting pot for gender, race, and class relations'.[5] For example, rugby 'test matches' between the African and Coloured 'national' teams took place every year between 1950–59, while black cricket associations formed the South African Cricket Board of Control in 1952.[6] Changes in the structure and ideology of black South African amateur football organisations paralleled the transformations of racially aligned political movements into a mass-based, multiracial Congress Alliance.

THE STRUGGLE FOR SPORT SPACE

Durban was the epicentre of major changes in South African football in the 1950s, and Durban's African officials assumed prominent administrative positions in provincial and national soccer institutions. Henry Posselt Gagu Ngwenya emerged as a leading power broker in domestic football. Ngwenya was president of the Durban and District African Football Association (DDAFA) as well as its parent body, the South Africa African Football Association (SAAFA). He represented amateur soccer's entrepreneurial appeal to black men who were denied not only a formal political voice, but virtually all legal means of accumulating wealth.

On the playing field, the prodigious Durban Bush Bucks were led by the formidable trio of 'Kalamazoo' Mokone, Petrus 'Halleluya' Zulu, and Herbert 'Shordex' Zuma, who excited the crowds with their winning soccer. At the representative level, Durban defeated teams from Mozambique and Southern Rhodesia. Natal sides composed of Durban players won seven Moroka-Baloyi Cups. All-Durban sides represented 'African' national teams in 1956 and 1958. With the help of an expanding black popular press, local heroes like Mokone, Darius Dhlomo, and Vusi 'Stadig' Makhathini became household names in the townships of Durban, Johannesburg, and Cape Town. In the early 1950s, soccer matches in Durban, as in Johannesburg, attracted crowds of 5 000 to 10 000 people on a regular basis.[7] But by the end of the decade, top Durban teams Bush Bucks, Wanderers, Zulu Royals, and City Blacks were drawing 20 000 to 40 000 spectators to Somtseu Ground – a facility designed to accommodate at most 15 000 people. These were considerably larger crowds than those found at Bantu Sports and Wemmer in Johannesburg.[8]

The lack of sources makes it impossible to determine the exact composition of the crowd or people's motivations for attending football matches in such great numbers. These limitations notwithstanding, a contemporary researcher pointed out the working-class, male character of African sport in the Cape Town area, where 'the biggest demand [for sport] comes from the younger men working in factories, as well as from men and women employed in domestic service in Cape Town and Suburbs'.[9] In Durban, as in Johannesburg, Cape Town, and other cities and towns, the game was incorporated into the daily popular discourse of urban Africans. 'From the day the fixtures are out,' sociologist Bernard Magubane pointed out, 'the important matches of the weekend are discussed in the buses, on the pavements during the lunch hour, and in the long queues where Africans wait for hours in the morning and afternoons to be carried to their destinations.'[10] Fans recounted memorable individual moves and goals, debated questionable refereeing calls, or second-guessed coaches' decisions. Thanks to football, Magubane believed, the 'drudgery which their life imposes on them is temporarily forgotten. Arguments range from the form of the respective players, to their prospects of winning the match, and past encounters are assessed. This preoccupation with football makes life worth living despite its frustrations.'[11]

Official sources illustrate that the vertiginous rate of increase of African soccer teams in Durban followed almost exactly that of the overall African population in the city. As the number of Africans in Durban more than tripled from 43 750 in 1932 to about 150 000 in 1949, the DDAFA's membership increased threefold from 45 clubs in 1934 to 140 clubs in 1950 – 130 organised and run by Africans themselves, and 10 by private businesses.[12] This direct correlation between demographic growth and the proliferation of soccer clubs continued throughout the 1950s so that in 1959, when the approximate African population reached 205 000, the DDAFA boasted 264 registered teams and at least 5 000 registered players.[13]

The expansion of black football in the early years of apartheid was an extraordinary phenomenon given the abysmal sporting facilities available to black athletes.[14] Research studies conducted in the mid-1940s and early 50s highlighted the extreme need for increased provision of sporting facilities for Africans in urban residential areas. For example, Cape Town's official population of 44 300 Africans had access to only 30 acres of playing fields instead of a recommended 220 acres. Typically, Sunday soccer and rugby matches started at 9 a.m. and continued uninterrupted as long as visibility permitted. The situation in Cape Town was representative of a national trend. Official data reported that Durban's 150 000 Africans had access to only six standard size soccer fields in 1950 – three at Somtseu, two at migrant workers' hostels, and one in Durban North.[15] This shortage was described by municipal authorities themselves as 'an acute shortage of playing fields'.[16]

By contrast, during this period white sport in Durban received generous city council funding for the construction of state-of-the-art stadiums at the New

Kingsmead Ground. The municipality provided loans of £257 300 and approved 'non-recoverable works' totalling about £227 980 for the construction of the rugby, cricket, and soccer stadiums.[17] In Pietermaritzburg, Natal's provincial capital, a similar longer-term trend revealed how the city council expanded white sports facilities in the 1920–60 period by giving public land, loans, and grants-in-aid, while, at the same time, it failed to provide sporting facilities for black residents, particularly in the African townships.[18]

The Durban city council's enthusiastic embrace of urban segregation under the 1950 Group Areas Act and the 1949 riots between Africans and Indians led to a local government initiative that funded housing, sport, and recreation for Africans, a move designed to improve some of the rigours of black urban life.[19] In this way, the city council sought to address the lack of adequate places for leisure, entertainment, and sport available to the majority of the city's black residents. It also included new sporting facilities in the plans for the new African townships of KwaMashu and Umlazi – the show-piece of apartheid social engineering in Durban. As with the inadequate supply of African housing, however, the Durban city council's construction of football grounds – nineteen existed by 1959 – did not come close to meeting the expanding needs of African players and fans. The scarcity of facilities and other material resources severely constrained black athletes' ability to attain the highest standard of play.[20] Even so, an important consequence of the new funding for African leisure led to substantial renovations at Somtseu Ground, namely, the construction of five additional grass fields, eight ticket offices, eleven turnstiles, a fence, and a brick wall to enclose the complex.[21] The enclosure made the collection of the council's 15 per cent share of gate receipts more reliable and efficient. The wall also blocked off the predominantly African crowds at Somtseu from the neighbouring municipal barracks for Indian workers. With tensions high in the wake of the deadly Indian–African riots of 1949, the council saw the barrier as 'prevent[ing] possible friction between the two races'; but the wall also captured the Durban authorities' enthusiastic endorsement of 'separate development'.[22]

African officials, fans, and players welcomed the improvements to Somtseu. The new fields eased pressure on playing space. The DDAFA benefited economically; it consolidated its prominent position and retained financial autonomy from the city council. Municipal documents described the renovated Somtseu Ground in the following way: 'The main ground in this group of fields has raised bankings which can accommodate a crowd of 15 000 spectators' and 'tiered seating . . . with a combined accommodation for about 6,000 spectators. The original grandstand has now been doubled giving accommodation for 500 people.'[23] Fans who had previously been forced to stand five or six deep on the sidelines finally could sit on the embankments and have a clear, expansive view of the action on the field, a factor likely to have played a major role in the rising attendance figures in the second half of the decade. The players enjoyed the new surroundings, especially the well-maintained grass pitch. According to the Durban city council, Somtseu was 'one of the premier Native recreational grounds in South Africa'.[24]

Durban officials lead players onto a pitch (1950s).

Leo Kuper, *An African Bourgeoisie: Race Class and Politics in South Africa* (Yale University Press, 1965)

DURBAN BUSH BUCKS: A PARALLEL WITH ORLANDO PIRATES

The Bush Bucks Football Club became the most entertaining, popular, and winning team performing on the Somtseu stage in the late 1940s and early 50s. Jackson Ngidi was the chief architect behind the glittering success of one of the oldest surviving clubs in South Africa, one founded on an American Board mission station in 1902 (see Chapter 3). At a time when family ties were an important motivation for affiliation, Jackson Ngidi followed in the footsteps of his father, a former Bucks goalkeeper, and joined the club in 1934.[25] After a decade playing for the Bush Bucks, Ngidi became the team's manager and trainer in 1944. He spearheaded what *Drum* magazine, the popular illustrated monthly that focused on black urban cultural life and functioned as a 'social barometer of the decade', in July 1956 described as the 'meteoric rise' of the gold-and-blue Bucks to football 'fame and fortune'.[26] In no uncertain terms, the portly Ngidi saw football as a key to his self-conception and his personal development. His comments also reveal the extent to which football was perceived to be a road to higher status and social prestige: 'I had built up the Bush Bucks to a wonderful team and had created a wonderful discipline and I felt myself very important . . . I was a demi-god.'[27]

The presence of a charismatic, knowledgeable strategist and trainer in the Durban club is reminiscent of the significant role played by Bethuel Mokgosinyane and Andries Mkwanazi in the early history of Orlando Pirates (see Chapter 6). There are several additional parallels linking the histories of Bush Bucks and Pirates. Both clubs established themselves in the country's football pantheon in the first years of the apartheid era. The Bush Bucks proved virtually unbeatable between 1948 and 1953 as they captured numerous league and cup titles in Durban and Natal.[28] Moreover, the success of Bush Bucks had its roots in Ngidi's studious approach to the game – one that resembled the thorough technical analyses observed earlier in the case of Orlando Pirates. But Ngidi, unlike Pirates tacticians Mokgosinyane and Mkwanazi, relied much more on British football literature – popular magazines, coaching manuals, player biographies – to teach his players the craft of football. A *Drum* story in July 1956 portrayed Ngidi's Tuesday evening training sessions as:

> classes where his players are lectured on dribbling, passing, ball-control, team-work . . . . And there you see Jackson in action, demonstrating what his ace inside-right, Herbert Zuma, reads from a book. Zuma will read on Stanley Matthews, the English soccer maestro; Ted Ditchburn on goalkeeping; Jackie Milburn and Stan Mortensen on method of attack; Leon Lenty on ball control; Billy Wright on tackling and Roy Bentley and Neil Franklin on heading.

The former Bucks forward Stephen 'Kalamazoo' Mokone described Jackson Ngidi as:

> one of the best trainers in South Africa. A hard-driving man, he strove for perfection, never satisfied. Though he could be kind and gentle, rarely were these facets of his personality displayed. He was feared by all players . . . no other team was trained as hard or as well as the Bucks. We did our road work on the beach. We were trained by every book in print.[29]

Under Ngidi's supervision, books supplemented the skill, grit, and guile of stars like midfielder Petrus Zulu and the forward trio of Mokone, Zuma, and Geoffrey 'Ace' Moeketsi. These leading South African footballers electrified the crowds with dazzling plays executed with well-rehearsed precision and near-mechanical consistency. Over the years, Bush Bucks provided key players to the Natal teams that monopolised the Moroka-Baloyi Cup in the 1950s – winning seven of the eight competitions completed during the 'fabulous decade'.[30]

In 1948 the charismatic Ngidi became a full-time salaried coach, a unique position for either black or white South Africans at the time. To the talented, yet inexperienced, nineteen-year-old Mokone, then a high school student at Ohlange, Ngidi underlined the importance of thoughtful movements and instilled a deeper appreciation of spatial relationships on the field. Ngidi told his confident young striker:

> One can play a great game without having touched the ball once. Playing an offensive position does not mean just scoring goals. It means creating goals. This means creating space for your teammates to utilise by taking up intelligent positions. It means moving about the field so as to pull a defender out of the middle area with you, creating an opening for a teammate.[31]

Ngidi often dispensed this wisdom during physically demanding practices held at Somtseu Ground on the day of the match. Ngidi's source of inspiration for holding these training sessions was his predecessor, John Mchunu, whose dedicated team, it was reported in *Drum* of July 1956, 'walked a two-day journey, sleeping on the way from their Umtwalumi home to Adams Mission station, which had the only soccer ground on the Natal South Coast'.

Ngidi was an ambitious self-made man and a visionary manager. 'He had very good insight into the essence of football. He was a talent . . . . I looked at him with respect,' Darius Dhlomo told me in an interview.[32] 'Bush Bucks and City Blacks were strong rivals. Our matches were always sold out. We [City Blacks] were more centred on playing attractive football; juggling, misleading and making fun of the opponent,' said Dhlomo. 'We were easygoing, but with the Bush Bucks that would never ha[ve] happened. Bush Bucks said: "No! We must score more goals!" Bush Bucks were more practical.'[33]

Riding their wave of widespread popularity among Durban's football fans, Bush Bucks – like Orlando Pirates – became a popular barnstorming team. Itinerant teams used the income from challenge matches to cover their operational expenses. Barnstorming tours not only benefited the club, but also individual players. One of the ways in which football provided an avenue for self-improvement was through 'under the table' payments to top players. Mokone said:

> Though an amateur, I was paid five pounds a week by the Bucks. It was a lot of money in those days – more than most men made working in factories, more money than men with large families made. It was also more money than I'd ever handled; I didn't know what to do with it . . . I spent all of my money on clothes and developed a reputation as a snappy dresser.[34]

'Jackson had his view of how to run his own club,' Dhlomo remarked. 'He used a certain reverend and rich, middle-class people to bring in some money and that's how he could buy some good players like Steve Mokone, Godfrey Moeketsi, Shordex Zuma and others. The fans loved it because they were confronted with different styles of playing soccer. It was attractive!'[35] Although illegal payments to amateurs had been occurring for at least two decades, the more intense competition of the 1950s led to an expansion of the practice into a widely acknowledged system of 'hidden professionalism'. Contemporary researchers discovered that:

> players of promise are frequently paid a salary from the treasury of the team as a means of keeping them. If a skilled player has had difficulty in finding employment, it is incumbent on all members of the team to find suitable and well-paying employment for the star. So involved are the efforts of teammates to keep them happy that star players are known to pass from club to club for the 'best deal'.[36]

In the case of Durban Bush Bucks, money raised from tours also helped to endow a scholarship fund for student-athletes. This scheme granted access to status and education – a rare opportunity for self-advancement and social mobility. Herbert Zuma, for example, used this financial aid in the 1950s to complete a teacher-training course at the Mariannhill Catholic mission school in Pinetown, between Durban and Pietermaritzburg.[37]

The Bucks's profitable tours provoked their suspension from the Durban and District African Football Association in 1953 for engaging in an 'unauthorised' match against an Indian team at Durban's Curries Fountain Stadium.[38] This does not appear to have been a racist incident but, rather, an attempt by the DDAFA to assert its power against an increasingly autonomous football club. The suspension released Bucks from league and cup commitments, so they staged remunerative matches in Johannesburg, Pretoria, Bloemfontein, and Maseru (Lesotho), entertaining huge crowds and garnering even greater fame.[39] Late in 1953 the Natal African Football Association appeals board overturned Bucks's suspension and reinstated the club.

After renewed success from 1954–56, Bush Bucks lost the Durban title to Wanderers after a tense match in 1957. While the president of Wanderers, John Khambule, attributed the team's success to first-class training under their new white coach Bobby Reed, groups of infuriated Bush Bucks supporters blamed poor officiating for their team's defeat. Fans forced referee John Mabizela to barricade himself in the dressing room. The *Golden Post* of 3 November 1957 reported that 'Police reinforcements arrived in time to save Mabizela from a milling, angry crowd that threatened to storm the stall if he was not released to them. Forty policemen escorted Mabizela to his home through the shouting crowd.' This incident illustrates how hidden professionalism's higher stakes and football's fealties in an increasingly violent society helped to spark incidents of soccer hooliganism. Much more research needs to be done on male associations, youth and ethnic gangs, and urban criminals – social groups that often associated 'sport' with public displays of collective violence – before we can fully understand their relationship to the tide of 'all these incidents of riots and fighting on the sports fields' reported with increasing frequency in the black press in the 1950s.[40]

SPORT AND ENTREPRENEURSHIP

The presence of thousands of black spectators at weekend matches across the country made the game increasingly attractive to private manufacturers, retailers, and African entrepreneurs. As early as 1923, black newspapers carried advertisements for football and rugby equipment aimed directly at sporting 'Natives'.[41] Since those early years, sporting goods outlets, owned mostly by white businessmen, tried to capitalise on the popularity of sport among the black population. Urban slums, townships, and industrial compounds offered a valuable new market for greater numbers of boots, stockings, jerseys, shorts, balls, and caps. Competition in the sporting goods market catering to black athletes in Johannesburg appears to have been stiff from the beginning; three different outfitters advertised on the front page of a March 1933 issue of the Chamber of Mines weekly newspaper *Umteteli Wa Bantu* (The Voice of the People).[42]

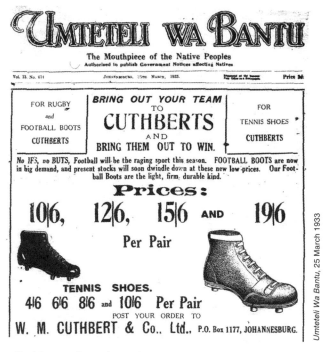

Cuthberts advert (1933).

Large white businesses also eyed the growing legions of devoted black fans as potential customers. In the 1930s, for example, the Durban biscuit manufacturer Bakers Ltd. was among the first private companies outside the mining sector to support black soccer competitions. Its owner, J. Lynch, saw sponsorship as a way both to advertise his products and recruit a more stabilised non-migrant labour force.[43] The United Tobacco Company (UTC, now British American Tobacco, BAT) sponsored competitions of the Johannesburg African Football Association since at least the 1940s. UTC also employed well-known African football players as cigarette salesmen in black residential areas.[44] For example, the president of the Johannesburg Bantu Football Association, Henry Percy Madibane of Sophiatown, worked for UTC.[45] Tobacco products were specifically marketed to black people thanks to advertising on billboards and posters located in frequently travelled areas in the townships, as well as on the radio and in newspapers and magazines catering to black audiences.[46] Black players like 'Kalamazoo' Mokone endorsed UTC products, helping to project an image of tobacco consumption as the glamorous, healthy, invigorating, fashionable pastime of famous black cultural icons.[47] Darius Dhlomo from Durban was another pioneer in sports marketing aimed at township consumers. Pictured in a high-flying shooting pose in one advertisement in the May 1958 issue of *Drum*, Dhlomo's endorsement declared: 'I'm never without my Wilson's Three-X Mints. They are Good and Strong.'

For the skilled African footballer there were some material advantages to playing football. Since the 1930s, and increasingly so in the 1940s, prestigious and enterprising clubs poached athletes from smaller, less well-known ones by providing better wages or a full-time job. Former player and manager Peter Sitsila recounted that 'with soccer skills a player could get a job, easily too! Even the association, not just his own team, the association would join forces with his team and try to look for a job for him because the association would be making use of that good player,' and benefiting from his performances.[48] Covert payments to amateurs outraged some Africans. As early as 1935, detractors of 'unprofessed professionalism' were decrying how the 'soccer game has so advanced among Non-Europeans that it has become commercialised, and its enclosed grounds are becoming reservoirs of accumulated wealth'.[49] For these critics, the model of European professional football was simply the 'horror of selling and buying players . . . wholesale slavery of humans under the guise of sport'.[50] Of course, many African footballers did not see it that way. Football talent, for example, allowed individuals to obtain passes at a time when the Union government and local authorities were trying to limit the growing influx of black people to urban areas.[51] Anthropologists Monica Wilson and Archie Mafeje recounted the case of a Sotho-speaking player in Langa township who said he was recruited by the predominantly Xhosa-speaking Transkei Lions team, 'who welcomed him warmly and organized a pass for him'.[52]

Some black entrepreneurs sought to profit from football. In the Vereeniging area in the Transvaal, a man named N. Molafo became famous for organising 'ox competitions' in the 1950s.[53] The winning teams received a beast, which they either sold at the grounds for cash or carried back home in the back of a lorry for a fundraising function or a neighbourhood feast.[54] This kind of communal consumption showed the continuing importance of established, agrarian values of solidarity and reciprocity in an industrial capitalist environment. Ben Malamba, arguably the best African cricketer of the 1950s, remarked in an interview that township sporting events were occasions when 'people sold fruits, drinks, food – unauthorised

Mbanya Guinness advert.

business! The matches were attractive, there weren't many opportunities to get so many people together.'⁵⁵ Women carried out one of the most profitable trades, illegally brewing and selling beer and alcoholic concoctions to spectators or in shebeens (drinking dens) adjacent to the grounds (see Chapter 5).

The intensity of popular interest and the revenue generated by the soccer movement in general in the 1950s paved the way for Durban entrepreneur Henry Posselt Gagu Ngwenya's development of an elaborate patronage network linked to an emerging system of hidden professionalism.

NGWENYA'S PATRONAGE MACHINE

Elected president of DDAFA in 1952, Ngwenya possessed entrepreneurial skills that put Durban soccer on a sound organisational and economic footing. He used his considerable influence, visibility, and access to association funds to build a powerful clientship network which he directed with growing authoritarianism. Ngwenya used this local power base as a stepping stone to become a leading South African football entrepreneur. The Durban soccer chief's advancement was part of the broader historical development of 'football patronage . . . whereby "big men" were able to grant favors in return for allegiance, so enhancing their prestige and status in the township community'.[56] The government's severe restrictions on black political and social activity exacerbated the tendency of 'big men' to assume positions of considerable power and control within sporting organisations.[57]

A former official of Zulu Royals, the team that split from Wanderers in 1939, but not a former player, Ngwenya symbolised a new generation of educated, petit bourgeois administrators who were not involved solely 'for the love of the game' as had been commonplace in the inter-war period. Born in Harrismith (Orange Free State) in 1899, the son of a Methodist preacher and a school teacher, Ngwenya attended various prestigious mission schools. He opened a restaurant in Durban's central business district in 1934, a rare dining establishment catering to black patrons. In 1942 he joined the African National Congress (ANC), rising through the ranks to the national executive committee in 1948, a position he held until 1950.[58] It is likely that Ngwenya's formal political career succumbed to the radicalisation of the movement that resulted from the adoption of the Congress Youth League's Programme of Action in 1949. The precise character and function of the links between soccer and ANC politics in Durban at the time remains nebulous. We do know that Albert Luthuli was the patron of the Natal Inter-Race Soccer Board when he was elected to the ANC presidency in 1952, and that an ANC Youth League member and the treasurer of the ANC Natal branch sat on the five-man DDAFA executive committee in 1953.[59] In fact, as the next section will show, political organisations were in the process of becoming actively engaged in sporting matters.

Ngwenya encouraged the development of an entrepreneurial ethos in amateur football. He made admission charges a standard feature at Somtseu and, as a result, gate receipts became an expanding source of revenue for the association. Before 1952 the association charged a 6d. admission price only for important matches, but Ngwenya capitalised on African workers' willingness to spend hard-earned income on football.[60] DDAFA's budget quickly became the largest of any African sporting organisation, increasing from about £4 000 in 1953 to more than £12 000 by the end of the decade.[61]

Ngwenya used DDAFA revenue in unprecedented ways, such as the organisation of foreign tours to Southern Rhodesia and Mozambique, the purchase of a bus, and the employment of a professional coach for the association's representative team. These innovative decisions captured the fans' imagination and received ample coverage in the press and municipal documents. This kind of functional consumption and lavish spending on football showed blacks, as well as whites, that Africans were capable of organising themselves effectively and autonomously. It also significantly enhanced the public image of DDAFA and, of course, the standing and visibility of Ngwenya himself.

FOREIGN TOURS: 'NATAL SOCCER IS NOW THE COUNTRY'S SHOW-PIECE'
Foreign tours were an important factor in crafting Durban's reputation as 'the strongest African football center in the Union'.[62] In July 1953, a Durban select team accompanied by Ngwenya, the coach Jackson Ngidi, and several other officials flew to Salisbury (Harare) in Southern Rhodesia (Zimbabwe), at a cost of more than £1 000, for a tournament commemorating the centenary of Cecil Rhodes's birth.[63]

George Thabe, *It's a Goal!* (Skotaville, 1983)

DDAFA players and officials who toured Southern Rhodesia (1953).

Durban's first match was against a representative side of the Salisbury African Football Association in front of an estimated crowd of 10 000 spectators in Harare township. The visitors struggled to cope with the hosts' fast, kick-and-rush style and the hard, turfless ground.[64] An injury to the starting goalkeeper forced the eclectic midfielder Darius Dhlomo (born in 1931) – YMCA social worker, professional cruiserweight boxing champion, cricketer, tennis player, jazz drummer, and blues singer – to replace him between the posts, where he made a series of remarkable saves.[65]

The star of the Harare match, however, was Vusi 'Stadig' Makhathini (born c.1933), 'a crowd pleaser with his showmanship and an excellent footballer noted for his lightning speed, goal-scoring averages and an uncanny dribbling ability'.[66] A chauffeur who lived in Lamontville township in Durban and captained Union Jacks, Makhathini was one of South Africa's finest pure dribblers. He had received his nickname in a game in Johannesburg at the tender age of fifteen, when his 'dashing around the field, wriggling, feinting as grown men fell easy prey to his virtuosity, [a fan] shouted in Afrikaans: "Stadig My Kind" (slow down my baby [sic]). Halfway through the game practically all the spectators were shouting: "Stadig . . . Stadig My Kind". This was later abbreviated to Stadig.' In the Salisbury match, Stadig started with the ball out on the left flank, wove through the Rhodesians' defence, and scored to give Durban a comeback 3-2 victory in the closing minutes of the contest.[67] At the Harare Ground the next day, 'the largest crowd to assemble at a soccer match in Southern Rhodesia' saw Durban attack through 'complicated short passing movements' and exploit their superior fitness to defeat Southern Rhodesia, known as 'Red Army', 3-1 and claim the Rhodes tournament title.[68]

The Southern Rhodesian teams at the time consisted of players from Salisbury, Bulawayo, Umtali, and Mrewa. The average age of these men was about 27, and they shared a privileged working-class or elite background common among the best African athletes at the time. Among them were three teachers, three policemen, three drivers, two welfare workers, two traders (probably team officials), a court interpreter, a tailor, and five 'general' workers.[69] One of the leading Red Army players was centre-half Just Rize, nicknamed 'Kontrola' for his crafty ball control. According to historian Ossie Stuart, Rize was born in Northern Rhodesia (Zambia) in 1921 and learned the game on the industrial Copper Belt, where he worked as a company Sports Organiser.[70] In 1944 he migrated to a Southern Rhodesian mine, but soon moved to Bulawayo – the largest and most successful football centre in that colony. In Bulawayo he played for the Northern Rhodesia Football Club as well as the city team and the Red Army from 1944–53. Rize's career shows the close relationship between soccer and migrant labourers' social networks reinforcing ties to their home areas. Foreign tours bolstered the game's links to wider processes of industrialisation, urban migration, cultural change, and the construction of social identities throughout southern and central Africa.

George Thabe, *It's a Goal!* (Skotaville, 1983)

The victorious DDAFA team.

In June 1957 Durban again journeyed abroad, this time to the Mozambican capital of Lourenço Marques (Maputo) for a three-game series against local teams. Durban municipal documents described the opponents as 'coloured', but according to the Union Native Affairs Department's racial classification at least one of the local teams, the Grupo Desportivo Nova Alianca, had seventeen 'coloured' and twenty-seven 'Native' members.[71] The Durban team featured four players from Wanderers, three each from Bush Bucks, City Blacks, and Zulu Royals, one each from Union Jacks, Home Tigers, and United Jumpers.[72] Travelling by ship, the South Africans arrived in the Portuguese colony port city on a Saturday morning; they then defeated Nova Alianca (1-0) and Suburban Lourenço Marques (11-0!) in a gruelling Saturday-afternoon doubleheader. Durban completed a clean sweep the following day with a 4-3 win over a combined Lourenço Marques team.[73]

In September 1957 Durban hosted the Matabeleland (Southern Rhodesia) pick team in front of an estimated 45 000 fans – the largest crowd in the history of Somtseu Ground.[74] 'The fans keep the turnstiles clicking whenever Natal plays,' the *Golden City Post* of 17 July 1955 reported. Besides local passion and loyalty, three more factors help to explain the record crowd for this contest. Firstly, 'international' matches captured the imagination of southern African soccer fans.[75] Secondly, an amicable rivalry had arisen between South African teams and their northern neighbours as a result of reciprocal visits, as well as Southern Rhodesia's affiliation to SAAFA and its participation in the 1954 Moroka-Baloyi Cup. Thirdly, the knowledgeable Durban fans went to watch the likes of Gibson Makhanda (born 1927?), a brilliant centre-forward and court interpreter from Bulawayo, who had impressed South Africans in previous years. The South African black press hailed Makhanda as 'one of the greatest center forwards to visit this country in recent times. His body-swerving and sure-footed power house kicking is something that thrilled the fans.'[76] That Sunday afternoon, however, Herbert Zuma of Bush Bucks upstaged Makhanda: Zuma scored two goals as Durban defeated Matabeleland 3-2 to the delight of the huge partisan crowd.[77]

Ngwenya's hiring of Topper Brown, a former professional with Arsenal in England, played an important role in Durban's continued success. Brown had replaced Jackson Ngidi as coach of the Durban and Natal teams in 1955. The charismatic Ngidi had fallen out of favour with the DDAFA leadership in the wake of both the suspension of Bush Bucks and Natal's loss to Transvaal in the 1953 Moroka-Baloyi Cup. Most Africans did not seem to object (at least not publicly) to a white man's coaching of the team, perhaps recognising Brown's hand in the string of victories and the attractive football performed by Durban and Natal sides.[78] The competent Brown selected Natal sides stacked with Durban players he knew well. This selection strategy gave Natal the 1954 and 1955 Moroka-Baloyi Cup and the 1955 S.L. Singh Natal Inter-Race titles. According to one of his former players, Topper Brown was a 'good Englishman . . . a wonderful coach. We learned quite a lot from him. What made him so unique was that he didn't want to bring the English style; he made some possibilities for our creativity. He had played in England and when he looked at how we played soccer in the streets he developed an in-between system and approach. We were unbeatable.'[79] The Indian press reported that Natal Africans 'indulged in some of the finest artistic soccer . . . ever seen. Their ball control, deft touches, the accuracy of their passing, and their ability to find the open gaps was indeed amazing.'[80] Brown's Natal teams exhibited 'purpose, well thought-out plans and counter tactics, and a generally superior knowledge of the game', so that the appreciative black sporting press declared: 'Natal soccer is now the country's show-piece.'[81]

THE DEMISE OF THE DDAFA

Ngwenya used Durban's triumphs on the field to expand his power base. In 1954 he won the presidency of the South Africa African Football Association, an electoral outcome motivated, perhaps, by a misplaced collective hope that DDAFA's economic resources would revive the cash-strapped national association.[82] During this period Durban also controlled provincial soccer. DDAFA executive committee member I.J. Motholo was president of the Natal African Football Association from 1951 through to 1958, the year Natal again won both the Moroka-Baloyi Cup and the S.L. Singh Natal Inter-Race trophy. Ngwenya, however, seemed less interested in helping the national organisation than in using his new role as the head of the largest African sporting institution in the country to boost both his personal power and DDAFA's reputation. Over the course of the decade, he bolstered his authority through clientelist practices and the politics of fear.

Football notoriety benefited Ngwenya in economic terms. Located near Somtseu Ground in the central business district, his restaurant flourished. The president was not only a popular host, he also awarded himself catering contracts for the provision of meals to visiting teams and delegations – a lucrative deal that produced nearly £700 in net profit one year.[83] Ngwenya's hand-picked gate attendants defrauded the association by deliberately, and consistently, failing to document ticket sales. After matches, these men delivered cash to the president who, instead of depositing the funds into the DDAFA bank account, stuffed the cash into envelopes, which he sealed and locked in his office desk drawer together with the treasurer's financial records.[84] In this way, thousands of pounds from gate receipts – economic resources that could have otherwise been invested in the sport – were diverted to a presidential 'slush fund' from which Ngwenya paid association officials cash allowances ranging between £1.10s and £5 for work they had previously done gratis.[85] Thanks to this fraudulent scheme, he dispensed material benefits that secured him the loyalty of many delegates in annual elections. The football patronage machine of Ngwenya exemplified how urban black entrepreneurs built local networks of power, and sometimes wealth, that were only tangentially connected to, or even in competition with, the aims of contemporary formal political organisations like the ANC.

The government's denial of political rights and economic opportunity to black people exacerbated competition for power and money in soccer. As Bernard Magubane pointed out, the DDAFA 'provide[d] scope for political ambitions of Africans frustrated in the wider society. [Africans] seek to satisfy the desire for recognition of their talents and abilities [in sport] since there are no opportunities in the service of the state'.[86]

In Cape Town, Monica Wilson and Archie Mafeje observed identical processes among African soccer and rugby officials in Langa township: 'To the white man the secretaryship of a rugby club may indeed be a burden, not willingly undertaken, but to most Africans office in almost any organisation carries prestige – far more than in a corresponding white club – and it is sought for that reason. "People in Langa cling to positions as tenaciously as if they were careers".'[87] Coplan has also pointed out how '[t]raditionally, personal prestige had been the most important incentive for productive activity beyond the necessary minimum. In the towns, social status depended on Western education, occupation, urbanization, and wealth.'[88] This social context aggravated tensions between Ngwenya's cabinet, known as the 'Russians', and an opposing group of educated, petit bourgeois men known as the 'Japanese'.

Fierce conflicts within DDAFA led to public disclosure of Ngwenya's unbridled corruption. The catalyst seems to have been the crash of the association's bus near Grahamstown on 29 September 1957, an incident which Ngwenya used to eliminate his opponents in the DDAFA executive committee. According to a DDAFA report, several players and officials were seriously injured in the accident on the way to a match in Port Elizabeth. There was speculation that the driver,

DDAFA official Zephaniah Dhlomo, may have been intoxicated at the time of the crash. Shortly after the accident DDAFA suspended Dhlomo for stealing £50 from the association. Members were prohibited from 'mingling' with Dhlomo until he repaid the organisation.[89] Charging that executive officials had met surreptitiously with Dhlomo in Albert Park, at the Dalton Road migrant worker hostel, and around greater Durban, Ngwenya called an emergency meeting in November. At this meeting, the house suspended six executive members by a vote of 228-20. The only officials who escaped unblemished were the treasurer, M. Mota, and Ngwenya, to whom, revealingly, the assembled delegates awarded extraordinary powers.[90]

Having victimised his opponents, Ngwenya slid into spiralling authoritarianism that precipitated a split in the Durban association. Banned from DDAFA in early 1958, officials and sympathisers of the 'Japanese' group founded the Durban and County African Football Association, or 'Tokyo', between 1959 and 1960. The black daily *World* of 15 February 1958 provided details of the chaotic atmosphere surrounding the 1958 annual general meeting:

> a riotous crowd stood outside the J.L. Farrell Hall hoping to enter the hall but in vain. All the people who were allowed to enter were Mr. Ngwenya's supporters. Mr. Ngwenya said he did not want to see a single reporter or photographer. Delegates from many clubs who were refused admission tried to gate-crash but they were stopped by the security corps with big sticks.

The *Golden City Post* of 23 February 1958 referred to these stick-wielding men as 'Ngwenya's Gestapo'. Unsurprisingly, the incumbent president secured re-election, though the press reported widespread dissatisfaction among the delegates regarding the conduct of the elections.[91] The sports columnist Theo Mthembu excoriated Ngwenya, comparing him to Shaka Zulu.[92] In the hyperbolic words of Mthembu in the *Golden City Post* of 23 February 1958:

> Can it be that the ghost of Chaka ka Zulu, one of the most despotic rulers in the history of the Africans, has come back to life in the person of Mr. H.P. Ngwenya, president of the DDAFA? His handling of the Association's recent annual meeting and election of office bearers for 1958 makes the ancient Zulu despot look tamer than a Salvation Army lass at an all-in wrestling show.

Ngwenya's abuse of power at the end of the decade suggested a larger breakdown in the administration of African football. He symbolised how hidden professionalism, racially aligned associations, and poor administration stymied the organic development of the game. He earned severe criticism for inexplicably overturning Eastern Transvaal's victory over 'his' Natal in the final of the National Shield knock-out competition in November 1958.[93]

Matters came to a head at the 1959 Durban annual general meeting. A delegate rose to speak and said: 'The President says that he has pimps [referring to the hand-picked gate attendants] he pays from the association funds. I am surprised that at the gates we are charged such exorbitant sums to pay these pimps. Now what I ask is that we be given the best way of voicing our dissatisfaction and that is the vote.'[94] The house voted 133-57 to appoint a commission of inquiry into the allegations of embezzlement and corruption against the president. In less than four months the five-man commission conducted 37 meetings, interviewed two dozen witnesses, and issued a 39-page report blasting Ngwenya.

The commission, which was chaired by DDAFA's elder statesman Edward C. Jali, discovered substantial evidence of deliberate wrongdoing. These findings were unusual in the South African context because no other African sporting association had DDAFA's money and because people were reluctant to give the authorities an opportunity to intrude on an African association's relative autonomy. In its detailed report, the commission denounced the executive's 'naked dereliction of duty' as an enabling factor for the failure of Ngwenya and treasurer Mota to prepare financial statements for 1958 and their inability to account for £7 772.[95] The report stated that more than £5 330 was paid to gate keepers, the key cogs in the president's patronage machine. It also pointed out that Ngwenya failed to discuss the association's £7 800 purchase of a 54-acre farm for new playing fields in the Inanda reserve, north-northwest of Durban centre, which, for reasons unknown, were never built.[96] The president admitted to placing cash from gate-takings in sealed en-velopes 'and put[ting] these away for safe-keeping until the persons for whom the payments are intended call for them'.[97] Amidst other somewhat minor misappropriations, Ngwenya used unauthorised Durban funds to pay for SAAFA travelling expenses and to 'loan' £200 to SAAFA. The commission found damning evidence that Ngwenya paid a £100 bribe to the driver of the bus involved in the accident, in exchange for providing evidence favourable to DDAFA in connection with a legal case arising from the bus crash in the Eastern Cape.[98] The Jali commission's report recommended that DDAFA eliminate 'gate payments'; document finances properly as required by its own constitution (that is, with the full participation of the executive committee); and cease the practice of paying allowances to executive members.[99]

Ngwenya rejected the report. He suspended the five members of the commission of inquiry and others he deemed political opponents.[100]

The once-powerful Durban and District African Football Association was crumbling. 'The [1960 annual general] meeting ended in an uproar, and the President, on the advice of the police, declared the meeting closed. The police escorted him from the hall accompanied by shouts of "We don't want you!" and "You must resign!"'[101] Later that afternoon, the 'Japanese' opposition met at the YMCA hall on Beatrice Street to elect interim officials of the Durban and County African Football Association. Following a court interdict, the DDAFA held a second annual general meeting in May 1960, which the 'Japanese' boycotted. At this meeting, the shrewd Ngwenya spoke in Zulu instead of English. This decision seems to have been a populist attempt to woo Zulu-speaking working-class delegates to his side. This appeal to ethnic consciousness exposed class divisions among the African population, which Ngwenya sought to exploit to his advantage in order to marginalise the educated, comparatively affluent, English-speaking backers of the 'Japanese' faction.[102]

Ngwenya employed rural and biblical imagery that resonated with both working-class Christians and with people who maintained spiritual and material connections to the densely inhabited rural reserves near the city. In a speech in which he 'declared both his dispensability and his indispensability', Ngwenya said: 'You chose me like an old man would do when he chooses his herdboy. He will choose him not because the boy will be better than others but because he likes the way he looks after the sheep.'[103] However, by this time, the soccer patriarch was overwhelmed by larger changes in soccer and society which brought sport, race, and politics closer together.

FOOTBALL ACROSS THE RACIAL DIVIDE
Football attracted considerable political interest in South Africa because it was played and watched by the majority of South Africans. In the 1950s domestic and international challenges to apartheid in football amplified the game's vanguard role within black popular culture and made it the most contentious sport in the country.[104] In ideological terms, black soccer institutions' demands for a nonracial, inclusive national association and a national team selected on merit politicised a vast majority of local athletes and fans while sensitising international opinion to the broader struggle against apartheid.[105] Football and political organisations – alternative institutions created by and serving the interests of black people – underwent similar, significant changes in the 1950s. Racially defined groups formed a multiracial alliance with domestic and international links, adopting a universal, non-sectarian political programme that gradually grew more radical over time.[106]

Historians Robert Archer and Antoine Bouillon correctly characterised South African football's balkanised organisation on the eve of apartheid as a 'wasteful system. There were up to four national federations in each sport, each with an independent organising body, separate finances and facilities and competitions. Administrative and financial costs were quadrupled while the level of competition was reduced by a similar factor.'[107] If the standards of play suffered from segregated football, so did the stability of administration and the quality of facilities available to different racial groups. There were structural causes for divided sport because residential (and social) segregation and apartheid social engineering hindered co-operation and competition across the colour line. But it is important to note that personal conflicts, as well as individual and group patterns of settlement and association also produced internal divisions within black sport. For example, the Cape District Football Association in Cape Town, a Coloured organisation founded in 1929, explicitly barred Muslims from joining its ranks.[108]

Despite these tensions within black football, some black officials began to question the *status quo*. Some administrators started to 'visualize the possibilities of gaining international honors' for black players.[109] In 1948 A.J. Albertyn, vice-president of the South African Coloured Football Association and president of the Western Province Association Football Board in Cape Town, attended a meeting in Johannesburg with the South Africa African Football Association. The delegates agreed 'in principle [to] the formation of a federation of the Coloured, Indian and African Associations'.[110] In a friendly match that coincided with the high-level negotiations, the Coloured 'national' team defeated (5-2) the African 'national' side. As a result of the positive atmosphere engendered by the events in Johannesburg, Albertyn and Dan Twala, secretary of SAAFA, organised a second round of talks and a rematch for May 1950. In this game played at Wynberg, Cape Town, the Coloureds won again (3-1), but, more importantly, delegates of the two associations formed the 'Federation of South African Football Associations', which appointed Twala president and Albertyn secretary and gave them the task of drafting a constitution.[111] Then, in April 1951, the Indian association attended an important meeting in Johannesburg where all three 'national' sporting institutions approved the Federation's constitution.

Finally, in a momentous conference held in Durban on 30 September 1951, African, Coloured, and Indian officials founded the South African Soccer Federation. Barring nobody on the grounds of race, colour, or creed, the Federation (SASF) was the largest soccer organisation in South Africa.[112] It brought more than 46 000 members of the African, Coloured, and Indian national associations into one multiracial umbrella body opposed to apartheid in football. Only the small 'Bantu' group, probably fearing a loss of power and visibility, and the racist white association (with 20 000 members) remained outside the Federation.[113] 'Long Live Federation, the football of the future!' Albertyn proclaimed to the press.[114]

As the links between sport and nationalism were reinforced, both personal and instrumental aspects of the evolving relationship between football and black politics came to the fore. These dynamics were captured in an article published in the November 1953 issue of *Drum* under the headline 'Political Football!' The 60 000 readers of *Drum* read about banned leaders of the liberation movement playing a 'Veterans versus Youth' soccer game on a farm outside Johannesburg.[115] It seems extremely likely that Rand soccer impresario Dan Twala, the game's referee, organised the event given that he was both a member of the ANC Youth League and a frequent contributor to *Drum's* sports pages.[116] Communist Party leaders Yusuf Dadoo and Moses Kotane were described as 'very comfortable at inside left and left back'. One of Bob Gosani's photographs portrayed Oliver Tambo, ANC Youth League co-founder and Nelson Mandela's law partner, playing for the Veterans in trousers, suspenders, and a beret, with his eyes focused on a football nestled at his feet. Many black nationalists enjoyed the game as a momentary physical and mental release from political organising. In the words of a former Robben Island prisoner:

'You can only sit around and read about Marxism and imperialism for so many hours a week, then you've got to have some fun!'[117]

Indeed, football was enjoyable, but it also projected an image of black politicians in touch with the social worlds of black workers. The ANC may have aimed to benefit from *Drum*'s coverage to counter charges from poorer people that it was losing touch with the popular constituency, a sensitive matter that was connected to the Western Areas Removals Scheme and the destruction of Sophiatown by the apartheid state.[118] ANC Youth League founder Walter Sisulu recognised the opinion-making role of Jim Bailey's magazine in the 1950s:

> The press was absolutely hostile to us. [. . .] When *Drum* came up, and later *Golden City Post*, it more or less took a different attitude. I think they had men who were able to read the situation. Men like Anthony Sampson [editor] and Bailey [publisher], that combination, they were able men who could see things better than the rest of the press. So they were not hostile, they were shaping things.[119]

Football evolved with and influenced the politics of South African liberation movements. In 1952 the ANC elected Chief Albert Luthuli, long-time football administrator and then president of the Natal Inter-Race Soccer Board, as its new president. That year, the ANC joined forces with the South African Indian Congress (SAIC) and members of the banned Communist Party to launch the Defiance Campaign, an 'essentially demonstrative' operation of mass civil disobedience against 'unjust laws' that popularised the anti-apartheid movement.[120] In 1955 the Coloured People's Organisation and the white Congress of Democrats joined the ANC and the SAIC in the Congress Alliance that adopted the Freedom Charter at the Congress of the People in Kliptown, outside Johannesburg. The co-operation and involvement of black South Africans on a mass scale inspired hope among proponents of a multiracial society. A similar process took place in football.

INTER-RACIALISM AND CHANGES ON THE PLAYING FIELDS

In 1952 A.I. Kajee, a pre-eminent Muslim Indian businessman and conservative Natal Indian Congress politician from Durban, donated a £500 trophy to SASF for a biennial competition between African, Coloured, and Indian 'national' teams.[121] The first Kajee Cup superseded anything ever seen in the friendly matches and inter-race board contests in earlier years. Staged in front of huge mixed crowds in Johannesburg, Durban, and Cape Town, the Kajee Cup games captured the imagination of the soccer-loving public. The expanding black press built up popular interest and stoked the fires of collective trepidation.[122] In October 1952, more than 15 000 enthusiastic spectators attended the Kajee Cup final between the Coloured and African 'national' teams at Wembley Stadium in a 'white' area of Johannesburg.[123]

The legendary 1952 final offers a glimpse into the social make-up of Federation soccer. Midfielder David Julius led a 'blue-collar' Coloured team comprised of carpenters, painters, construction workers, and other working-class players from Cape Town, Johannesburg, and Bloemfontein. (Later in the decade, Julius went to play professional football for Sporting Lisbon and obtained Portuguese citizenship.) Forward Prince Mabila captained a 'white-collar' African side of teachers, clerks, and messengers from Durban and the Witwatersrand. Mabila was a primary school teacher of history and Afrikaans from Eastern Native Township (George Goch), where he starred for the well-known Eastern Brothers club.[124] Among Mabila's team-mates were famous Durban stars like 'Stadig' Makhathini, Darius Dhlomo, Bush Bucks' 'Ace' Moeketsi and 'Halleluya' Zulu, as well as Gibson 'Danger' Makatelele – a clerk, boxer, 'muscular, agile, tough' defender for Alexandra Rangers who had an unsuccessful trial for Wolverhampton Wanderers in England in the late 1950s.[125] Also in the side was Grant Khomo, another teacher, described by *African Sports*, a black sporting monthly magazine published in 1953–54, as 'the best all-rounder that South Africa has ever produced'.[126] Khomo's career reflects the privileged, 'respectable' working-class background of many of the top African players of this period. Born in Potgietersrus in the northern Transvaal (1922?), Khomo played soccer at Khaiso High School and then during the war attended the South African Native College at Fort Hare where he excelled in soccer, rugby, tennis, golf, and athletics. Like many former Fort Hare students, including Nelson Mandela and Oliver Tambo, Khomo moved to the Rand, where he began teaching history at Orlando High School in 1944. Outstanding physical fitness and stamina complemented his all-round skills. Khomo won the South African Bantu Lawn Tennis Union men's singles, doubles, and mixed doubles titles in 1953, was an African Springbok in rugby, showed promise as a batsman, wicket-keeper, and slip fielder in cricket and, of course, performed admirably as a versatile midfielder for the African 'national' football team.

The novelty of the Kajee Cup and African and Coloured teams' reliance on contrasting playing styles contributed to the enthusiasm surrounding the 1952 final. The African team used the short-passing 'Motherwell' positional style while the Coloured team employed a more physical, direct, English kick-and-rush style.[127] The Cup final entertained the large yet disciplined crowd with a 'mixed diet of brawn and brain'.[128] Trailing 2-5 and seemingly desperate, the Africans threw caution to the wind and launched a wave of attacks. In a thrilling finish, three goals from Solomon 'Buya Msotho' Nkuta, a classy centre-forward from Alexandra with a 'terrific shot', a 'tactician and strategist' who had scored both of his team's goals, tied the game at 5-5.[129] Buya Msotho's memorable five-goal performance exhilarated fans and provided ammunition for the many fans, players, and officials who believed in the need for racial integration under the aegis of the multiracial South African Soccer Federation.

Even though a starkly ghettoised society greatly complicated the practical pursuit of inter-racial sport, occasional friendly matches between white and black teams took place in Durban, Johannesburg, and Cape Town during the first half of the decade. In Durban, a white team captained by a Springbok midfielder named

Howell could not contain 'Kalamazoo' Mokone whose hat-trick led Adams College Shooting Stars to an impressive 5-2 victory. In 1955 a mixed crowd in attendance at the Princeton Ground in Wynberg, Cape Town, watched a Coloured Western Province Association Football Board team managed by Cape District Football Association president William Herbert and captained by Basil D'Oliveira – future professional cricketer in England – trounce (5-1) the white Currie Cup winners Western Province team.[130] Growing government opposition to inter-racial sport, however, made it increasingly difficult to organise such exciting matches. After a black Pretoria Methodist team crushed a white Johannesburg Texas Rovers 9-0 at Wemmer Ground in Johannesburg in 1954, the municipal Non-European Affairs Department informed the organisers that 'under no circumstances whatsoever are European teams to play on council grounds allocated to you without my permission in writing'.[131] South African police detectives questioned 'certain football people' about the game; 'apparently, the detectives wanted to know who the Europeans were, and who made the arrangements for the match'.[132] Repressive police tactics and hardening urban segregation made it harder (and more costly) to play football across the apartheid colour line. But *Drum*, probably voicing the opinion of most South Africans, crafted an alternative vision in December 1955: 'Just imagine a team drawn from the pick of the Coloured, African and Indian leagues, as well as from the Whites. What an unbeatable Springbok side that would be!'

CHAPTER 8

No Apartheid Here

Anti-racism and Professional Football in the 1960s

On Saturday, 6 April 1963, thousands of fans gathered outside the Natalspruit Indian Sports Ground in Johannesburg to attend matches staged by the South African Soccer League (SASL). But the gates were closed. A handwritten notice posted by the Johannesburg city council's NEAD announced the cancellation of the games.[1] Intrepid spectators and organisers climbed over the corrugated iron fence, only to discover that the prescient municipal authorities had removed the goalposts from the playing field! A group of supporters then transported a set of goalposts from a nearby ground and lifted them over the perimeter fence. The *World* of 8 April 1963 reported that vice-president Dan Twala exclaimed in a defiant tone: 'We told the council we would play on our ground.' That afternoon, a crowd of over 15 000 people watched Alexandra's Real Fighters defeat Transvaal United 1-0 and Moroka Swallows crush Blackpool United 6-1. Why had the city council shut out the predominantly black crowd from Johannesburg's most popular soccer stadium? What was the defiant – and that day successful – SASL, who backed it, and how significant was its role in the broader social and political history of South African football?

THE INTERNATIONAL POLITICS OF FOOTBALL

As we saw in Chapter 7, the South African Soccer Federation's competitions were an integral part of broader trends in contemporary South African sport. Between 1948 and 1960, many racially defined black federations forged unified national sporting institutions in protest against apartheid. These multiracial bodies represented the majority of South Africans and 'their demand for recognition on terms of equality with other (white) sportsmen was contrary to Government policy, threatened the power of the white federations and embarrassed the international sports bodies'.[2] In response to these developments, the Pretoria regime articulated the first apartheid sport policy in 1956. In so doing, it asserted the Afrikaner-led government's steadfast opposition to inter-racialism. Pretoria's heavy-handed intervention and the entrenchment of apartheid bureaucracy persuaded black athletes, spectators and organisers that demands for meritocratic sport were inextricably connected to the struggle for a free and democratic society.

The SASF fought a bitter struggle for recognition within FIFA. Led by George Singh, a progressive (Hindu) Indian lawyer from Durban, the SASF in June 1954 applied for membership to the world soccer body (which permits only one association per member nation), claiming to be the legitimate representative of South Africa with 82 per cent of its registered players. The white South African Football Association (SAFA), which had been hastily accepted into FIFA at the 1952 Helsinki Congress, represented only 18 per cent of South African players.[3] At a heated meeting in Johannesburg in November 1954, the Federation rejected the white association's offer of affiliate membership without voting rights. Then on 8 May 1955 the Federation won a relatively easy, though significant, battle at FIFA. The world body's Emergency Committee concluded that the white association 'does not comprise and control all the clubs and the players in South Africa and therefore it has not the standing of a real national association that can govern and develop football in accordance with provision of art. 3 of the Statutes of FIFA'.[4] While this important official statement gave black football some confidence, as well as the high moral ground, FIFA did not extend the offer of membership to the Federation because the latter did not include whites.[5] The following month SASF once again offered to merge with SAFA on equal terms, but the white body, showing no intention of modifying its racist stance, rejected the offer.

June 1955 was a milestone in South African political history as the Freedom Charter was presented to the Congress of the People, but 1955 was also an important year for South African sport. Dennis Brutus, a teacher, poet, journalist, sportsman and activist from Port Elizabeth, founded the Co-ordinating Committee for International Recognition of Sport (CCIRS). In a letter to the *Golden City Press* published on 5 August 1956, Brutus, who had been classified 'Coloured' under the provisions of the Population Registration Act, stated that the CCIRS 'based itself on a single, simple principle: That, all South Africans should be allowed to represent their country – if they are good enough.' Even though, according to Brutus, the CCIRS succumbed quickly to police intimidation, it 'established that all-white teams were not entitled to describe themselves as South African'.[6] This important achievement by the short-lived organisation invigorated the Federation's campaign at FIFA and inspired the founding of the anti-apartheid South African Sports Association in East London in 1958.[7]

Soccer's vanguard role in challenging white South Africa was reflected in the fact that the first international delegation to visit the country for the purpose of addressing apartheid-related disputes was the 1956 FIFA commission of inquiry.[8] K.L. Lotsy, a former colonial officer in the Dutch East Indies, headed the delegation that included Joseph McGuire (United States of America), Abdelaziz Abdallah Salem (Egypt), and FIFA's Swiss secretary Kurt Gasunann.[9] After hearing from officials of SAFA and SASF in January 1956, the Lotsy commission confirmed the FIFA executive's earlier findings that SAFA represented a minority group and did not properly constitute a national association. However, the FIFA commission dealt Federation a major setback by agreeing with SAFA that football segregation was a

South African 'tradition and custom', and it recommended further negotiations between the whites and Federation. The Lotsy commission highlighted the ways in which white South Africans' lobbying efforts in favour of the *status quo*, and the evasive actions of conservative international federations, hindered black sport from making more substantial progress in the apartheid era.

In an attempt to create confusion while remaining indifferent to apartheid in soccer, the white association deleted the offending racially exclusionary clause from its constitution at its annual meeting in March 1956. SAFA then renamed itself the Football Association of Southern Africa (FASA) to create the perception of substantive change while keeping an all-white status.[10] In response to this subterfuge, the Federation reiterated its demands for complete racial integration; it also announced a plan to merge the rival 'African' and 'Bantu' groups who, in the interim, formed an 'All-Blacks' team coached by Topper Brown in the 1956 Kajee Cup.[11] In this evolving scenario, Pretoria denied passports to the Federation's delegates planning on travelling to the FIFA Congress in Lisbon in June 1956; with the consequence that the renowned white intellectual Harold Bloom argued the Federation's case instead.[12] Despite Bloom's best efforts in Lisbon, FASA's deletion of the racist clause in its constitution preserved its membership in FIFA.

World football's governing body revisited the South African issue at its Stockholm congress in 1958 and again advised that SASF and FASA find a compromise.[13] It is interesting to note that the debates about apartheid South Africa in Lisbon led to a decision by Egyptian, Ethiopian, and Sudanese officials to form the Confédération Africaine de Football (CAF). Diplomatically, the African officials invited Fred Fell, president of FASA, to attend the founding meeting of CAF in Khartoum in 1957: the white South African accepted. According to Darby, the founding of CAF was of great political significance because 'it lent considerable weight to the use of the game as a tool for asserting national and pan-African identity . . . on a global basis'.[14]

THE SOUTH AFRICAN GOVERNMENT'S RESPONSE

As the nonracial cricket, weightlifting, and rugby federations joined the Federation in applying for international recognition, the South African government invaded the playing fields.[15] In a statement to the Afrikaans press on 27 June 1956, the Minister of the Interior, Dr T.E. Dönges, announced that sport within the borders of South Africa had to be practised in accordance with the principle of 'separate development'.[16] The Dönges declaration, as historian Grant Jarvie stated, 'incorporated the area of sport and of non-racial sport for the first time into the political domain of the state'.[17] The sport policy stipulated that:

> Whites and blacks should organise their sporting activities separately, there should be no inter-racial competitions within the Republic's borders, mixing of races in [South African] teams should be avoided and sportsmen from other lands should respect the country's customs, as she respected theirs. Within that

framework, non-White sportsmen from [the] outside world should not be debarred from entering South Africa to compete with non-Whites.

The Government would prefer Non-White sports organisations seeking international recognition to do so through the aegis of White associations already enjoying such benefits. It would not support Non-White sporting divisions by any process of squeezing White South Africans out of international competitions. No travel facilities would be granted to people guilty of such subversive intentions.[18]

The Dönges policy strengthened the Federation's case at FIFA. Inside the country, Pretoria's direct intervention in sport and the removal of Coloured people from the Common Voters Roll in 1956, fostered firmer unity among black footballers against the common enemy of apartheid.

Between 1956 and 1958 the central government avoided further actions that might have jeopardised white athletes' participation in international sporting events. The state relied on existing legislation (particularly the Native Urban Areas Act of 1923 [amended in 1945], the 1950 Group Areas Act, and the 1953 Reservation of Separate Amenities Act) to make truly nonracial sport effectively impossible. White officials blamed segregation in domestic soccer on internal divisions in black sport and blacks' inferior standard of play *vis-à-vis* whites, and even claimed mixed sport led to racial tensions.[19] In addition to blaming the victims of apartheid, FASA dismissed the Federation's calls for integration as 'political' rather than concerned with sport: 'the *political agitators* who are now ruling the Federation behind the scenes, are merely using soccer as a catspaw for their own selfish ends' (emphasis added).[20] Of course, it had been the Dönges policy that explicitly politicised sport in South Africa.

In an attempt to protect and preserve white South Africa's international affiliation, municipal authorities and FASA shifted tactics in 1958. They cajoled some local black associations into accepting non-voting 'associate membership' in FASA. In collusion with local city councils, FASA offered both the carrot of stadiums, coaching, and foreign tours and the stick of possible ostracism from township facilities.[21] This paternalistic touch of trusteeship ideology divided black sport. It also deluded members of FIFA who were sympathetic to South Africa into thinking that the white association, having dropped the racial exclusivity clause from its constitution in 1956, no longer practised racial discrimination. Africans were most vulnerable to co-optation because they – unlike Indians and Coloureds – were denied the right to own land in urban areas and, consequently, were dependent on the munificence of local authorities for provision of, and access to, sporting facilities.[22]

The Johannesburg Bantu Football Association (JBFA) and the United (Coloured) Football Association in Cape Town were the first to accept subordinate membership in the white association in 1958.[23] While the co-optation of a minor Cape Town group comprising 12 teams was mainly symbolic, the affiliation of the JBFA's 253 teams with the white Southern Transvaal Football Association was of much greater significance.[24] JBFA officials agreed to co-operate at a meeting with officials of the Southern Transvaal and the Johannesburg Non-European Affairs Department (NEAD) held in February 1958. Dave Snaier, chairman of the Southern Transvaal and vice-president of FASA, and W.J.P. Carr, the NEAD manager, argued that 'it would be in the interest of the JBFA to affiliate and enjoy the advantages offered'.[25] The benefits included international matches, coaching, lectures for referees, training literature from overseas, and access to the Orlando Stadium under construction in Soweto. After securing the support of Bethuel P. Morolo, president of the South African Bantu Football Association, in Kimberley in October 1958, Harry Madibane officially announced the JBFA's affiliation with the white association in his presidential report at the annual general meeting held at the Jubilee Social Centre at Wemmer Hostel in March 1959.[26] The SABFA followed suit in May. The rewards were immediate. Orlando Stadium, which had cost £36 000 (£21 000 came from private companies and £15 000 from the city council) to build, was opened by Daan C. de Wet Nel, Minister of Bantu Administration and Development, on 2 May 1959, and promptly allocated to the JBFA.[27]

This orchestrated co-optation campaign and Pretoria's refusal to grant passports to SASF officials facilitated FIFA's decision to confirm FASA's standing as the legitimate representative of South African football in 1958.[28] At the Stockholm congress, president Fred Fell and vice-president Dave Snaier appeared for FASA, while Ivor Montague, president of the International Table Tennis Board and a strong ally of the anti-apartheid movement, represented the Federation. Following the setback in Stockholm, the Federation issued a proudly defiant press statement: 'the refusal of full status by FIFA was preferable to the acceptance of subservient, associate membership through FASA and that the Federation would continue to fight for international recognition'.[29] But in order for its position to be as persuasive as possible before the FIFA meetings scheduled in Rome in 1960, the Federation needed to reorganise its racially aligned – African, Coloured, and Indian – 'federal' structure and finally transform itself into a fully nonracial organisation.

The reluctance of some black football associations to desegregate, as well as the opposition of the government and the white sporting establishment, complicated the realignment. The South African Indian Football Association (SAIFA), for example, excluded non-Indians from its ranks until the late 1950s, when it permitted four per team in the Sam China Cup, the Indian 'national' tournament. Forming a small minority *vis-à-vis* Coloureds and Africans, some Indian officials feared that opening their football competitions to athletes of all races would erode their personal status and power and also dismantle a proud ethnic tradition established in 1903. In other words, as David Black and John Nauright noted with reference to black rugby in South Africa, 'white policies were not the only factors in the creation and maintenance of social divisions . . . historical agents in local communities also profoundly shaped local [sport] cultures'.[30]

As the Federation began to address these cumbersome organisational problems, a group of weightlifters led by Dennis Brutus formed the South African Sports

Association (SASA) in October 1958. SASA injected new life into the Federation's domestic and international struggle. Supported by the ANC and white liberals such as Alan Paton, the SASA 'promoted nonracial sport and lobbied international sports federations to withdraw recognition of whites-only South African affiliates'.[31] Football represented about 50 000 of the 70 000 members; the other athletes came from weightlifting, athletics, cycling, boxing, table tennis, lawn tennis, netball, baseball and softball, rugby and cricket.[32] With ten Federation officials on its executive committee and George Singh a co-author of its constitution, football played a vital role in the development of SASA.[33]

Football scored one of SASA's very first successes. In 1959 a well-organised campaign forced the cancellation of a football match in Cape Town between the white Western Province team and Portuguesa, a professional Brazilian club *en route* to Mozambique. To comply with apartheid policies, the Brazilian club (presumably its white members) had offered to drop several black players and field an all-white side against the South Africans. After receiving an official protest from SASA objecting to this acceptance of racism, the Brazilian president Juscelino Kubitschek cabled the Portuguesa men in Cape Town and prohibited them from competing in South Africa.[34]

With the Portuguesa incident showing the benefits of the football/SASA partnership, the time seemed right for Federation to make the transition from a

The truth about soccer apartheid.

multiracial to nonracial organisation. In January 1960 the Capetonian A.J. Albertyn submitted an official proposal to transform Federation into a fully nonracial institution, 'as a means of hastening and ensuring our eventual recognition in the international sphere'.[35] Albertyn advocated the elimination of the national African, Coloured, and Indian units that constituted the SASF and called for their replacement with new, nonracial provincial units. Before the motion could even be tabled at the biennial meeting in Durban, Federation obtained two major victories in the international arena. In August 1960 the FIFA Congress in Rome passed with overwhelming support a resolution that stated: 'a National Association must be open to all who practise football in that country whether amateur, "non-amateur" or professional and without any racial, religious, or political discrimination'.[36] FIFA also demanded that FASA abide by the Rome resolution within twelve months or face expulsion from international football. At a separate meeting in Rome, CAF went ahead and expelled white South Africa. FIFA suspended South Africa on 25 September 1961.[37] Football sanctions were among the very first international indictments of the apartheid regime. At the same time that apartheid South Africa came to dominate the international politics of sport, the game transformed itself into a life-blood for black South Africans living in the grim context of grand apartheid's bantustans, labour bureaus, and internal security machinery.

THE FORMATION OF THE PEOPLE'S LEAGUE

After year-long discussions regarding the organisation of a professional league, ten African, Indian, and Coloured football administrators officially established the South African Soccer League at a meeting held in February 1961 at the home of Lucas Khoza, in Alexandra Township, Johannesburg.[38] These educated professionals and businessmen had decided to break away from the South African Soccer Federation which was opposed to professionalism.[39] The executive tightly controlled League affairs, its power unchecked by a constitution that awarded individual executive members ten electoral votes while individual clubs had the right to only one each. The fledgling 'People's League' was not a democratic organisation, but its leadership produced widespread support for nonracial sport while ably tackling serious financial difficulties and growing opposition from white authorities.

As an alternative institution, the SASL did not see itself as a political organisation, but its attractive games and meritocratic, colour-blind ideals had mass appeal and, therefore, potential political implications for white-minority rule. The Pretoria regime and the white soccer establishment came to view the integrated SASL as a pernicious force because there was no law in South Africa prohibiting racially mixed team sport.[40] The government's neglect of sporting infrastructure in black communities, coupled with the authorities' increasingly aggressive dedication to strict racial segregation in sport, provided incontrovertible proof to black athletes and fans that sport and politics were inseparable. The struggle for survival of the SASL influenced decisively FIFA's decision to uphold the suspension of the racist white Football Association of South Africa (FASA) from international football after 1961.[41]

The possibility of organising football on a professional basis in South Africa had been the subject of debate since the 1930s. As already noted, money was no stranger to black football. In the 1920s slumyard teams in Johannesburg competed for cash prizes and, since at least the early 1930s, mines, factories and local associations offered employment and preferential treatment to workers who exhibited outstanding footballing skills (see Chapters 3 to 5). It was common knowledge that in the 1950s top clubs such as Orlando Pirates and Moroka Swallows in Johannesburg and Durban Bush Bucks paid their best players 'under the table' by distributing portions of the club's share of gate-takings at big matches (see Chapters 6 and 7). Patron-managers and administrators reaped the lion's share of the direct and indirect material profits trickling out of the game, not least because amateur players, by definition, had no right to claim compensation for their sporting performances.[42] The main consequences of hidden professionalism were inefficient administration, sub-par standards of play, unequal distribution of financial rewards and seemingly hopeless segmentation of black football along racial and ethnic lines.

The founding of a white professional league proved to be a catalyst for black football in South Africa. In June 1959, journalist Vivian Granger, businessman Lubbe Snooyman, Johannesburg councillor Dave Marais, and others, mostly English-speaking whites linked to the United Party, launched the National Football League (NFL).[43] The NFL secured financial support from wealthy corporate sponsors, most notably British Petroleum (BP), South African Breweries (SAB), as well as the United Tobacco Company (UTC). Encouraged by the backing of municipal authorities, big business, and the media, the NFL attracted sizeable crowds in Durban and Johannesburg, and later in Cape Town as well. SAB sponsorship linked the white Football Association Cup final to a popular beer by naming it the Castle Cup. Because white soccer rarely generated widespread enthusiasm, whites and blacks were surprised when Castle Cup finals at the city council-owned Rand Stadium between Johannesburg Rangers and Germiston Callies in 1959, and Durban City and Johannesburg Ramblers in 1960, drew 16 238 and 22 524 spectators respectively.[44] Crowds at white games were generally small although championship matches could be exceptions, as in 1946 when 40 000 spectators attended the Challenge Cup final between Boksburg and Rangers at the old Wanderers Ground in Johannesburg.[45]

Drum magazine picked up on the achievements of the NFL. In the August 1959 issue an article entitled 'Why shouldn't we start our own Pro Soccer?' publicly raised the question many were now discussing in private: what might happen if there were a nonracial, professional league run by black people? 'Remember that soccer is just another game to the whites. Rugby gets the crowds. Soccer gets what is left. Now, for non-white South Africans, soccer is the National Game,' *Drum* pointed out; 'Why shouldn't WE start our own professional inter-racial Soccer League? . . . We've asked these questions the past few weeks, and, from clubmen and sports officials, the answer every time has been, "Yes, let's try."'

Theo Mthembu, a leading sports reporter for the *Golden City Post* in the 1950s and 60s, explained in an interview that an additional factor driving popular demand for nonracial professional soccer was the widely publicised knowledge that top black South Africans were being recruited for trials and signing contracts in European leagues. 'Players and officials were very much in favor [of pro soccer],' said Mthembu. 'It had been done in many parts of the world, they had their own players going out of the country [pauses] Dhlomo, Zuma, Mokone, they had been successful.'[46] Pretoria's Stephen 'Kalamazoo' Mokone was the first black South African footballer to play professionally in Europe when he signed a contract with Welsh club Cardiff City in the English Third division in 1956.[47] Two years later, Mokone moved to Dutch Second division club Heracles, where he was joined by Durban superstars Darius Dhlomo in November 1958 and Herbert 'Shordex' Zuma the following season. Dhlomo pursued a second career in professional boxing and both players remained in the Netherlands after their sporting careers ended.[48] Early in 1961, top English club Leeds United signed Albert 'Hurry-Hurry' Johanneson, an exceptionally fast winger who had caught the eye of English scouts when he led the Coloured 'national' team to Kajee Cup triumphs in 1956 and 1960.[49] Players' international experiences inspired fans. In Mthembu's words, 'those things made them feel that they had to do something to get up; but it wasn't everybody who could go overseas so why not start it at home? Let's play professional soccer right here!'[50] The SASL aimed to satisfy the voracious appetite for top-class soccer in black communities around the country.

The League's perpetual struggle to secure playing grounds and economic capital underlines the profound connections between sport and the political economy of apartheid. From its inception, the SASL fought to keep sporting dreams and financial investments alive by openly challenging racism in sport. The SASL encouraged those athletes classified by the apartheid regime as African, Indian or Coloured to compete in racially mixed teams. SASL's principled and unwavering commitment to nonracialism, a stance motivated by a combination of moral principle, political consciousness, and market-driven interests, represented a direct challenge to Pretoria's master plan of separate development. As a result, the organisation came into conflict with white sporting officials, municipal authorities, and the apartheid state.

For the oppositional SASL, carving out a nonracial sporting space at a time of unprecedented state repression entailed compliance with some apartheid regulations. For example, the SASL always applied to local Group Areas Boards for permits to gain access to municipal sporting facilities.[51] Initially, white authorities allowed these SASL matches to take place. At least three factors explain this governmental lassitude. Firstly, the state was dealing with serious political challenges from the liberation movements and social unrest in the early 1960s, so that the operations of an unproven, renegade football league were of secondary importance.[52] Secondly, the League was perceived as a 'non-European' affair. There were only a few whites involved, and those usually occupied positions of authority as coaches and referees. Finally, the SASL matches presented local governments with an opportunity to collect entertainment taxes at rates of 15 to 20 per cent, which would provide additional revenue for municipal treasuries.

Nascent pro clubs grappled with grave financial insecurity. Investments by Durban entrepreneurial groups, including Indian textile manufacturers, retailers in the central business district, organised crime syndicates, and boxing promoters supplied an initial injection of capital for individual clubs. Durban Aces United, for example, received the financial and technical support of Daddy Naidoo, a boss in the notorious Crimson League gang, as well as a promoter of professional boxing fights at Durban City Hall.[53] In Cape Town, Bennie Katz, a Jewish night club owner with a passion for thoroughbred racing, provided financial backing for the formation of the Cape Ramblers Football Club.[54] The resources of powerful men like Naidoo and Katz covered neither the operational costs for individual clubs nor the national League's expenses. And so the meagre resources available to black entrepreneurs meant that the SASL also needed corporate sponsorships to survive. Dan Twala approached the UTC, a corporation with a long-standing connection to African football. Eager to attract black consumers, UTC agreed to a sponsorship deal with the SASL worth R2 000 in 1961, a partnership renewed each season of the League's existence. The UTC–SASL deal was mutually beneficial. The tobacco company gained access to vast township markets and the League obtained prize money for its competitions.

THE LEAGUE'S EARLY SUCCESS

The SASL competition that kicked off on 9 April 1961 ushered in a new era in the history of South African football. Avalon Athletic, Berea, and Aces United from Durban, and Moroka Swallows, Transvaal United, and Blackpool United from Johannesburg competed in the first season.[55] A dazzling performance by 23-year-old left-winger Joseph 'Excellent' Mthembu of Pietermaritzburg, unofficial Footballer of the Year in 1959 according to the *World* newspaper, highlighted an explosive debut for the SASL. Mthembu scored four goals in Durban Aces United's 6-1 rout of Blackpool United at Curries Fountain. A paying crowd estimated at between 7 000 and 8 000 people watched the inaugural contest for a reported gate-taking of R1 240.[56] Transvaal United from Noordgesig, the Coloured township in Soweto, claimed the inaugural League championship. United narrowly missed winning the 'double,' losing the UTC Cup final to Cape Town Ramblers. In a spectacular match that drew over 20 000 spectators to the Green Point Track in Cape Town, the hosts won 4-2, with Basil 'Puzzy' Jansen scoring a hat-trick.[57]

Consistently large crowds bear out the League's extraordinary success in comparison with the amateur era. The average paid attendance in 1961 was 6 598 for R45 335 in gate-takings at Durban's Curries Fountain, Johannesburg's Natalspruit Indian Sports Ground, and Cape Town's Green Point Track.[58] However, contemporary

SOUTH AFRICAN SOCCER LEAGUE

presents

R2000 United Tobacco Co. Knock-Out Cup Final

CAPE RAMBLERS

vs.

TRANSVAAL UNITED

GREEN POINT TRACK

SATURDAY, 14th OCTOBER, 1961

at 3.30 p.m.

№   1636

5c

Edited by D. N. BANSDA for and on behalf of the W.P. Soccer League

With Compliments and Best Wishes for a Memorable Cup-Final

from

OHLSSON'S CAPE BREWERIES LTD.

Basil Jansen

Official Match Programme, South African Soccer League Cup Final (1961).

newspaper reports and interviews with former players, club directors, and League officials pointed out that the official attendance figures were grossly misleading. In Johannesburg, for example, thousands of fans scaled the fence or watched games from surrounding mine dumps.[59] Tax evasion also encouraged the underreporting of match attendance. It is reasonable to conclude that the average crowd at SASL games was about 11 000 spectators.[60]

Despite meagre financial resources and substandard facilities, the SASL overcame government opposition and rose to national prominence. After a successful first season, the SASL expanded by adding Soweto's Orlando Pirates, Maritzburg City, and Lincoln City from Pietermaritzburg and Durban Hearts. The League also created three provincial Second division leagues with 46 clubs in the Transvaal, Natal and the Cape. Teams joined the League for a range of reasons. The promise of financial gain appealed to organisers and players denied most (legal) economic opportunities. The League's integrationist stance also garnered popular support. The affiliation of Orlando Pirates to the SASL, for example, was largely attributed to the efforts of their charismatic captain, the late Eric 'Scara' Sono, a populist and an ardent opponent of racism in sport.[61]

For many participants the human desire to compete at the highest possible level trumped political considerations. Doug Lomberg, captain and secretary of the Cape Ramblers, stated he 'knew so little of the underlying political turmoil'. Personal development and professional success were more immediate motivations. In Lomberg's words: 'I chose to dedicate myself to promoting the game of soccer, to the success of the Cape Ramblers organisation, to those wonderful team-mates of mine who sacrificed so much to elevate soccer to the relatively great heights we accomplished.'[62] The SASL's remarkable capacity to resonate with individual ambitions and collective needs, while entertaining thousands of people on a regular basis, were fundamental to the League's growing popularity. In addition, an expanding black popular press provided extensive coverage of the SASL's entertaining games, thereby helping to entrench football deeper into South African popular culture before the advent of state television in 1976.[63]

With expansion in 1962, SASL attendance increased 177 per cent from the previous year.[64] According to the available data, integrated professional football at its peak may have attracted about 17 per cent of the black population living in urban areas.[65] Professionalism improved playing standards tremendously and the popularity of the SASL owed a great deal to the exciting quality of the football on display.

EARLY SCIENTIFIC FOOTBALL AND THE BLACK WORKING-CLASS STREET GAME

The fitness and tactical aspects of the game saw the most dramatic change in the way in which black football in South Africa was played after 1960. In *Drum* of May 1961, Doug Lomberg described the impact of professional training on amateur footballers in unambiguous terms:

When we trotted out on the pitch for our first training spell, I thought we were a pretty slick bunch of soccer players. Brother! Did I have a lot to learn. An hour with a pro trainer and we were breathing like a lot of cart-horses. When I look back and see what he's done for our game I realize what a long way it is from amateur to pro. Our game is unrecognizable. We're rippling fit, and our whole approach to the game is more serious.

Keen followers of the League appreciated the dynamic new brand of football performed. 'The best feature of these boys, besides their superb ball control and accuracy, was their workout to a rigorous schedule,' stated a reporter in *The Leader* of 30 June 1961 after watching the Cape Ramblers in training. 'I was more than impressed by the seriousness with which they took their exercises.' This new emphasis on fitness turned physical conditioning into a regular feature of domestic football. With so few proper training facilities available, a growing number of footballers worked out with pro boxers who willingly shared their knowledge and experience in maintaining rigorous, regimented fitness training routines. Footballers and boxers, the black working-class athletes *par excellence*, ran together through township streets in the early mornings and evenings, and trained in gyms lifting weights and strengthening both the upper and lower body.[66] Sparring was kept to a minimum, probably not at the boxers' insistence.

By the 1963 season, almost every SASL club employed a physical trainer, typically an individual borrowed from bodybuilding or boxing circles. Many teams were coached by whites, among them R.F. Young at Maritzburg City, Koos Brandsma at Lincoln City, Bobby Reed at Berea, and Norman 'Jock' Samuels at Cape Ramblers. Twenty-two-year-old Clive Barker, future coach of the South African team that won the 1996 African Nations' Cup and qualified for the World Cup finals for the first time in 1998, took his first steps in the coaching profession with Coastals, a club based in the Clairwood section of Durban. Fielding Indian, white, and Coloured athletes, Coastals competed in the Natal Second division of the SASL and were later promoted to the First division.[67] White coaches brought different experiences and approaches to SASL clubs, but they all shared an emphasis on fitness, discipline, and teamwork.

Many black athletes shared white coaches' enthusiasm for physical conditioning. Napoleon 'Kallie' Page of Blackpool and Eric 'Scara' Sono of Orlando Pirates were among the athletes who worked out regularly, alternating days with weights in the gym, to morning roadwork (running) and late-afternoon practice with the ball.[68] Other players, however, criticised the approach of white coaches. One player argued in *The Leader* of 6 July 1962 that, 'apart from ordinary physical training routines they [whites] don't seem to teach us much theory. I feel they're holding back on us.' The unwillingness (or inability) of some whites to modify European coaching methods and philosophies to suit the strengths of black players stunted the development of a creolised South African style of play.[69]

Given some of the difficulties in dealing with white coaches, black professionals often 'learned more about football through reading overseas magazines'.[70] Without access to either formally trained coaches in the townships or televised matches, black players educated themselves by reading and circulating British football magazines and coaching manuals.[71] For example, Edward 'Fish' Neku of Moroka Swallows, one of the top black goalkeepers in the 1950s and early 60s, told reporter Sy Mogapi, for the *Golden City Post* of 23 September 1956, that he 'read a lot about the techniques of 'keeping from books written by well-known goalies'. The distribution of European football films also influenced the adoption of new methods of play. On the Rand, football enthusiasts paid a 25c admission fee to watch the Real Madrid vs Eintracht Frankfurt 1960 European Cup final at an overcrowded Kings Theatre in Alexandra township on 9 August 1962.[72]

Keeping pace with global changes in the game that led to the rise of 'scientific football', a tactical revolution occurred in the local game. The introduction of the attacking 4-2-4 system, popularised by Brazil in Pelé's first World Cup triumph in 1958, was among the most important changes. The arrival of the 4-2-4 scheme in South Africa attenuated the dominance of the older tactical formations, such as the 2-3-5 'pyramid', the Italian *metodo*, and the English WM.[73] Avalon Athletic of Durban was one of the first clubs in South Africa to use the physically demanding 4-2-4 system. The League's most successful club employed it with stunning consistency, winning League championships in 1962 (shared with Aces United), 1963 and 1964, and UTC Cup titles in 1963, 1964 and 1965. In general, SASL teams shunned the English long-ball game because, according to one knowledgeable source in *The Leader* of 30 June 1961, 'the short-passing Continental type of play is much en vogue and is paying better dividends'.

The structural neglect of sport in black townships complicated the adoption of new tactics and styles of play. SASL players developed their skills as youths in the narrow and uneven spaces of street football. In the streets and patches of open ground in schools and townships, ball control, individualism, toughness, and improvisation outweighed the importance of moving without the ball, creating and using space, combination passing, and field vision. Lack of fundamentals was apparent in the SASL, where 'positioning, defensive play, how to finish off forward moves, what to do with the ball when hard pressed, how to tackle properly and how to beat a man were all elementary points that were sadly neglected by our top teams'.[74] These kinds of local dynamics seem to explain the SASL's 5,11 goals per match average (1961–65), which was twice that of contemporary European professional leagues and World Cup tournaments.[75]

Material poverty hindered the organic development of the SASL in other ways. SASL players could not afford to live by football wages alone. Athletes earned R16 (£8 at the time) per match *played*; some enterprising owners also offered incentive bonuses of R2 for a draw and R4 for a win.[76] Team members who trained regularly but did not participate in official matches received no money at all. Modest wages and nonsalaried contracts meant that football emoluments could only supplement wages from regular employment in a variety of higher and lower working-class occupations. Work commitments limited the amount of time athletes could devote to training. Practice sessions were held two or three times a week, with players scrambling to reach the designated ground in the late afternoon after work and paying for transport costs out of their meagre wages. If players earned little more than pocket money, then club directors and investors hardly fared better. The case of Transvaal United in 1961 synthesised the gargantuan financial difficulties facing early professional football clubs. Despite winning the League championship and reaching the UTC Cup final, Transvaal United barely covered its expenses at the end of the 1961 season. Players who participated in each of the club's thirteen matches earned R208 (£104). In 1975, the average monthly wage of Indian workers was R246, while Coloured and African labourers earned R172 and R105 respectively.[77]

Struggling to make ends meet, supporters identified closely with players with whom they shared not only an irrepressible passion for football, but also workplace subordination and a profound antipathy of apartheid's restrictions. Football heroes and favourite clubs brought joy to disenfranchised fans, allowed them to transcend monotony and gain self-validation, and defined black people's belonging and identity. Among the most acclaimed popular heroes in the SASL were Eric 'Scara' Sono of Orlando Pirates and Difference 'City Council' Mbanya of Moroka Swallows. Scara Sono's popularity was such that, despite breaking his leg in August 1962 and missing the last three months of the season, the two most widely circulated weekly and monthly publications among black readers, *Post* and *Drum* (April 1963), crowned him, respectively, 'Sportsman of the Year' and 'Footballer of the Year'. Scara's extraordinary physical strength (he was also a fine boxer), exquisite ball control, uncanny sense of anticipation, and legendary work ethic made him the consummate township football artist.[78] 'What a marvelous player man. I get goose bumps thinking about that player,' remembered Vince Belgeums, a powerfully built six-foot-two-inch fullback who marked Scara Sono man-to-man on several occasions while playing for Cape Ramblers. 'What a clever player. The man had flair, flair. A pleasure to watch at all times. It's difficult to mark this man. He plays off the ball; he's fantastic. He's all over. He's on the left hand side; he switches to the right side; he comes through the center; he was a terror!'[79] Scara's national reputation and his crafty style of play personified the SASL's success. The entertaining brand of football on display, combined with the trickle-down effects from the high economic growth of the 1960s, brought more African, Coloured, and Indian women and nuclear families to the SASL matches.[80] As crowds became increasingly diverse, official supporters' clubs appeared.

THE SOCIABILITY AND DEMOCRACY OF SUPPORTERS' CLUBS
The founding of official supporters' clubs across the country was a unique development of the SASL years. These social institutions, which featured not only adult men but also many women in prominent positions, functioned as small-scale participatory democracies and represented the conviviality and sociability of

Enthusiastic Pirates supporters.

Bailey's African History Archive

soccer.[81] Supporters' clubs provided moral support for teams and transportation of fans to away matches. Members also organised social events in the tradition of African mutual aid societies like *stokfels* and *manyano*s (women's rotating credit associations and prayer groups).[82] Through the activities of supporters' clubs, South Africans forged and maintained new individual and social identities and networks that cut across gender, generational, class, ethnic, regional and religious lines.

The proliferation of SASL supporters' clubs eroded the differences between fans and supporters by broadening the meaning of supporter to include a much wider spectrum of people than during the amateur era.[83] Before the SASL, fans and supporters had different standing, privileges and power within clubs. Fans had been voyeuristic outsiders in the affairs of amateur African clubs. They were primarily working-class men aged 20 to 40 who enjoyed the game and expressed their identification with a neighbourhood, location, or migrant worker network by purchasing match tickets out of their modest wages and cheering (or jeering) their side at the sports grounds. Supporters, by contrast, were active insiders. Financially insecure soccer clubs depended on the efforts of a small number of middle-class men (and some women) aged 35 to 50 who donated their time, money and organisational skills. These patrons bought new uniforms for their team, boots for individual players, and provided transportation to and from sports grounds by shuttling players around the townships in flashy automobiles. By virtue of their (relative) wealth and resources, supporters, unlike fans, were offered associate and even full membership into the football club itself. Transformations in fan culture in the early 1960s rendered such distinctions less meaningful.

Supporters' clubs were established across the country. The Berea group formed in Durban in 1961 seems to have been the first; but it was soon followed by similar clubs linked to Orlando Pirates, Moroka Swallows, Blackpool, Real Fighters, Durban Aces and Maritzburg City.[84] The activities of supporters' clubs were so popular that meetings of the Maritzburg City group attracted over 400 people.[85] Likewise, supporters of Pirates were so numerous that their meetings were held in the township's largest indoor hall.[86] Money was so scarce that groups spent significant time raising funds. By way of example, there was one case in which Alexandra Real Fighters supporters offered a portable radio, a case of beer, and a half bag of sugar as top prizes.[87] Generally, club meetings ostensibly functioned as forums for conversation, dissemination of news, and discussions about the team's performances. An important feature was the promulgation of travel plans for an upcoming away game. Buses and cars travelling between Johannesburg and Durban typically left on Friday evenings or Saturday mornings and returned immediately after the match on Sunday night.[88] Apartheid laws forced supporters to obtain travel permits from the authorities before embarking on their journeys.

The visibility of teams competing in the SASL tended to broaden their support base. This process was particularly evident in the case of the more popular sides. For example, Swallows fan clubs emerged in Durban and even in Mbabane (Swaziland). Clearly, the nature of fandom was changing. Followers were no longer drawn solely from the usual parochial networks, but from national and regional sources. In fact, there were so many organised fan groups associated with the SASL by January 1963 that some of them, as reported in *The Leader* of 1 February 1963, called for the creation of a 'federation of soccer supporters' clubs of South Africa . . . [for the] promotion of true sportsmanship, friendship, and better understanding among its members . . . and to protect [them] from abuse'.

One of the outstanding features of supporters' clubs was the active participation of increasing numbers of women. Female organisers and actors filled simultaneously progressive and conservative roles.[89] Fan groups represented a social space in which black women excluded from sporting activities could exercise informal power in a deeply patriarchal South African society. For example, the Berea organisation featured a female-dominated executive board.[90] These women were part of a group of about 30 Indian women supporters travelling with the team to Johannesburg in August 1961. The women from Durban watched Berea lose a thrilling match against Moroka Swallows (2-3) before the largest crowd of the year at Natalspruit.[91] This vigorous interest in football was not restricted to Indian women. African women had also involved themselves more directly in soccer. For example, young female fans of Orlando Pirates '[c]lad in black and white uniforms . . . became renowned for their fierce loyalty and inspirational singing and sloganeering at matches'.[92] Two powerful women, Betty Nkosi and Edith 'Moipone' Moorosi, influenced Pirates's internal affairs to such a considerable extent by the late 1960s that men in the club referred to them disparagingly as an 'apron government'.[93]

While women's participation generated gender tensions, it also recorded notable attempts at levelling the playing field. In Soweto, a group of educated young women led by Jessie Maseko made an unsuccessful attempt to run an Orlando Pirates Women's Football Club in 1962.[94] A similar short-lived effort took place in Cape Town, where Mother City Girls played SASL curtain-raisers and competed successfully against high school boys and mixed teams. Male reporters, noted one scholar, appeared 'genuinely impressed with their skills. Indeed, their sexual attractiveness is heightened by their abilities on the pitch in contrast to much discourse that would categorize their skills and aggressive play as distinctly unfeminine and hence, unattractive.'[95] In another important development, Jeanne Pottier, an employee in the SASL's Durban office, became the first South African woman to be certified by the National Referees' Examination Board in 1963.[96] Pottier refereed at least one curtain-raiser to a SASL match in Cape Town in August 1963. While far too little is known about women's involvement in men's sports, its nature and impact appears contradictory.[97] On the one hand, women supporters challenged men's tenacious grip on football but, on the other, they also organised events that reproduced patriarchal representations of gender.

Supporters' clubs served a social purpose in black communities. Saturday-evening football parties, dances, and braais (barbecues) sustained the social and cultural lives of urban black people and enhanced the reputation and status of teams and players. Soccer gatherings created a social sphere in which individual and collective desires could be fulfilled. Functions hosted by Pirates and Swallows followers in Soweto, for example, were important dates in the social calendar of black Johannesburg. These parties offered a chance to make or rekindle relationships and to 'be seen' in the company of glamorous athletes, singers, intellectuals, gangsters, *shebeen* owners and other socialites. At more formal events, women provided a catered dinner, prominent members of the African community gave speeches, and live jazz, swing, dixie, *kwela*, or *mbaqanga* bands supplied musical entertainment while men and women danced into the night. Female supporters also arranged and starred in beauty pageants and fashion shows.

The intensity of rivalries between clubs like Pirates and Swallows seemed to hinder co-operation in planning social events and sharing the revenue.[98] And yet the

Sekola Sello, *Chiefs: 21 Glorious Years* (Skotaville, 1991)

Chiefs players carry Chiefs' director Gilbert Sekhabi's coffin (April 1980).

unwavering loyalties and fierce competition engendered by football did not prevent people from co-operating in extraordinary circumstances, such as organising League functions or making funeral arrangements. Most notably, Soweto rivals Moroka Swallows and Orlando Pirates established a 'Jeppe Tragedy Fund' in co-operation with the SASL in order to provide some financial assistance to the families of the eleven victims killed in a stampede at the Jeppe train station after a Swallows–Pirates match at Natalspruit in 1962.[99]

In addition to their sporting and social functions, organised fan groups played a democratising role in the post-Sharpeville period.[100] The danger associated with joining banned political organisations led black South Africans to channel their aspirations for power, status and prestige increasingly into social and cultural organisations, especially sports clubs and associations.[101] By paying small annual dues, fans received a membership card granting them the right to vote and to present themselves as candidates in elections for sought-after offices in the executive board. In many ways, supporters' clubs partially filled the vacuum left by the apartheid state's draconian repression of mass political movements after April 1960. In short, individual participation in the cultural production of professional football was fraught with political implications.

The SASL's firm ideological commitment to nonracial sport strengthened the democratising impulse in football. Supporters became political actors largely because supporting the 'People's League' meant taking a stance against state-enforced racial discrimination. When the South African Sports Association (SASA), the vanguard of the sport boycott movement, launched 'Operation Support Only Nonracial Events In Sport' (SONREIS) in June 1961, the SASL and the overwhelming majority of its fans enthusiastically backed the campaign.[102] The objectives of SONREIS were twofold. Firstly, it attempted to curtail black people's attendance at white sporting events, especially Indians' support of NFL matches in Durban.[103] Secondly, it called for a boycott of racially exclusive associations propped up by the apartheid establishment. In 1961–62, for example, people on the Rand deserted matches organised by the National Professional Soccer League (NPSL). This rival of the SASL was set up by a small group of African officials led by Seth Mzizi, Sydney Sepanya, and Willy Baqwa with the financial and ideological assistance of white authorities. But the successful SONREIS boycott of the NPSL signified a popular rejection of the inferior quality of racially-segregated football *vis-à-vis* the SASL; it led to the rapid demise of the pro-apartheid league.[104]

ROWDY MASCULINITY

The League's huge popularity had its costs. Overcrowding at matches staged in inadequate, unsafe facilities created conditions in which fans' participation easily derailed into violence. Football grounds open to blacks had no fences, walls, or moats to keep fans off the pitch, and there were very few policemen on duty. These conditions made burgeoning crowds difficult to control, and violence in and around SASL's venues became more frequent. Excessive liquor consumption, rivalries between hard-core fans, and poor refereeing sparked fights, pitch invasions, stampedes, and riots at several SASL games. Incidents of football hooliganism were often linked to organised gangs and loosely linked groups of young black men. This motley social constituency tended to be unemployed and with dim hopes of taking remunerative jobs in the near future. 'Gangsterism and sports provided possible routes to fame and stardom outside the drudgery of education.'[105] Accordingly, township youths took their football very seriously and steadfastly refused to join official supporters' clubs.

Ardent followers of Orlando Pirates, for example, scoffed at their own team's supporters' club, which they perceived as older, soft, and middle-class. Instead, Pirates *tsotsis* (urban toughs, petty criminals) from Soweto staked out territorial claims behind one of the goals at Natalspruit Indian Sports Ground and carved out an autonomous 'Pirates-only' area that they called 'Congo'.[106] The absence of physical constraints in the stands, and the assertive autonomy inherent in the occupation of this section of the grounds, turned 'Congo' into a potent source of topophilia (love of place) for Pirates fans, a term coined by the British geographer John Bale.[107] A loyal supporter named Boy Shogwe was so profoundly involved with Pirates that he chose to celebrate his wedding at the stadium. He recalled with distinct pride his days as a passionate Pirates supporter at Natalspruit: 'The Mecca of Soccer! Oh my God, I got married there! You know, it was the "in-thing." Man, it was my life. There was a place we called the Congo, after the Belgian Congo you know, it was the roughest place because it was *Ours*. Pirates, Pirates, Pirates.' Once inside, Shogwe said, the young men would assert their territoriality and drink copious amounts of beer. 'We would sneak in beer bottles and once we get drunk we would fill the bottles with urine – hey, it was a rough place. Congo, at Indian Sports Ground, it was the only pavilion that was *Ours*. If you sit there by mistake, conform or [silence] . . . We fuck you up!'[108]

An additional factor behind the rise in football violence was the widespread practice of high-stakes gambling on matches. Although much more research into football gambling needs to be done, some preliminary evidence indicates that it was widespread and highly visible. The Durban Indian newspaper *The Leader*, for example, reported on 13 March 1964 that during a SASL match in Pietermaritzburg in 1964, 'armed non-white policemen at the [Royal Agricultural] Showgrounds last Sunday . . . turned a blind eye to an Orlando Pirates official waving bank notes as he shouted odds against a Lincoln City victory'. After Pirates defeated Aces 2-0 at Natalspruit in July 1964, the *World* reported that it 'was a great win for Pirates but the happiest man in the huge crowd was Mr. Freddy Shabangu, of Standerton, who won R200 in a side bet', nearly twice the average monthly wage of an African worker.[109]

According to Shogwe, gambling caused several riots at Pirates SASL matches. Shogwe himself resorted to hooliganism to avoid a costly gambling loss in May 1964: 'I struck a bet with the Moroka Swallows president that Avalon [Athletic of Durban] would not win. Problem, I had no money. I was working with Scara [Sono] at the Stock Exchange and on Friday afternoon my boss gave me money to bank. We decided to keep it for the bet. On Monday we would have doubled it and my boss would have his money.'[110] Football being an unpredictable sport, Shogwe grew increasingly anxious as the match wore on: 'After halftime . . . 2-1 Avalon! Ten minutes to go! . . . I stood up. I signal to Scara, he shrugs. Man, the place was full, the margin of the ground was spectators, I just jumped over them. I said "Ruka!" which means "to cause havoc."' Shogwe then punched the Avalon goalkeeper, Denzil Easthorpe, who was forced to leave his position between the posts. The situation spiralled out of control. 'He moved and stood on the touchline, which was packed with people,' Shogwe said:

> Somebody gave me a gun, a P.38. I thought, 'hey, if I shoot this man in public – *public murder*, no, no, no.' I showed him the gun, and he ran away . . . . Then I heard, 'Goal!' and I asked the linesmen if it was official. It was a draw! I ran out of the stadium, collected my money and was gone. On Monday my boss got his money.

Studies of West Indian cricket culture suggest other ways in which sport's quasi-religious ceremonies could take a turn for the worse in a matter of seconds.[111] An unacceptable result or event on the pitch would suddenly break the magical spell of a joyous communal ritual channelling the emotions of the audience. Supporters transformed a disciplined, symbolic identification with their team into violent, *real* conflict at the grounds. As in the case of Caribbean cricket, the development of football into a mass phenomenon in South Africa in the 1960s coincided with an intensification of fans' emotional attachment to their particular clubs and beloved idols. Defeat became unacceptable to young devotees and thugs who formed their sporting culture in the poor, aggressive, male-dominated street culture of South African townships.

Ironically, the increase in violent incidents coincided with women, children, and families attending matches in greater numbers than ever before. Rowdy and assertive male youths self-consciously differentiated themselves from organised fan groups and the growing number of women and families who joined the traditional adult male football constituency at the grounds across the country. In a letter to the black newspaper *World*, a Soweto fan writing under the pseudonym 'Fullback' captured poignantly the impact of changing crowd behaviour and disorder in the mid-1960s:

> My wife and I are both keen sports fans, and have a lot of pleasure watching soccer matches at the many Reef grounds. But now a lot of that joy has gone out of our lives, because we are becoming afraid to watch now. So much so that my wife, who is now pregnant, says that she won't go to any more matches . . . It is all because of the way certain people behave when they get to the soccer grounds. Don't these people who throw stones, use sticks and swear at people realise that in the excitement of a soccer game it takes very little to start big trouble and spoil the game for thousands of people who have come along, not for trouble, but because they love the game and want a good afternoon's entertainment?[112]

Violent and non-violent football fans in the 1960s became, for good or ill, powerful expressions of popular culture that formulated political critiques of apartheid society by aligning themselves with nonracial sport. Ultimately, violence at SASL venues presented white authorities with a convenient excuse to crack down on the oppositional organisation. Aided by the propaganda of print and broadcasting media, the white alliance waged 'a war of attrition' against the 'facilities, spectators, and finances of nonracial professional football'.[113]

THE STRANGULATION OF THE SASL
The white political and sporting establishment perceived nonracial sport as threatening and sought to eradicate it from the social geography of apartheid.[114] Johannesburg NEAD manager William Carr and NFL chairman Viv Granger fired the first salvos in the war of attrition in 1962 when they conspired to shut out the SASL's Transvaal Second division clubs from municipal grounds.[115] The Minister of the Interior Jan de Klerk publicly supported Granger's and Carr's move to squeeze out the 'People's League' from municipal grounds in September 1962. From then on, the government declared that: 'the use of all stadia and fields for Native football . . . [was] reserved for use by Associations affiliated to the Football Association of South Africa'.[116] By tightening the noose around SASL's neck the

white soccer establishment (professional NFL and amateur FASA) wished to achieve three main goals: attract black fans to 'Non-European' stands of its segregated stadia; gain full control of domestic football; and get South Africa's FIFA suspension lifted. To this end, it tried to convince world football's governing body that supporters of nonracial soccer were political agitators.[117] White South Africans also sought to (mis)represent the affiliation of pro-apartheid African, Coloured, and Indian associations as evidence of progressive change within the country.

In this quickly evolving context, a Durban court's acquittal in May 1962 of members of SASL's Lincoln City Football Club charged by the state with violating a provision of the Group Areas Act by playing mixed soccer triggered the white political and sporting establishment's all-out assault on the SASL.[118] Judge J.L. Pretorius ruled that since Lincoln City's Indian, Coloured, and white players had indeed played football together at Curries Fountain Stadium, but had not entered any building to socialise or share refreshments as intended by the Group Areas Act proclamation concerning social clubs, their actions were not illegal.[119] This decision – upheld by the Natal Supreme Court in October 1962 – confirmed what the SASL and the anti-apartheid sport movement had argued vociferously at home and abroad: there was no law prohibiting mixed sports teams in South Africa.[120] This legal triumph, however, turned out to be a pyrrhic victory for the SASL because it motivated white authorities and soccer administrators to suppress the League. FASA actively co-operated with the government by, among other things, 'send[ing] SASF letters addressed to them to the Government in the hope that action will be taken against SASF officials' and by 'writ[ing] to all Municipalities throughout the country, to prohibit the use of playing fields to SASF units [especially the SASL]'.[121] Members of the security branch and the South African police attended meetings to intimidate and take notes of speeches by officials of nonracial sport.[122]

A LORRY BRINGS POSTS

A lorry waits outside the Natalspruit Indian Sports Ground with goal posts brought from Kliptown. But these posts were found unsuitable, so some fans went to an adjoining ground and got some other posts. These were lifted over the corrugated iron fence — and two S. A. S. L. matches went on !

World, 8 April 1963

Lorry brings the posts.

Therefore, the NEAD's removal of Natalspruit's goalposts on 6 April 1963 – the incident reported at the start of this chapter – was part of an overall strategy to strangle the SASL and suppress nonracial soccer. Denied access to Natalspruit, the SASL could not survive for long given that the facility was home to the League's

Johannesburg-area teams. Soweto giants Orlando Pirates and Moroka Swallows had gained a national following and accounted for nearly a third of SASL's total attendance and income.[123]

In a meeting with SASL representative Reggie Feldman, Viv Granger described white officialdom's brutal attack unambiguously: it was 'a war to the death . . . we're doing our best to obliterate you'.[124] A prolonged, costly legal battle resulted in the Supreme Court in Bloemfontein taking Natalspruit away from the Johannesburg Indian Sports Ground Association (which leased it to the SASL) and turning it over to the Johannesburg city council in 1964.[125]

The League survived one more year playing a truncated schedule. Deprived of suitable grounds in Johannesburg, the SASL staged its Rand matches at Kliptown near Soweto, on or near the open ground where the historic Congress of the People had taken place in June 1955.[126] Despite the spartan playing conditions, a crowd estimated at between 16 000 and 20 000 watched Pirates defeat Swallows 2-1 at Kliptown in November. Ironically, the gradual suffocation of the SASL in Johannesburg coincided with Moroka Swallows winning the 1965 League title – the first national championship ever claimed by a Sowetan side.[127]

Moroka Swallows players with 'retro' jerseys.

George Thabe, *It's a Goal!* (Skotaville, 1983)

Swallows's victory inspired the first known South African music recordings about soccer. According to Gallo Music archivist Rob Allingham, unknown artists (probably session musicians) recorded an instrumental song in 1966 entitled 'Up the Birds'.[128] That same year a group called the Jabulani Quads recorded the single 'Okongo Mame', a song that praised a famous Swallows player named Kongo Malemane. The League's tight connections with black popular culture, however, could not prevent a final government eviction from Kliptown,[129] and the SASL – unquestionably the most important force in the history of football in South Africa before 1976 – finally folded ahead of the 1966 season for lack of playing grounds.

Epilogue

The strangulation of the South African Soccer League (SASL) by the state and its allies, and the country's suspension from international soccer from 1961 to 1992 (with a one-year reprieve in 1963) exacerbated apartheid's stunting effect on the South African game. Ostracised from World Cup and African Nations Cup tournaments, and unable to play friendly matches with FIFA members, South Africa – black and white – maintained tenuous links with the organisational, technical, and economic transformations that revolutionised world football in the 1970s and 80s.[1] This epilogue briefly highlights the most important developments in the domestic game between 1971 and 1992 in order to bring the story of South African soccer closer to the present.

The 1970s witnessed the white regime's coercive re-imposition of strict racial segregation on the pitch. An Africans-only National Professional Soccer League emerged with the backing of the government and South African Breweries (SAB). Corporate sponsorships of black football spiked after the launch of state television in 1976, as companies looked to exploit the game to gain access to township consumers. Commercialisation and the social and political turmoil that followed the 1976 Soweto uprising effected a gradual de-racialisation of professional soccer. School and amateur soccer, which comprised more than 95 per cent of players, remained strictly segregated until the 1980s. Beginning in the latter half of the 1980s, as the ANC and the National Party laid the foundations for a negotiated end to apartheid, antagonistic football associations discussed the formation of a single, nonracial controlling body. This 'unity' process accelerated in the late 1980s and led to the creation, in December 1991, of an integrated South African Football Association. With this development, FIFA welcomed South Africa back into world soccer in 1992. A new era had begun.

REVITALISATION EFFORTS: 1966–71

Without a professional league between 1966 and 1971, black South African clubs survived by competing in challenge matches and occasional weekend tournaments for small cash prizes. SAB and the United Tobacco Company (UTC) re-evaluated their long-standing sponsorship of black soccer. White authorities denied Orlando Pirates and Moroka Swallows access to municipal stadiums because of the Sowetan sides' earlier commitment to the nonracial SASL. This gloomy scenario complicated revitalisation efforts in domestic football.

Nevertheless, in 1969 Orlando Pirates and Highlands Park, the white league champions, organised a match to determine the 'true' South African champions. The contest was planned for 31 August in Mbabane, Swaziland, and received FIFA's blessing. The black popular press ignited a feverish build-up to the match with daily coverage. As the day of reckoning approached, the *World*, the most popular black daily, of 13 August 1969, revealed in 'Rush On for Big Swazi Game' that 'excitement is mounting among soccer fans and there has been an unprecedented rush for passports by soccer fans wanting to see the soccer game of the year'. But two weeks before an expected mass exodus to Swaziland, S.L. Muller, Minister of Police, announced that the match would not take place because it contravened government policy.[2]

Intense conflicts within Pirates surfaced in the run-up to the Highlands Park match. Ultimately, these resulted in the formation of Kaizer Chiefs – presently the most popular club in South Africa. Legendary Pirates striker Kaizer Motaung and flamboyant team manager Ewert 'The Lip' Nene headed a breakaway faction that formed an invitation side in January 1970 initially called Kaizer XI. The immediate cause of the split was the expulsion of Nene and three players – Edward 'Msomi' Khoza, Thomas 'Zero' Johnson, and Ratha Mokgoatleng.[3] Motaung renamed the team Kaizer Chiefs in 1971, after his American team – the Atlanta Chiefs of the fledgling North American Soccer League (NASL).[4] The corporate model of American sport deeply impressed the enterprising Motaung: 'I had seen how professional clubs are run abroad and suggested that we should adopt the same concept at Pirates. Nobody cared to listen. But, I got wind of the fact that if we wanted to go on with our "thing" then I could take the expelled guys.'[5] Amakhosi (Chiefs in Zulu) and their many new supporters adopted the V peace symbol, Afro hairstyles, colourful broad-collared shirts, and bell-bottom trousers. Known as 'hippies' because of this counter-cultural identity, Chiefs joined Pirates and Swallows in the pantheon of South African soccer.[6]

The return of rigid racial segregation in South African football tempered the excitement generated by the rise of Kaizer Chiefs. The white soccer establishment and its political allies in 1970 ordered the South African Bantu Football Association to expel Coloureds and Indians from African clubs.[7] Faced with the false choice of either disbanding or accepting this racist ultimatum, virtually every township team, including Pirates and Swallows, capitulated. This coercive 'Africanisation' of black professional soccer was intended to halt, even reverse, the integrationist gains that had been won over time by the inter-race boards in the 1930s and 40s, the Federation in the 1950s, and the South African Soccer League in the 1960s.

ANTI-RACISM ENDURES: THE FEDERATION PROFESSIONAL LEAGUE
Anti-racist football survived, albeit in a sharply curtailed form. In 1969 the amateur South African Soccer Federation established a six-team Federation Professional League (FPL). It absorbed several of Natal's defunct SASL clubs (Avalon Athletic, Berea, Maritzburg City, and Aces United) and garnered most of its support in the

coastal areas. Much of the FPL's leadership came from the SASL. Most notably, R.K. Naidoo, SASL's only president, served as the FPL's first chairman (until 1978), and Ramhori Lutchman and Charles Pillay sat on the executive committee. Sponsorships were hard to come by for outspken opponents of apartheid in sport, amounting to a paltry R15 000 for the 1972 season.[8] Forced to rely on gate income for its operational funds, the FPL signed exceptional Coloured and Indian players victimised by SABFA's racist purge, which helped to attract sizeable crowds to its games.

The career of Bernard 'Dancing Shoes' Hartze provides a glimpse of the effects of racialisation in the 1970s. Born in 1944, Hartze grew up in Marabastad, a poor but racially diverse area in Pretoria, where he learned the game in the streets.[9] After playing for amateur clubs like Mohawks and Pretoria City, Hartze revived a moribund club called Sundowns in 1964, with the help of his friends and neighbours. Hartze, Ingle and Melvin Singh, Rashid Khan, Vincent Julius, Joey Lawrence, Lawrence Chauke and Smiley Moosa formed the core of Sundowns – a successful barnstorming team managed by Hartze's older brother Reginald.[10] In 1967 Orlando Pirates signed Hartze from Sundowns. A skilful and speedy inside forward, Hartze's exhilarating dribbling and sensational scoring ability mesmerised township fans, who nicknamed him 'Dancing Shoes'. Sadly, the segregationist order of 1970 truncated Hartze's career at Pirates.

After a short, unfulfilling return to Sundowns in a regional Coloured league, Hartze accepted an offer to play for Cape Town Spurs in the nonracial FPL. The Western Province Association Football Board, which owned Spurs, paid Hartze R200 monthly, less than half of what he earned at Pirates.[11] In his first season,

Sekola Sello, *Chiefs: 21 Glorious Years* (Skotaville, 1991)

From left: Kaizer Motaung, Bernard Hartze and Ewert Nene.

'Dancing Shoes' helped Spurs to win the 1971 FPL championship, and he set a South African goal-scoring average record for a professional season that still stands: 35 goals in 16 matches.[12] Four years and many trophies later, Hartze went to the United States, where he won the 1975 NASL title with Tampa Bay Rowdies. After this brief American experience, Hartze returned to Cape Town to close his illustrious career. By the late 1970s, thanks to the exploits of players like Hartze and others, the FPL had developed a devoted fan base among Indians in Durban and Coloureds in Cape Town. Unlike its predecessor in the 1960s, however, the conspicuous lack of African participation, especially the absence of the Soweto 'big three' (Pirates, Chiefs, and Swallows), coupled with inadequate corporate sponsorships, prevented the League from capturing the national imagination.

THE CASTLE LEAGUE AND 'MULTI-NATIONALISM'
In stark contrast to the Federation Professional League's struggle for survival, African clubs received a major boost from United Party members, white soccer, and big business as SABFA's National Professional Soccer League (NPSL) launched the Keg League in 1971.[13] FASA president and United Party MP Dave Marais worked behind the scenes to secure business and government backing for the League.[14] SAB provided R30 000 in sponsorship money.[15] Originally, the League had thirteen teams: Kaizer Chiefs, Moroka Swallows Big XV, Orlando Pirates, Pimville United Brothers, Real Katlehong City, Bantu Callies, Mamelodi XI, Vaal Professionals and Witbank Black Aces from the Transvaal; Bloemfontein Celtic from the Orange Free State; Kimberley Dalton Brothers from the Cape; and Lamontville Golden Arrows and African Wanderers from Natal. The NPSL's co-operation with the white establishment brought tangible rewards. For example, the Keg League (later renamed the Castle League, after a popular brand of beer) gained access to municipal grounds, including Orlando Stadium, where Soweto derbies regularly drew crowds of 50 000 spectators and more.

South Africa's expulsion from the Olympic movement in 1970 motivated Prime Minister B.J. Vorster's new policy of 'multinationalism'.[16] Introduced in 1971 to gain readmission into world sport, multinationalism tinkered with apartheid by allowing for the possibility of integrated national teams abroad and by permitting occasional matches in South Africa between representative teams from different racial groups – defined as 'nations' by apartheid orthodoxy. These cosmetic changes were part of Pretoria's broader effort to project an image of substantive reform to the outside world while maintaining apartheid intact. The popularity of soccer among the African majority placed it at the forefront of the government's multinational policy.[17] The soccer competition at the 1973 South African Games, for example, attracted immense popular interest. On 27 March, 45 000 fans crammed into the segregated stands of the 32 000-capacity Rand Stadium in Johannesburg to watch a black (African) versus white game. The whites won 4-0. Four days later, the two sides clashed at the same venue in the gold-medal match – the whites won again (3-1).

The following year the government approved the Embassy Multinational Series, a football tournament sponsored by the United Tobacco Company (Embassy was a cigarette brand). In a highly controversial match on 20 April 1974, the whites defeated the Africans 2-0 at a dangerously oversold Rand Stadium. Squeezed in behind barbed wire fencing opposite white spectators, black supporters erupted in celebration when Macdonald 'Rhee' Skosana scored the game's opening goal in the 43rd minute. But the white referee disallowed it for a dubious offside infraction. Black supporters showered the pitch with stones, bottles, and other missiles, forcing the white referee to blow the half-time whistle early and beat a hasty retreat into the dressing room. This injustice seemed to symbolise black life under white minority rule: 'They will not let us win,' said Pirates striker Ephraim 'Jomo' Sono, 19-year-old son of the late Eric 'Scara' Sono, in the locker room at the break.[18] After a lack-lustre second-half performance, the Africans suffered a demoralising 0-2 defeat. Reflecting on the game, the white team's captain, Martin Cohen, recognised that: 'Something had to happen. That game made it impossible to suppress people for the rest of their lives.'[19]

Multinationalism continued to evolve. In 1975 the American auto maker Chevrolet sponsored a government-sanctioned 'Champion of Champions' competition between white and African clubs. Cape Town-based Hellenic, a white club, won the trophy and collected R14 000 in prize money winning a two-leg final against Kaizer Chiefs 5-2 on aggregate.[20] In a tense return match at the Rand Stadium, a missile-throwing incident and near riot ensued when Hellenic scored the opening goal from an apparent offside position. In the end, unruly spectator behaviour during both the 1975 Chevrolet 'Champion of Champions' and the 1974 Embassy series illustrated how multinational football was 'a festering time-bomb that is ready to explode at any time'.[21] Seemingly unperturbed, however, Pretoria extended multinationalism to club sport in September 1976, only weeks after South Africa's exclusion from FIFA.[22]

AFTER SOWETO: TOP-DOWN INTEGRATION AND CONSUMERISATION

In the wake of the township uprising that began in Soweto on 16 June 1976 – a watershed event in South African history which, eventually, led to the capitulation of apartheid – Pretoria gradually de-racialised the professional game, hoping to use football as a stabilising force in tumultuous times. In October 1976, the new Football Council of South Africa under the leadership of George Thabe brought together whites, Africans, and two minor Indian and Coloured organisations.[23] An authoritarian leader unsympathetic to apartheid's critics, Thabe was undoubtedly the most powerful soccer official of his time. He controlled both the amateur South African National Football Association (it had dropped the derogatory term 'Bantu' in 1973) and the NPSL.

Many white clubs viewed the Football Council as a means to revive waning interest in the NFL. 'Even at their own [white] grounds,' the black sporting press pointed out, 'you cannot find more than a thousand spectators who attend the game.'[24] Only 48 000 spectators paid to watch the seven NFL clubs in the Transvaal during the entire 1971 season. 'More people,' the *African Soccer Mirror* of May

1972 noted wryly, 'watched one game between Kaizer Chiefs and Orlando Pirates at KwaMashu recently.' Declining attendance at NFL games was partly the result of Proclamation 225 of the Group Areas Act issued in 1965, which prohibited interested blacks from attending white matches, and partly the consequence of white spectators' flight from stadiums entertaining racially mixed audiences watching 'multinational' sport.[25] Co-operation with blacks and the Football Council offered a lifeline to white clubs drowning in a sea of debt and indifference.

By this time, private firms had cast their lot with black clubs in order to market their products to millions of township consumers. The Mainstay League Cup represented the Football Council's first attempt at 'reforming apartheid'. Launched in 1977 with the backing of a R70 000 sponsorship from the Stellenbosch Farmers Wineries (Mainstay is a cane spirit), it featured 27 teams drawn from the white NFL and the African NPSL.[26] The government allowed teams to field up to three players from another racial group, but only on a loan basis so as to prevent black clubs from buying white players – a notion offensive to apartheid ideology. Ultimately, ineffective management, Group Areas legislation, high travel costs, and spectator violence forced the abandonment of the first Mainstay Cup. In spite of that, Stellenbosch Farmers Wineries raised its sponsorship for the 1978 edition of the Cup to R100 000.[27] The company's public relations officer spelled out the logic behind this commitment to black sport: 'There's a definite spin-off from black consumers. They identify your product with the game and support it. Football's helped us retain our market share in a competitive industry.'[28] In a surprising turn of events, Wits University, a white team, won the 1978 Mainstay Cup final against Kaizer Chiefs. The survival of the 'multinational' Mainstay Cup sealed the fate of the NFL, which folded after the 1977 season. Facing extinction, some white clubs affiliated to the FPL. 'I'm gambling by joining Federation,' Norman 'Silver Fox' Elliott, director of white Durban City, explained; 'I'm hoping the crowds will improve by our taking this step.'[29] The anti-apartheid South African Council of Sport (SACOS) viewed this *ad hoc* alliance as collaboration with apartheid and so it expelled the Federation from its ranks in 1979, though this penalty was rescinded a few months later.[30] By the end of the 1970s, 'multinationalism' and the increasing influence of corporate sponsors on soccer had severely damaged the FPL and made the NPSL's popular Castle League the dominant force in the professional game.[31]

Television sparked soccer's commercial boom. The state-owned South African Broadcasting Corporation (SABC) only launched its television service in January 1976. SABC-TV first showed football matches in 1977 and then began to broadcast live games in October 1981. When the SABC added a second channel in 1982, its palimpsest featured a tape-delayed 'match of the day' on Saturday nights and a dozen live matches, the rights to which the NPSL sold for R250 000.[32] Companies relished the advertisement potential of soccer on television – a mass medium that allowed potential access to millions of black households. SAB more than tripled its Castle League sponsorship from R15 000 to R50 000 in 1976, then to R75 000 in 1978, R200 000 in 1979, R250 000 in 1980, and R325 000 in 1982.[33] New investments in football sponsorships came not only from alcohol and tobacco firms, but also from energy companies, the auto industry, clothing, food, and consumer electronics retailers. Vigorous corporate support and rising gate income in 1982 generated gross revenues for the NPSL of R3 185 956, with a profit of R321 000.[34] While ticket sales accounted for most of the income, sponsorships (excluding TV rights) reached R742 000 – 23,3 per cent of total revenue in 1982. On its fiftieth anniversary, SANFA, the NPSL's parent organisation, boasted an accumulated income of R225 656,26.[35]

The game's financial growth benefited the most popular clubs to a far greater extent than ordinary ones. Kaizer Chiefs signed a five-year sponsorship deal in 1979 with the Premier Milling Company, manufacturers of Iwisa maize meal, worth at least R350 000.[36] The following year, Orlando Pirates and Fruitree agreed to a three-year R160 000 pact, and in 1986 Moroka Swallows secured a R450 000 five-year commitment from Mobil Oil.[37] Less popular teams branded themselves with corporate names to survive, as in the case of Arcadia Pepsi (later Flouride), Dion Highlands, and Casio (and later Sanyo, and Jade East) Dynamos. Clubs struggled to stay afloat at the same time that Castle League sponsorships exceeded R1 million for the first time in 1983.[38] An outside review of the League recognised that 'the majority of Clubs in the League suffer from liquidity problems. Some clubs were reported to be in such a negative cash flow situation that they would have to cease operating at the end of the current season.'[39] This gloomy scenario created entrepreneurial opportunities for black capitalists. Most notably, in 1983 Jomo Sono bought Highlands Park, a white football powerhouse, for R100 000 and renamed it Jomo Cosmos.[40] This momentous event signalled growing black power in South African soccer.[41]

THE NSL, UNITY AND THE END OF APARTHEID

Cracks in the edifice of apartheid emerged in the mid-1980s. Simultaneously, in football, autocratic leadership, corruption, poor management, and the unequal distribution of income in the professional ranks had bitterly divided the elite game. George Thabe ruled by decree and surrounded himself with 'yes-men'. Critics high-lighted major problems with the NPSL: deeply flawed accounting procedures, inefficient fixture planning, administrative inadequacies, dangerous arenas, and a lack of training of coaches and referees.[42] Furthermore, dissident officials and many clubs objected to the disproportionate profits that SANFA and the NPSL amassed from ticket sales, sponsorship revenues, and the sale of television rights. In a typical case, gate-takings of R67 038,09 for the second leg of the 1981 BP Cup final at Orlando Stadium earned finalists Kaizer Chiefs and Casio Dynamos R4 846,96 each, while SANFA received R8 000 and the NPSL an unspecified but probably similar sum of money.[43] The stark contrast between the parent organisation's healthy bottom-line and the modest profits made by leading sides like Kaizer Chiefs, or the losses crippling small clubs, bitterly divided professional soccer.

Conflicts over money and power came to a head in the summer of 1985. On 1 February, Chiefs' chairman Kaizer Motaung, former NPSL public relations officer Abdul Bhamjee, NPSL general-secretary Cyril Kobus, and every Castle League club (except Moroka Swallows) declared their independence from the NPSL.[44] SAB announced a R400 000 sponsorship deal granting the newly named National Soccer League full control of the lucrative eighteen-team Castle League. SABC-TV secretly bought the broadcast rights for R450 000. The NSL broke ties with its predecessor by adopting nonracial principles and by backing the sport boycott movement. 'There is tacit recognition by the broad liberation movement,' argued Federation vice-president Danny Jordaan at the time, 'that the NSL is supported by a large percentage of its members. Workers who belong to COSATU and NACTU [union confederations] frequent matches of the NSL to support their favourite teams.'[45] The rise of the populist and autonomous NSL heralded fundamental changes in soccer, politics, and society.

In the mid-1980s old enemies began to consider the creation of a new integrated football association. Declining attendance, escalating violence, and organisational disarray led to meetings between the SANFA and Federation in December 1985 and January 1986.[46] These initial 'unity' talks broke down due to SANFA's unwillingness to commit to an anti-apartheid agenda.[47] Then, in October 1988, a delegation composed of NSL officials (including Kaizer Motaung) and its amateur affiliate, the Soccer Association of South Africa (led by Solomon Morewa), travelled to Lusaka, Zambia, to discuss the future of football with the ANC in exile.[48] Thabo Mbeki, then the director of public relations for the ANC, met the group at the airport.[49] In a joint communique, the ANC, NSL and SASA agreed that apartheid had to be eliminated before South Africa re-entered world football; they also resolved to 'strive for the establishment of a unitary, non-racial controlling body and integrate soccer at the grassroots level'. Meeting in Lusaka the following month, the ANC and the Federation reviewed 'unity' plans in detail.[50] In April 1989 in Durban, the Federation joined SANFA, and NSL/SASA for another round of high-level discussions.

Finally, after State President F.W. de Klerk unbanned liberation movements and freed Nelson Mandela and other political prisoners, thus clearing the way for the 'negotiated revolution' that dismantled apartheid, black and white football officials accelerated the process of *rapprochement*. Once again, transformations in sport and politics paralleled each other. In December 1991, the same month that formal negotiations for the transition to democracy began at the Convention for a Democratic South Africa outside Johannesburg, the unification process in soccer culminated in Durban with the founding of the nonracial South African Football Association (SAFA).[51]

As a result of this development, FIFA accepted South Africa back into world football in 1992. On 7 July 1992, at a jam-packed Durban's King's Park rugby stadium, South Africa played its first official international contest in three decades.

At the launch of SAFA (December 1991) are, from left, Tony Wilcox, Rodger Sishi, Danny Jordaan, unidentified official, and Mluleki George at the podium.

South Africa vs Cameroon in Cape Town (9 July 1992).

An integrated national team, nicknamed *Bafana Bafana* (Zulu and Xhosa for 'The Boys'), defeated Cameroon 1-0, thanks to a Doctor Khumalo penalty kick.[52]

With the country poised for its first democratic elections in April 1994, South African football could finally take advantage of the opportunities segregation and apartheid racism had long denied it. Nevertheless, the legacy of the past has not been forgotten. Looking back on his experiences as a young professional in the 1960s, and speaking for the lost generations of soccer stars, former SASL player Vince Belgeums reflected on his wrecked sporting dreams:

> In my heart I am also cross for the government for not giving us that scope to develop . . . In those times, those were my youth, and my goals were to go play against Pelé and to show that South Africa has also got a Pelé, or even better. Because we never had sponsors, and we never really got the right act to be recognised or to be taken overseas to give you that break, today I'm still cross. I feel I could have been in a better position today through soccer because this was my career. I was born to play soccer. And I was really robbed.[53]

Appendix

Scholarly Considerations and Sources

This book builds on existing scholarship on the South African social history of sport, as well as upon the emerging literature on leisure in Africa. As Emmanuel Akyeampong and Charles Ambler noted in a recent essay, the study of leisure in African history reveals everyday historical experiences and underlying social processes.[1] A poignant example of the significance of leisure as a field of personal and social autonomy, football is located within a growing literature on leisure and popular culture in Africa that includes music, radio, film, theatre, dance, alcohol use, fashion, and other visual and verbal arts.[2] In the South African context, materialist scholars sensitive to culture and ideology, such as David Coplan, Veit Erlmann, Patrick Harries, and Paul la Hausse, have examined popular cultural production.[3] This work originated from the revisionist (radical) 'school' of South African historiography of the 1970s and 80s, which aimed 'to "give voice" to the experience of previously marginal groups and to recover the agency of ordinary people'.[4] A major accomplishment of this interdisciplinary school was the demonstration that black men and women were agents of their own destiny to a significant extent.[5] Some of the earliest attempts at historicising black South African football emerged out of this radical interpretation of South African history. Tim Couzens outlined in brief, yet insightful, ways the diffusion and development of the game in cities, mines, and villages;[6] Ian Jeffrey's penetrating case study on Sharpeville township, south of Johannesburg, noted how football shaped community identities, rivalries, and social networks in black townships.[7]

Laduma! extends the literature on the role of sport and recreation in struggles over time and space in a colonial, industrial capitalist context. It underscores Phyllis Martin's conclusion about colonial Brazzaville that African sport spawned everyday struggles over access to leisure space and the meaning and use of free time.[8] Martin's analysis expanded on the work of Keletso Atkins, Fred Cooper and E.P. Thompson, which stressed the material, social, and cultural ways in which workers contested, negotiated, and shaped capitalist and, in Africa, colonial attempts to impose strict controls over their lives.[9] Leisure time was transformed into a terrain of struggle in South Africa in the 1920s and 30s. African footballers coped creatively with attempts at 'moralising leisure time' orchestrated by white missionaries and philanthropists, government officials, and employers.[10] Conflicts over time manifested themselves in other ways, such as black athletes experiencing constant difficulties in obtaining permission from their employers to take time away from work for travel to competitions. For those relatively privileged African workers participating in company-sponsored teams, it was not unusual to be denied compensation for wages lost due to sport-related activities.[11]

Conflicts over space occupy a prominent role in South African urban historiography, and several valid analyses have shed light on the complex relationship between black popular culture and the politics of legal and illegal leisure space.[12] Among the writers who have worked specifically on sport and social control, Cecile Badenhorst, Alan Cobley, and Goolam Vahed examined how Africans (and their allies) in Johannesburg and Durban fought constantly with the white government, the mining companies, and manufacturing firms over the provision and control of sporting facilities.[13] Playing and watching football in cities, towns, and mining compounds engendered prolonged popular struggles, largely because African sport was bound up with the pursuit of urban racial segregation in the twentieth century.[14]

COMPARATIVE ANALYSIS

If sport in Africa is an important field of research, it is also a useful platform for comparative analysis, which *Laduma!* pursues on two levels. Firstly, it attempts to move beyond the fiercely local approach that dominates South African urban historiography.[15] This parochial focus is reflected in the University of the Witwatersrand History Workshop's voluminous work on Johannesburg and the Transvaal; the ongoing development of Natal Studies at the University of KwaZulu-Natal in Durban; and, finally, in the engaging Western Cape history projects conducted at the University of Cape Town and the University of the Western Cape.[16] This increasingly sophisticated and richly textured scholarship has greatly enhanced our knowledge and understanding of South African urban history in many different ways, but it has also complicated attempts at synthesis. By analysing the social history of soccer in South Africa's three major metropolitan areas – Johannesburg, Durban, and Cape Town – I seek to transcend regional boundaries without sacrificing too much local specificity and depth.

On a second level, this study of black South African sport opens a productive new terrain for comparative studies of colonial societies.[17] Sport historians have already demonstrated the value of examining the diffusion of Western sports and the variegated impact of this process on indigenous people under colonial rule. The literature on this topic falls into two dominant categories. The first set illustrates the ways in which male athleticism and white sociability contributed to the production and reproduction of imperial cultural bonds in distant African, Asian, and Caribbean colonial territories.[18] The second category applies Gramscian hegemony theory, world systems analysis and, to a lesser extent, James Scott's concept of the 'weapons of the weak', to evaluate sport's role in the power relations between dominant elites and subordinate people, rich metropoles and poor peripheries.[19] Overall, these penetrating discussions of the comparative dimension of sport share a tendency to downplay the distinctive features of specific colonies and do not assess adequately the impact of local agency on modern sport's diffusion and globalisation. The partially autonomous development of South African football described in *Laduma!* underscores the limitations inherent in reading its sport history primarily in terms of cultural imperialism and colonial capitalist exigencies. Instead, an emphasis on indigenous African initiatives, including open accommodation, selective adaptation, and active resistance, and their existence in a global setting shaped by colonialism and the development of industrial capitalism seems to be a more fruitful way to examine local historical change.[20]

DOCUMENTARY AND ORAL EVIDENCE

The analysis in *Laduma!* is based on documentary evidence unearthed in public archives in South Africa, personal collections and manuscripts, published and unpublished sociological surveys, autobiographies, and the black popular press. In addition to the secondary literature, interviews conducted by myself and others were critical sources in reconstructing football's past. In the absence of a scholarly synthesis on the subject, the research process proved painfully difficult and, at times, frustrating. Primary sources were few and hard to obtain. In general, sport history in South Africa is greatly hampered by a lack of funds, staff, and initiative in storing and compiling records of sport organisations. Local authorities kept very few records of sport due, among other reasons, to lack of staff and interest. Moreover, sports bodies tended to store 'minutes, reports, results, programmes, correspondence . . . in private places like homes, even garages',[21] or, as I discovered, under a mattress in a Soweto home! The fragmentary nature of the evidence is compounded by the fact that the records of black football associations, when they were kept, frequently disappeared, were lost, or destroyed.

Bearing these challenges in mind, documents in the State Archives repositories in Pretoria, Cape Town, Pietermaritzburg, and Durban shed some light on the material worlds of black sport, though overwhelmingly from the perspective of local municipalities and the South African government. White authorities' lack of interest in African, Coloured, and Indian sport until the 1930s compounds an acute shortage of resources on the late nineteenth- and early twentieth-century period. The governmental Native Economic Commission (1930–32), which recommended the provision of sport and recreation in segregated African residential areas, stimulated the introduction of welfare and recreation programmes under the supervision of municipal Native Affairs Departments (NAD) in the 1930s. These programmes are relatively well-documented for the period between 1930 and 1960 in NAD reports, mayoral minutes, and minutes of Native Affairs Committees. The municipal files provide information on the lack of suitable sporting facilities, regulation and control of urban space for African recreation, and taxation of township sport. After the Afrikaner National Party's electoral victory in 1948, the onslaught of apartheid legislation and the creation of a gargantuan bureaucracy ensnared black soccer teams. Consequently, there is some archival evidence from the 1950s and 60s that sheds light on the racial, occupational, and generational profiles of teams. This information appears in applications for temporary travel permits and pass exemptions with the appropriate Native Commissioners, Directors of Native Labour, and the Department of Native Affairs.

Historians cannot unearth the sporting pasts of the majority of South African athletes – well-known and revered figures in the townships – by relying on government sources alone. The experiences and voices of black protagonists were gleaned from many different written and oral sources. The voluminous set of research notes and interview transcripts found in the private papers of Monica Wilson and Leo Kuper, located at the University of Cape Town's Manuscripts and Archives Library and through the Collaborative Africana Microfilm Project at the Center for Research Libraries in Chicago respectively, provided a valuable set of primary sources for this study. The records of the Bantu Men's Social Centre, the South African Institute of Race Relations, and the papers of J. Howard Pim and the Reverend Ray Phillips, housed at the University of the Witwatersrand's Cullen Library, were helpful in delineating developments in Johannesburg football during the inter-war period. Only a few written documents and a handful of photographs related to football are found in the papers of the American Board of Commissioners for Foreign Missions at Harvard University's Houghton Library. However, the American Board papers reveal the prominent role of Ray Phillips – an organiser of football for Africans in the 1920s and 30s – in its urban missions in South Africa. Richard Maguire generously provided access to the original minute books of Orlando Pirates Football Club (1945–61) donated to him by former members of the club. The papers of Durban's conservative populist African leader A.W.G. Champion, housed at the University of South Africa's Documentation Centre for African Studies in Pretoria, contained an interesting brochure of the Durban and District African Football Association's fiftieth anniversary celebrations in 1967, as well as samples of Champion's correspondence with city soccer officials. Copies of the Dennis Brutus papers at Yale University's Sterling Library and the Sir Stanley Rous papers at the University of Brighton's Falmer Library recorded important details of the domestic and international struggle against apartheid soccer that were not available in South Africa. The unsorted records of the Western Province Association Football Board, held at the University of the Western Cape's Mayibuye Archive in Belville, contained a wealth of information on the institutional history of nonracial soccer in the Western Cape in the 1970s and 80s. However, this collection shed little light on earlier years – the period with which *Laduma!* is primarily concerned.

The outstanding newspaper collection housed at the National Library of South Africa in Cape Town was of inestimable value.[22] Not only was the black popular press an indispensable source for the social history of township sport, but it also illustrates the ways in which black media shaped local football culture. For example, newspapers and magazines offered reverent coverage of football players and proved generally sympathetic to organisations fighting for equal rights and opportunities in sport. Prior to the 1950s, the black press reported mostly on the social lives of elite or aspirant middle-class people who wrote, bought, and read the newspapers. Therefore, in order 'to reconstruct some of the ideas and perceptions of working men,' as Tony Mason noted in his path-breaking studies of football and English society, 'we have to view them through the sometimes narrow and often misty lens of what middle-class observers thought and felt and said about them.'[23] With the major shift to a sex, crime, and sport format made famous in the 1950s by *Drum*, *Golden City Post*, and *Bantu World/World*, circulation increased and the quality of football (and boxing) coverage improved noticeably.[24] After the apartheid regime's violent crackdown on opposition movements and the subordination of the black press and periodicals to white commercial interests in the 1960s, newspapers catering to township residents significantly expanded their sport sections.[25] Valuable as they are, however, these newspapers provide an incomplete record of League and Cup competitions due to frequent, and often inexplicable, lapses in their reporting of critical matches and events. While a statistical history of football in South Africa is desirable for empirical purposes, clearly it is not feasible.

The limitations of official and media sources magnify the need for oral history techniques. As Charles van Onselen has stated, 'history lives on in the minds of people far more powerfully than the cracked parchment of its officialdom might know'.[26] My interviews with former players, fans, officials, and journalists – contacted through local football and university networks – were conducted in Cape Town, Pietermaritzburg, and Johannesburg during research visits in 1995 and 1997–98 and by Richard Maguire in Soweto and Johannesburg in 1991. The interviews, usually held in people's homes, provided personal memories and experiences that not only reflected wider social patterns, but unveiled particular narrative styles and conventions, and agency in remembering (or forgetting) the past.[27] Some of the people interviewed spontaneously opened their personal archives, which consisted of collected newspaper clippings, photographs, brochures, and magazines describing the sporting achievements of both the person being interviewed and his team(s). Overall, my outsider status seemed to encourage informants to speak openly about most topics, with obvious benefits for the success of the research project.

Oral testimonies opened a window on at least three unique elements of sport in South African history: the emotional dimension of soccer; its role in sustaining and giving meaning to people's social lives; and individuals' experience of sport.[28] Elderly men's accounts reflected how they used sport to wedge themselves into positions of greater power and visibility in their township community, workplace, and, in some cases, nation-wide. Interviews also afforded glimpses into informal inter-racial sport that rarely surfaced in archival or press sources. One man recalled with great pride and pleasure rugby matches as a youth in Cape Town: 'every free moment the white students [from the University of Cape Town] had, they used to come over and play rugby with us in Windermere. And they loved it! Because it was a chance to meet black people on their own turf, and we liked it, of course, because we saw them for who they really were.'[29]

Working with Richard Maguire's taped interviews with former members of Orlando Pirates Football Club was rewarding, though not without its challenges. Given the available research time and funding, these 30 hours of interviews proved of vital importance in developing a case study for Johannesburg. These tapes brought the 'hidden' past of one of South Africa's most popular teams to life. The most difficult challenge posed by the use of another researcher's oral history interviews was being an outsider listening in passively on conversations seven years after they took place. For example, Maguire's 'fact-checking' approach proved more useful in reconstructing statistical details than in exploring the implications of football for the informants' lives. Moreover, without the possibility of relying on visual cues, such as body language or the interview space, it was somewhat more difficult to interpret the narratives. Despite these difficulties, a recurring theme emerged from virtually every interview used in this book. In recalling the physical prowess, vigour, and popularity of days long gone, former players constructed romantic memories of the apartheid era. The men appeared nostalgic in remembering the 'good old days' of their youth. The darkest days of oppression were often remembered as personalised highlight reels of football memories.

Ultimately, the 'rediscovery of the ordinary'[30] documented in *Laduma!* explores a wide range of sources to uncover the specific ways in which the development of modern sport influenced, and was influenced by, the social, political, and economic experiences of black people caught in the web of segregation and apartheid.

Notes

INTRODUCTION

1. Brutus (1971: 144).
2. The term 'black' in this book refers to people classified African, Coloured, and Indian under the Population Registration Act of 1950. The collective racial terms are used only where appropriate. While the concept of 'race' is a social construction bound up with apartheid history, it is acknowledged that racial boundaries and identities were (and continue to be) relevant to South Africans themselves.
3. 'Messrs. Evans and Farrel Interest Natal Employers in Bantu Sport', *Bantu World*, 16 February 1935. City of Durban, Minute of Mayor 1958–59, 22; Kuper (1965: 347).
4. The 1939 figures are cited in Alan G. Cobley (1994: 222); 1959 figures derived from a letter by W.J.P. Carr, Manager of the Johannesburg Non-European Affairs Department (NEAD), to the Mayor's Secretary, 14 July 1959. This NEAD document is located in the (National Archives, Pretoria) files of the West Rand Administration Board, Welfare and Recreation Office (WRO), 138/8 v.4.
5. 'Business and Sport for a Team SA', *Business Day*, 4 September 2000; 'Beer Cash Bail-Out', *Daily Mail & Guardian*, 2 August 2002. The most recent Premier Soccer League sponsorship deal features a R500 million accord with the South African Broadcasting Corporation (length of contract unknown) and a R140 million pact with South African Breweries.
6. Alegi (2001).
7. For helpful definitions of popular culture in Africa see Barber (1997: 1–12); and Fabian (1978: 315–334). For a theoretical discussion see Barber (1987: 1–78).
8. Thompson (1967); Cooper (1983); Atkins (1993); and Martin (1995).
9. Wylie (2001); Scott (1998).
10. Booth (1998); Fair (1997); and Nauright (1997b).
11. Beinart (1991: 103–128); Bonner (1993: 160–194); Glaser (2000); Guy and Thabane (1987: 436–456); Kynoch (2000: 267–290); La Hausse (1990: 79–111); Van Onselen (1982: 1–73).
12. Clive Glaser (2000).
13. Definition of patriarchal masculinity adapted from Carton (2000) and Moodie (1994: 193–194).
14. Among the many discussions of sport and masculinity see Messner (1992); Messner and Sabo (1990); and Whitson (1990). For recent South African applications of these perspectives, see Morrell (1998, 2001).
15. Hargreaves (1997); and Saavedra (2003).

CHAPTER 1

1. Baker and Mangan (1987: viii).
2. Mandela (1994: 16).
3. Mandela (1994: 9).
4. Mandela (1994: 180).

5. Archer and Bouillon (1982: 26); Booth (1998: 14–15, 40–41); Nauright (1997b: 57–69); and Odendaal (1988: 200).
6. In a simplified explanation of more complex, changing dynamics, African men controlled the homestead's cattle, cleared fields for agricultural use, built houses and fences, and in the dry season engaged in craft-making and trade. Male leisure activities might include drinking beer, taking snuff, and smoking dagga (marijuana) with other men in the late afternoon and evening hours. Women, who took care of the children and their individual homes (*izindlu*), brewed *amabele* (sorghum beer) and performed heavy agricultural labour including planting, weeding, and harvesting crops, had considerably less leisure time than men, but still enjoyed story-telling, singing, and dancing. Girls helped senior and junior wives in collecting firewood, drawing water, and cleaning the home; and boys were responsible for cattle herding.
7. According to Omo-Osagie, a Nigerian author, 'work and leisure were so decisively physical that fitness and competitiveness, the twin pillars of sports, were easily achieved' by pre-colonial African societies (1987: 14).
8. Samuelson (1929: 372–376).
9. Guy and Thabane (1987: 445); Moodie (1994: 192).
10. Moodie (1994: 192–194).
11. Mager (1999: 129).
12. Rycroft and Ngcobo (1988: 12).
13. Mager (1999: 131).
14. On the praise poetry of migrant Basotho miners see Coplan (1994).
15. Samuelson (1929: 373–374).
16. McAllister and Deliwe (1996: 5). I am indebted to Dr Derick Fay for providing me with a copy of this study.
17. McAllister and Deliwe (1996: 5). Anthropologists Philip and Iona Mayer defined this process as 'socialization by peers' (1970: 159–189). For an in-depth account, see Mayer and Mayer (1972).
18. Akyeampong and Ambler (2002: 11).
19. Beinart (1992: 475).
20. McAllister and Deliwe (1996: 24–27, 34–38). The socio-cultural underpinnings of peasant opposition to state agricultural policies in the Transkei are explored in McAllister (1989: 346–368).
21. Clegg (1981: 164–198).
22. McAllister and Deliwe (1996: 22–23); Mager (1999: 134). These authors identify the growing difficulty in settling disputes due to the absence of older males (working as migrant labourers), increases in cattle theft, and changing ideas about youthful masculine behaviour as the main causes for the upsurge in violence connected to stick-fights.
23. Moodie (1994: 192).
24. Webb and Wright (1986: 294).
25. Erlmann (1991: 99). A similar point is made in McAllister and Deliwe (1996: 5).
26. Gluckman and Gluckman (1983: 203).
27. Samuelson (1929: 373). Ndukwana kaMbengwana told James Stuart in 1900 that 'in Cetshwayo's day a notable infringement of this well-known rule took place' in a bloody 1878 clash between members of the uThulwana and inGobamakosi regiments (Webb & Wright, 1986: 294–295). For analysis of the generational conflict that underpinned the attack by the older uThulwana regiment on the younger inGobamakosi, see Carton (2000: 38–39).
28. For twentieth-century political repercussions of British and French colonial administrations' creation of African 'customary' law see Mamdani (1996: Ch.4).
29. Mager (1999: 129).
30. Thompson (1990: 27). For these reasons Monica Hunter-Wilson stated that 'cattle raiding from neighboring tribes was a usual and honorable pastime' (Hunter, 1961: 132).

31. Cope (1999); Delius (1983); Eldredge (1993); Etherington (1978); Guy (1979); Hamilton (1995); Keegan (1996); Lambert (1995); Legassick (1969: 86–125); Marks and Atmore (1980); Peires (1987: 43–63); and Wright (1971).
32. Bonner (1982: 22).
33. Ashton (1952: 98).
34. Soga (1932: 371). For interesting descriptions of two cattle races see Soga (1932: 371–376). On J.H. Soga see Peires (1981: 178–179); on his father see Williams (1978).
35. Cook (1931: 120–121).
36. Cook (1931: 120–121).
37. Cook (1931: 120–121).
38. See, for example, Brownlee (1968, 2: 209–210) cited in Thompson (1990: 19).
39. Bryant (1949: 684–685); Samuelson (1929: 374).
40. Bryant (1949: 682).
41. On 'doctoring' of Zulu armed forces see Mpatshana's testimony in Webb and Wright (1982: 296–301).
42. Bale and Sang (1996: 63).
43. Kaeppler (1992: 196–197).
44. Omo-Osagie (1987: 14).
45. Ashton (1952: 95–99); Tracey (1952: 11–12).
46. Ashton (1952: 95–99).
47. Tracey (1952: 9).
48. Cook (1931: 87).
49. Cook (1931: 61, 68, 88).
50. Tracey (1952: 11–12).
51. Tracey (1952: 7). For an analysis of Zulu dance in Durban see Erlmann (1991: Ch.4).
52. Tracey (1952: 5).
53. Carton (2000: 24); Samuelson (1929: 374). Among the Swazi, the *incwala* first-fruit ceremonies, which fostered allegiance and legitimised the monarchy like the Zulu *umkhosi*, included an important homonymous dance. It was noted how 'the people dance with vigor; here more than at any other stage they keep their king alive and healthy by their own movements' (Hanna, 1977: 120).
54. Erlmann (1991: 101).
55. Erlmann (1991: 101).
56. Webb and Wright (1982: 306–307).
57. Clayton (1987: 117); Harris and Park (1983: 2–3).
58. Hanna (1977: 118).
59. Hanna (1977: 118).
60. Blacking (1987: 15). For more analyses of dance and sport in the African context see Gluckman and Gluckman (1983); and Mitchell (1956).
61. Bale and Sang (1996: 49–50).

CHAPTER 2

1. Holt (1989: Ch.4); Morrell (1996).
2. Lewson (1982: 19); Spies (1995: 66).
3. According to Burridge Spies, the new headmaster at Diocesan College (Bishops) in Cape Town, the Reverend George Ogilvie, brought the Winchester rules to the Cape in 1861 (Grundlingh, Odendaal and Spies, 1995: 66).
4. Archer and Bouillon (1982: 57). This ambiguity between rugby and soccer has distorted the history of football in the United States. The Rutgers vs Princeton football match that took place in New Brunswick, NJ on 6 November 1869, widely believed to be the first gridiron

(American) football match ever played, was more like a soccer game according to contemporary press accounts. This perspective is endorsed by McCabe (1999). I am grateful to Tom McCabe for providing me with a copy of this paper.

5. Hattersley (1938: 95–96).
6. Blades (1998: 8–9).
7. Gibson and Pickford (1906: 220).
8. Goulstone (2000: 135–143). On pre-industrial football in Britain also see Holt (1989: Ch. 1); and Walvin (1994: Ch.1).
9. Walvin (1994: 41–43).
10. Parker (1897: 82–84).
11. Mason (1995: 22).
12. Evidence of Corinthians tours from Creek (1933: 64–67, 207); Gibson and Pickford (1906: 226). For more details on the early period of white soccer see Parker (1897: 73–105).
13. Mason (1995: 18). According to Mason, the South African amateurs ('eight of them British and seven South African-born') were the first foreign team to play in Brazil. In their first match, the South Africans defeated Liga Paulistano 6-0 at São Paulo's Velodrome (1995: 18).
14. Nauright (1997b: 39).
15. This conclusion is made emphatically in Guttmann (1994). On sport and cultural imperialism see Bale and Sang (1996); Cashman (1988: 258–272); and Stoddart (1988: 649–673).
16. Morrell (1996: 101). Note that the British love of sport stood in stark opposition to the insignificant sporting culture of white South Africans of Dutch origin (Van der Merwe, 1988: 28–39).
17. Black and Nauright (1998); Morrell (1996: 91); Thompson (2001: 240–244).
18. Mangan (1986: 35–36).
19. Morrell (1996: 102).
20. Black and Nauright (1998: 24–29).
21. Morrell (1996: 91, 107). On Afrikaner rugby see Grundlingh in Grundlingh, Odendaal and Spies (1995: 106–135). In this illuminating study, Grundlingh shows how rugby's popularity in Afrikaner popular culture was 'in line with the wider Afrikaner quest for independent nationhood, the game came to be an integral part of the attempt to transform and transcend the imperial heritage by reformulating and modifying the values associated with it.'
22. Hardy (1990: 45–82).
23. Odendaal (1988: 200).
24. Cobley (1994: 213). See also, Archer and Bouillon (1982: 114–116); and Odendaal (1988: 207).
25. For more details on black migrancy and Kimberley see Worger (1987: esp. 64–109).
26. Willan (1984: 45).
27. Black and Nauright (1998: 49, 54–55); Odendaal (1995: 35, 39). This rugby organisation was made up of Africans, Coloureds, 'Malays' and Indians.
28. Mancoe (1934: 83).
29. Couzens (1983).
30. Freund (1995: 39). Freund goes on to say that the 'Bluebells, founded in 1884, were remembered as the first team' (1995: 39).
31. Couzens (1983: 203).
32. Campbell (2000: 47).
33. For details see, for example, reports by the war correspondent of the *Daily Telegraph*, McHugh (1900: 85). For an analysis of the effect of sport in British prison camps see Van der Merwe (1992: 439–454).
34. Plaatje (1990: 52, 58).

35. 'History of the Sam China Cup', *The Leader*, 8 September 1961. Among those present at the inaugural meeting of SAIFA were Sam China, P.M. Dawson, A.S. Dorasamy Pillay, and Joseph M. Peters of Kimberley, and David Ernest, Frank Benjamin Ernest, and Emmanuel A. Peters of the Transvaal.

36. Blades (1998: 18–19).

37. Evidence of permits issued to Indian football clubs by Natal authorities during this period is in the Pietermaritzburg Archive Repository (PAR), Ladysmith Town Clerk files, 1/LDS, 3/3/17 [L935A/1904], 28 June 1904.

38. 'History of the Sam China Cup', *The Leader*, 8 September 1961.

39. PAR, Natal Harbour Department files, II/1/22, HDE 875/1899. Over 5 000 African togt labourers, 28 per cent of Durban's African population, worked in the docks in 1904 (Maylam, 1985: 44). See also Atkins (1993: 100–114, 129–140).

40. Couzens (1983: 204). On African life in a Johannesburg slumyard see Hellmann (1948).

41. Cape Archives Repository (CAR), Town Clerk files, 3/CT 4/1/5/51 887/5: Letter from C.W. Yarney to Town Clerk, 25 May 1925.

42. Cobley (1994: 215).

43. Beinart (1992: 476). *Ingoma* (dance) teams and gangs of domestic servants known as *amalaita* rose to prominence in Durban, Johannesburg, and Pretoria; these were 'groups who shared a common set of mostly military symbols inherited from the pre-colonial past' (Erlmann, 1991: 103). See also Beinart (1991: 103–128); La Hausse (1990: 79–111); Van Onselen (1982: 1–73).

44. Mitchell (1956); Ranger (1975).

45. Ranger (1975: 15, 75). On the east African island of Zanzibar, historian Laura Fair observed a comparable process: 'Like competitive *ngoma*, football also provided an open ground on which existing hierarchies and social divisions could be challenged or reinforced, depending on the situation and the goals of the participants' (Fair, 1997: 228). Similarly, historian Phyllis Martin (1995) noted how urban Africans in Brazzaville seized on colonial forms of leisure that exhibited direct and indirect continuities with rural pre-colonial practices, normative values, and beliefs.

CHAPTER 3

1. Archer and Bouillon (1982: 100).

2. Van der Horst (1964: table 1, 19). The proportion of the urban population to South Africa's total population rose from 25 per cent to 37 per cent between 1911 and 1946.

3. Bundy (1979). Poor whites and Indians also moved to urban areas during this period. Between 1921 and 1936, the proportion of whites and Indians in urban areas rose dramatically from 56 per cent to 65 per cent and from 31 per cent to 66 per cent respectively (Van der Horst, 1964: 19).

4. Johannesburg's demographic statistics cited in Proctor (1987: 225–268). Official South African statistics are notoriously inaccurate and unreliable historical sources. For example, a white city councillor commented that 'the 93,000 Natives living in Johannesburg and on the Reef live by their wits, sleep with their friends at night, and are not included in the [1936] census' (Coplan, 1985: 90 fn.2). Nevertheless, official figures record the number of black people within the institutional reach of the state, and the mining and manufacturing industries, thus helping the historian estimate the size of the overall population.

5. Freund (2000: 148–155).

6. Durban demographics in *Durban Mayor's Minute*, 'Annual Report, Medical Officer of Health: City Health Department': 59; and Maylam (1985: 16). For further insight on the Indian population see Freund (1995).

7. Cape Town statistics from Western (1996: 36, 48); and Musemwa (1993: 28).

8. Thompson (1990: 166–178).

9. La Hausse's reliable estimate found that there were about 20 000 *kholwa* out of an African population of roughly one million in Natal and Zululand (2000: 11, 29 fn.38). Among the most insightful studies of *kholwa* are Etherington (1978); and Lambert (1995).

10. Marks (1986: 43). For more details on John Dube see Marable (1976).

11. Odendaal reported that *Imvo* had a 'sports editor' as early as 1887, and that teams issued challenges in its pages. Also, the interest in sport was such that advertising catered specifically to African athletes and clubs (1995: 33, 35).

12. *Ilanga Lase Natal*, vol.1, no.4 (1903).

13. The American Board of Commissioners for Foreign Missions (ABCFM) was organised by the General Association of Congregational Churches of Massachusetts in 1810. Beginning in 1812 missionaries were sent to Africa, North America (the United States and Canada), Mexico, China, Japan, India, the Pacific Islands, Balkans, Turkey, Syria, Persia, France, Spain, and Austria. The stated purpose of the ABCFM was 'to devise ways and means, adopt and prosecute measures, to promote the spread of the gospel in Heathen lands'. See the introduction to the accession guide to the *Papers of the American Board of Commissioners For Foreign Missions: Guide to the Microfilm Collection* (Woodbridge, CT, 1994), Harvard University, Houghton Manuscripts Library.

14. Hall (1994); Hopkins (1951); Mangan (1981, 1986).

15. United States President Theodore Roosevelt threatened to ban gridiron football in the United States in 1905 because of the large number of deaths among its players (Murray, 1996: 15). The history of the role of American missionaries in diffusing soccer around the world has yet to be written. According to historian Houchang Chehabi, Presbyterian missionaries based in Philadelphia, PA, played a key role in spreading the game to Iran in the early twentieth century (Chehabi, 'Football', *Encyclopedia Iranica*, vol.X, 79–80).

16. Collaborative Africana Microfilm Project (CAMP), Center for Research Libraries, Chicago, IL, Leo Kuper Papers (hereafter LKP): J. Ngidi, 'History of the Bush Bucks Football Club'.

17. Couzens (1983: 203).

18. The minutes of the meetings of the DDAFA mention the Victorians, but Ngidi refers to the Condors of the north coast. Here I privilege institutional records over individual memory. Note that *Dube* in Zulu means 'wild zebra', hence the nickname for Dube's Ohlange Institute team.

19. Edgar and Msumza (1996: 5). In addition to a teacher training college, Adams also had a high school and an industrial school.

20. Mangan (1986).

21. For an overview see Guttmann (1994). On India see Dimeo and Mills (2001); as well as Appaduraj (1996); Bose (1990); and James (1963). On the West Indies see Stoddart (1988: 649–673); and Stoddart and Beckles (1996).

22. Couzens (1983: 203).

23. Couzens (1983: 203).

24. 'On the Sportsfield', *Iso Lomuzi*, September 1931: 22–23. Additional information on Shooting Stars in this paragraph is culled from the same source.

25. UNISA, Documentation Centre for African Studies, AWG Champion Papers: 19.5.1.3, H. Ngwenya, 'Umlando Ngo D & D,' in Durban and District African Football Association 'Golden Jubilee Brochure': 22. Sithole (1983: 95). LKP: Transcript of interview by B. Magubane with John Khambule (1960?). While I have not been able to locate any evidence in this regard, it is possible that Mr Scotts was British.

26. The ratio of African men to women was 6,6:1 in 1921; 3,4:1 in 1936; 2,3:1 in 1951 (Maylam, 1996: 15); and Nuttall (1996: 178).

27. LKP: Transcript of interviews by B. Magubane with Douglas Evans, 4 July 1960, and with Khambule.

28. University of Cape Town Libraries, Manuscripts and Archives Department, Monica H. Wilson Papers: Archie Mafeje fieldnotes: 301–350.

29. Magubane (1963: 19).
30. Magubane interview with Khambule.
31. Sithole (1983: 95).
32. Couzens (1983: 203).
33. According to Douglas Evans, Berry presided over the drafting of a constitution before 1916. However, the clubs did not see any need to adopt it until they were ready to establish a formal association (Magubane interview with Evans).
34. Magubane (1963: 6). LKP: Magubane interview with D. Evans. According to J. Ngidi's 'History of Bush Bucks Football Club', Carleton died in 1918 trying to save his drowning son at sea.
35. For a critical analysis of the Durban town council's provision for, and control of, sport and leisure for Africans see Vahed (1998: 67–123).
36. La Hausse (1996: 33–66); Swanson (1976).
37. Maylam (1996: 6); Swanson (1976: 174).
38. LKP, Ngidi.
39. Magubane (1963: 8). Magubane was Leo Kuper's field researcher for the latter's study of Durban's black middle class; see Kuper (1965). Magubane went into exile shortly after completing his master's degree in 1963. After teaching for many years at the University of Connecticut in the United States of America, he recently retired and returned to Durban.
40. LKP: Magubane interviews with D. Evans and Edward C. Jali, Durban, March 1960.
41. Magubane interview with Evans; evidence also cited in Kuper (1965: 349).
42. Magubane interview with Evans; Magubane (1963: 7). On Pietermaritzburg as a centre of African radicalism see La Hausse (2000: 108).
43. LKP: Letter from Durban and District Native Football Association to D. Evans, 27 August 1923.
44. DDAFA Minutes, 7 June 1933; Magubane (1963: 7) and Magubane's interview with D. Evans.
45. For studies on the growing black radicalism of the segregation era see, for example, Bonner (1982: 270–313); Bradford (1987); Marks (1986); Vinson (2000); and Walshe (1971).
46. Magubane interview with D. Evans.
47. Letter from Durban and District Native Football Association to D. Evans, 27 August 1923.
48. Magubane (1963: 7).
49. An important study on this subject is Halisi (1999).
50. Data on clubs and registered players in Durban were culled from the following sources: LKP: Minutes of Meetings of the Durban and District Native Football Association (1924–1935); 3/DBN, 4/1/2/1165, 11/352: Report of the Native Welfare Officer, 25 April 1931; 3/DBN, 4/1/3/1606, 352 v. I: Letter from Douglas Evans, Bantu Recreational Grounds Association, to Councillor J.L. Farrell, Chairman, Native Administration Committee, 31 January 1935; Magubane (1963: 12).
51. Interview with Moses Molelekoa, Khayelitsha, 26 July 1995.
52. The term 'round-robin' describes a competition in which each team plays every other team at least once. The traditional 'point system' used worldwide awarded two points for victory, one for a draw, and none for a loss. It was revised in the 1990s when FIFA, world soccer's governing body, decided to give winners three points instead of two in order to encourage offensive play.
53. Sithole (1983: 95). Though Sithole states that Wanderers faced Union Jacks at the 1925 Kingsmead match, both H. Ngwenya (1899–1977), DDAFA president in 1952–64, and the *Bantu World* newspaper agree that the famous Union Jacks Football Club was formed out of a split from NGR in 1929. See *Bantu World*, 19 September 1936; and Ngwenya, 'Umlando Ngo D & D'.
54. Sithole (1983: 95).

55. Erlmann (1996a: 91). For more analysis of Durban beerhalls see La Hausse (1992: 78–114).
56. Speech made by Mr Howard of the Native Recruiting Corporation, quoted in DDNFA Minutes, 24 October 1930; also cited in Magubane (1963: 16). Howard spoke on the occasion of donating two company trophies to the DDNFA.
57. The 1913 Natives' Land Act limited the amount of South African land that Africans could own to 7 per cent; the 1923 Natives' Urban Areas Act mandated residential segregation for Africans in cities and towns (under certain conditions). In 1936 the amount of land available for African purchase was expanded to about 13 per cent, but, at the same time, ownership was restricted to rural labour reserves.
58. Erlmann (1996a: 89).
59. According to Paul La Hausse, Zulu workers gave Layman the nickname *Umthwazi* (monkey-rope) because of his reputation for martial toughness (2000: 115, 122 fn.87).
60. Led by Colonel Frederick Stallard, the Transvaal Local Government Commission (1920) declared in its published report of 1922 that: 'The Native should only be allowed to enter urban areas, which are essentially the white man's creation, when he is willing to enter and to minister to the needs of the white man, and should depart therefrom when he ceases so to minister' (Hindson, 1987: 37).
61. La Hausse (1989: 19–58).
62. Official figures reported one hundred and twenty injured and six dead – four black protestors and two white soldiers (La Hausse, 1989: 36–37).
63. On 16 December (Dingane's Day) 1930 police shot and killed Communist Party leader Johannes Nkosi and three other people involved in the pass-burning campaign at Durban's Cartwright Flats. The enactment of the 1930 Amendment to the Natives Urban Areas Act provided for the deportation of 'idle, dissolute or disorderly' Africans, while the DTC regulated the influx of African women in 1935. After the 1937 Native Laws Amendment Act, African workers were required to return to the countryside if they had not found employment within fourteen days of arriving in the city (Maylam, 1985: 51–54).
64. Municipal housing remained vastly inadequate to meet the demands of a growing black urban population who settled in expanding informal shack settlements in the city. The largest and best known in Durban was Cato Manor (Mkhumbane), whose estimated population rose from 2 500 in 1936 to more than 17 000 in 1943 (Maasdorp and Humphreys, 1975: 14–15). On Lamontville see Torr (1996: 245–273). For Cato Manor see Edwards (1989, 1996: 102–142).
65. La Hausse (1990: 108). See also Erlmann (1996a: 67–101); Vahed (1998: 67–123).
66. Maylam (1985: 56).
67. Maylam (1985: 56).
68. Durban Archives Repository, Durban Town Clerk files, 3/DBN, 4/1/2/1165, 11/352: Report on 'Native Recreation', J.T. Rawlins, Native Welfare Officer, to Town Clerk, 25 April 1931.
69. Vahed (1998: 70–73).
70. 3/DBN, 4/1/2/1165, 11/352: Report on 'Native Recreation'; LKP: Constitution of the Bantu Recreational Grounds Association; Magubane (1963: 16–19).
71. Paul Maylam showed that the Durban corporation in the first half of the twentieth century created and maintained a system of taxation without representation, which ensured that Africans paid, through their modest wages, for their own oppression. Adding insult to injury, Durban officials siphoned funds out of the Native Revenue Account to subsidise services available only to whites. For details see Maylam (1988: 69–92).
72. Data on municipal funding of African sport in Durban extracted from *Durban Mayor's Minute* and the Annual Reports of the Native Administration Department therein, 1930–33.
73. Maylam (1988: 84).
74. 3/DBN, 4/1/21165, 352: Notes of Interview between the Durban Town Council and the Durban and District Native Football Association, 15 November, 1930.

75. Luthuli's sporting career is examined in more detail in Alegi (26 May 2002).
76. 3/DBN, 4/1/21165, 352: Notes of Interview with Representatives of DDAFA, 15 November 1930.
77. 'Notes of Interview', 15 November 1930.
78. 'Notes of Interview', 15 November 1930.
79. DDAFA Minutes of Annual General Meeting, 11 March 1932. According to these minutes, the Natal association also changed its name to Natal African Football Association around this time.
80. Lodge (1983: 6).
81. For more insight on the name change issue, see P. Limb, 'SANNC to ANC: Reply', in H-SAFRICA, <h-safrica@h-net.msu.edu> (accessed on 30 October 2001).
82. Halisi (1999: 57).
83. In Johannesburg, African mine clerks previously involved with the Johannesburg Bantu Football Association and the moribund Witwatersrand and District Native Football Association founded the Transvaal African Football Association in 1930. In Cape Town, the Cape Peninsula Bantu Football Association, formed in 1927 in Langa township, transformed itself into the Western Province African Football Association in either 1936 or 1937.
84. Paul Maylam asserted that Durban's social programmes were a key factor in bringing about a relative calm in Durban's labour and race relations in the 1930s (1996: 12).
85. For more on the political conflicts over the provision of sport and leisure for Africans in the 1930s in Durban see Vahed (1998).
86. For example, in the early 1930s the DDAFA donated £25 'to help the cricket association out of its debts' (Magubane, 1963: 15).
87. 'Durban Municipality shows great Interest in Promoting Bantu Sport', *Bantu World*, 4 February 1933.
88. 'Bantu Sportsmen in Natal Know Only One Game – Soccer', *Bantu World*, 4 March 1933.
89. DDNFA Minutes, 2 September 1928 and 22 February 1929; 31 [*sic*] November 1930.
90. DDNFA Minutes, 2 September 1928.
91. DDNFA Minutes, 22 February 1929.
92. Durban Archives Repository (DAR), Durban Town Clerk files, 3/DBN, 4/1/3/1692, vol. 3, 30/467, Manager, NAD, 11 November 1936; La Hausse (1989: 21); Kuper (1965: 437 table 9).
93. Magubane (1963: 12); DDAFA Minutes.
94. The FA Cup format followed the diffusion of the modern game around the world, see Murray (1996). There is a rich literature on the history of English football, for example, see Cox, Russell and Vamplew (2002); Mason (1980); and Walvin (1994).
95. La Hausse (1993: 195–196).
96. Magubane (1963: 22–23 tables 2 and 3); Kuper (1965: 435 table 7).
97. During the 1924–60 period only 3,1 per cent of Africans completed ten years of schooling (South African Institute of Race Relations, 1960: 214).
98. 'Class' is defined here more in terms of status and respectability than material circumstances.
99. DDAFA Minutes, 10 June 1932. Painfully long meetings were not uncommon; on 20 May 1932, the meeting lasted from 7:45 p.m. until 4:45 a.m.
100. Magubane (1963: 15). For a thoughtful consideration of language, ethnicity, and the politics of African nationalism see Vail (1989: 1–19).
101. Magubane (1963: 21–22).
102. Interview with Ben Malamba, Langa, 26 July 1995. Nauright (1997b: 65).
103. The executive committee was composed of: T. Ngcobo (president), A.R. Ntuli (vice-president), J.E. Radebe (treasurer), F.E. Mwandla (secretary), S.J.J. Benghu (recording clerk), with Ngcobo, W.K. Luvuno, and W. Ngidi acting delegates to the Natal association (DDNFA Minutes, Annual General Meeting, 11 March 1927).

104. Hughes (1996: 303); La Hausse (2000: 172).
105. Magubane (1963: 9 table 1). Magubane must have incorrectly dated his table '1924–1932' because many of the people included served after 1932. The period is, most likely, 1924–60, during which fourteen out of thirty-one officials of DDAFA were on the NAB, six were ANC members, and at least five were members of NATA, ICU, and the Joint Council.
106. Luthuli (1962: 38).
107. Couzens (1983: 202–203).
108. Bonner (1982: 272–274); Bradford (1987: 13–16, 74–81); Cobley (1990); La Hausse (1989: 20).
109. Erlmann (1996a: 68); Marks (1986: 106).
110. Erlmann (1996a: 68).
111. Phillips (1936: 311).
112. Ballantine (1993: 50–51); Erlmann (1991: 104).
113. DDAFA Minutes of Annual General Meeting, 10 March 1933.
114. Magubane interview with Edward C. Jali.
115. La Hausse (1990: 107).
116. On *amalaita* in Durban see La Hausse (1990); on *ngoma* (traditional dancing) see Erlmann (1991: 95–111). For more on *amalaita* in Johannesburg see Van Onselen (1982: 54–60).
117. Morrell (1998: 623).
118. Magubane (1963: 12); DDAFA Minutes.
119. Magubane (1963: 12). For further discussion of *izibongo* see Cope (1968: 1–31); Gunner and Gwala (1991: 1–52).
120. Interview with C. Stuurman, Factreton, 25 February 1998.
121. Magubane (1963: 12).
122. Moodie (1994: 192).
123. Clubs were required to register players with the association at least seven days in advance of their participation in their first match. In a typical eligibility case of the period, DDAFA awarded the victory to Victorians over Callies in the knock-out Cup competition of 1932 due to the latter club's failure to register its players 'a clear seven days in advance'. Case cited in DDAFA Minutes, 29 April 1932.
124. Magubane (1963). On African legal traditions see Gluckman (1965b) and (1965a: esp. 169–215) as well as (1969).
125. For a brief account of modern-day stick fighting see Carton (2001: 137–139).
126. 'Rough Play Becomes Popular', *Bantu World*, 5 August 1937. The article stated that 'referees as appointed now are bound to have bias, for each referee comes from a registered club that competes'.
127. DDNFA Minutes, 24 July 1925 and 30 October 1925. The average wage for single male migrants (*izimpohlo*, bachelor in Zulu) was £2.8s. (La Hausse, 1989: 22).
128. DDNFA Minutes, 1924–31.
129. DDNFA Minutes, 1924–31.
130. On the emergence of African co-operatives, self-help schemes, and *umholiswano* (People's Banks) in Durban in the 1930s and 40s, see Edwards (1989: 59–104); and La Hausse (1993: 201–218).
131. 'Natal Soccer Optimistic', *Natal Mercury*, 1 March 1932.
132. For example, a Mr Cele was reported to have 'disappeared with £5.19s.10d' in 1925–26; cited in DDNFA Minutes of Annual General Meeting, 26 March 1926.
133. 3/DBN, 4/1/2/1606: Report of the DDAFA Commission of Inquiry, 22 February 1933 (Manyoni, 1933).
134. 3/DBN, 4/1/2/1167, 30/352: Secretary, DDAFA, to Town Clerk, 26 January 1934; information corroborated by *Bantu World*, 16 February 1935.

135. Cobley (1994: 224).
136. DDAFA Minutes, Annual General Meeting, March 1931.

CHAPTER 4

1. Couzens (1983: 203–204).
2. Couzens (1983: 203–204).
3. 'WDAFA Forges Ahead Despite Difficulties', *Bantu World*, 1 September 1934.
4. In the wake of the 1920 African mineworkers strike the 'Chamber warned, "that the native is advancing more rapidly than we had anticipated, and that we should take measures accordingly." [The Chamber feared] "that at no distant date further attempts will be made to organize strikes among the natives"' (Johnstone, 1976: 183).
5. In 1934, Graham Ballenden, manager of the Johannesburg Native Affairs Department, praised his efforts to gain control of African football in the city: 'The free fights and knifing episodes that were such a big feature of Native football matches played for money prizes on all odd pieces of ground before the creation of the Bantu Football Association, have almost completely disappeared.' Annual Report of Manager, NAD, 1933–34.
6. For additional evidence of Zulu mine clerk involvement in establishing soccer on the Rand see La Hausse (2000: 172–173).
7. Badenhorst (1992: 370–371). For details on the appalling working and living conditions of black miners on the Rand, see U.G. 34-14 (1914: 209).
8. For details on the Old Natalians, see *Bantu World*, 26 June 1937 and 4 April 1942.
9. Tribal dancing was part of mining companies' overall strategy to divide the migrant labour force along ethnic lines and reinforce rural roots. By 1949, however, it was clear that miners 'participated in the sport and leisure of their choice, despite the efforts of mine managers' (Badenhorst & Mather, 1997: 488). It should be pointed out that the majority of African miners around this time were 'foreign Natives', that is, migrant labourers from southern and central African colonial territories; see *Thirty-fourth Annual Report of the Transvaal Chamber of Mines: Year 1923* (1924: 161). On the migrant labour system on the Rand gold mines see Crush, Jeeves and Yudelman (1991); Wilson (1972).
10. Cobley (1994: 224).
11. Bonner (1992: 269–305). In an interview with Tim Couzens in 1978, Dan Twala pointed out the significance of football in the mining companies' attempts to separate the compounds and the urban locations (Couzens, 1983: 206). In practice, mine compounds and townships formed interlocking worlds that, according to Philip Bonner, 'defied all official attempts at control' (1992: 287). There were some exceptions to this pattern, however, as Mpondo miners were reluctant to enter the townships. Dunbar Moodie revealed that they preferred to stay in the mine compounds where they could take advantage of the sociability and security of home-based social networks (Moodie, 1994: 96–97).
12. 'Life in Mine Compounds', *Umteteli Wa Bantu,* 13 October 1923.
13. Crush, Jeeves and Yudelman (1991: 34).
14. Van Onselen (1976: 191). For scholarship on Britain see Holt (1986: 5–17); Jones (1988); and Korr (1978: 211–232).
15. Vundla (1973: 17). For more details on Philip Vundla's ANC activities during the Sophiatown removals, see Lodge (1983: 97, 105–106). Critics called attention to the bribery and corruption that surrounded the recruitment of workers with football skills by mines and municipalities; see, for example, 'Is it to be Professional or Amateur Football?' *Bantu World*, 30 November 1935.
16. *Bantu World*, 16 May 1936.
17. Alegi (1999: 55–74).

18. Moodie (1994: 181). Moodie concluded that there were two periods of relative labour peace on the mines in the twentieth century: 1921–37 and 1947–72.

19. Badenhorst (1992: 80–81). The Johannesburg NAD was renamed the Non-European Affairs Department (NEAD) in 1937. For further commentary on white liberals and African sport see Cobley (1994, 1997: Ch.1).

20. There is a substantial literature on the conflicts over leisure between white officials, private companies, missionaries, and African colonial subjects. See, for example, Akyeampong (1996: 215–236); Ambler (2001: 81–105); Fair (1997: 224–251); Martin (1995); Ranger (1987: 196–213); and Stuart (1996: 167–180). For an overview of the literature see Akyeampong and Ambler (2002: 1–16).

21. Cooper (1983: 7–8).

22. *Report of the Native Economic Commission*, para.572. Ballenden and Phillips joined forces in publicly espousing the 'recreation as social welfare' policy the following year at a conference of NAD managers and superintendents on 'Urban Native Affairs' in Durban, as reported in Atkinson (1933).

23. Cape Archives Repository, Cape Town Town Clerk files, 3/CT, 1/4/10/1/1/6: Minutes of the Native Affairs Committee (Cape Town City Council), 26 October 1932.

24. Phillips (1930: 58).

25. For more details see Couzens (1982: 314–337). Ray Phillips, one of the ABM's most prominent urban social workers, was an American lecturer who came to South Africa in 1918. He was invited by Dr Bridgman, director of the ABM in South Africa, a missionary who 'endeavored to undertake something constructive in a social way for the native – something in the nature of a YMCA'. This quote is from a Johannesburg newspaper clipping (*The Star*? 1923?) found in the microfilm version of the 'American Zulu Mission' files in the *Papers of the American Board of Commissioners For Foreign Missions*. As Badenhorst and Couzens pointed out, Phillips strongly believed that organised, controlled recreational activities were the only way to ensure that African leisure time could be '*moralized* in the correct way', and not for any other 'questionable activity' (see Badenhorst, 1992: 104–105; Couzens, 1982: 330). ABM records reveal that Phillips's salary was consistently the highest in the 'Zulu mission'; this support demonstrated the ABM's appreciation of his sport and recreation work in Johannesburg.

26. Badenhorst (1992: 94–95). The black-white Joint Council was a politically moderate organisation founded in Johannesburg in 1921 at the suggestion of Dr James Aggrey (Jamaica) and the Revd Thomas Jones (United States of America) during their visit to South Africa as members of the Phelps-Stokes Foundation Educational Commission. For more details see Horton (1972: 29–44); Rich (1984: 10–22).

27. University of the Witwatersrand, Historical Papers at William Cullen Library, Bantu Men's Social Centre Papers, Annual Report of the Bantu Men's Social Centre, 1929; Couzens (1985: 90). The religious and liberal ameliorative agenda was embodied in the BMSC's four-part programme crystallised in its initials: Body, Mind, Spirit, Character, as cited in BMSC Annual Reports, 1929–40. For the ABM's role in African girls' recreation see Gaitskell (1984: 222–264).

28. Badenhorst (1992: 146–150).

29. Pim and Hardy founded an accounting firm in Johannesburg after the 1899–1902 war. '[The Irish-born] Pim was a founder member of the Joint Council of Europeans and Africans and the South African Institute of Race Relations (SAIRR) . . . he was active throughout his life in politics, race relations and the condition of black people in South Africa' (Cunningham, 1976: v).

30. 'JBFA', *Umteteli Wa Bantu*, 11 May 1929; 'Rival Associations: JBFA–WAFA', *Umteteli Wa Bantu*, 27 August 1932; 'Review of JBFA's Rapid Progress', *Bantu World*, 4 April 1936; '1939 JBFA Annual Report', *Bantu World*, 13 April 1940. The actual number of founding JBFA clubs

is unclear. The article 'Johannesburg Bantu Football Association Forges Ahead', *Bantu World*, 10 November 1934, stated that there were nine original JBFA clubs, but this claim must be weighed with evidence that twenty teams joined the JBFA in 1929, as cited in *Umteteli Wa Bantu*, 11 May 1929.

31. The JBFA executive in 1929 also included vice-presidents D.M. Denalane, A. Tshabalala, R. Sondazi, and H. Kumalo as recording secretary; cited in 'JBFA', *Umteteli Wa Bantu*, 11 May 1929. On the establishment of the JBFA see also Couzens (1983: 206).

32. 'A New Football Association', *Umteteli Wa Bantu*, 25 March 1933.

33. Based in Benoni and Springs, the East Rand and District Native Football Association boasted 36 clubs in three divisions in 1934, see 'History of East Rand Football Association Crowded With Success', *Bantu World*, 15 September 1934.

34. 'Transvaal African Football Association Grows Like a Mushroom', *Bantu World*, 22 September 1934.

35. 'WDAFA Forges Ahead in Spite of Difficulties', *Bantu World*, 1 September 1934. Following the dominant trend, the reborn mine association dropped the term 'Native' and replaced it with 'African'.

36. Without consulting the JBFA, the Bantu Sports Club in 1932 lowered the admission price to attract larger crowds. According to Badenhorst, tensions between the BSC and JBFA leadership over control of gate-takings and decision-making had developed very early on. Viewed in this perspective, the JBFA's move to Wemmer was the final straw in what was, essentially, the BSC's opposition to the JBFA's dependency on the NEAD and the city council (Badenhorst, 1992: 293–295).

37. Delegates elected D.M. Denalane president, F.J. Modibedi and H.T. Kumalo vice-presidents, Godfrey Nchee secretary, and E.P. Hlope treasurer. D.M. Denalane was an *induna* – supervisor – at Robinson Deep Mine. He was also a leading figure in the Mine Clerks Association and the Bantu Dramatic Society, and a founding member of the JBFA; see 'Indunas Evidence', *Bantu World*, 19 June 1943; 'Successful Gathering at Bantu Men's Social Centre', *Bantu World*, 23 October 1937; Couzens (1985: 179).

38. 'A New Football Association', *Umteteli Wa Bantu*, 25 March 1933.

39. 'Transvaal Bantu Football Association, Annual General Meeting: Report of 1940 Season', *Bantu World*, 10 May 1941. The patrons of the TBFA in 1940 were J.R. Brent, Manager of Pretoria Asiatic and Native Administration; Graham Ballenden, Manager Johannesburg NEAD; E.J. Baker, Manager Springs NAD; J. Gold, Superintendent of Brakpan Location; B.P. Dodd, Manager Benoni NAD; E.G. Meyer, Superintendent of Germiston Location; Mr. Mackenzie, Acting Superintendent of Vereeniging Location, and P. Mansie, (unknown position) Krugersdorp. The JBFA held its meetings at the NAD offices at Wemmer, symbolising its close ties to white authorities.

40. Dr William Godfrey was an Indian physician and personal friend of Ray Phillips involved in a number of liberal causes in Johannesburg. The Godfrey Cup disappeared in the early 1940s, but re-emerged after the war without its white stewards. Under the guidance of the Transvaal Inter-Race Soccer Board, a new group comprised of reform-minded Africans, Indians, and Coloureds, made a first (timid) formal attempt to confront racial segregation in domestic football.

41. Leo Kuper Papers (LKP): DDAFA Minutes, 7 June 1933; T.H.D. Ngcobo claimed that DDAFA (not NAFA) and TAFA formed the South Africa African Football Association in 1931.

42. *Bantu World*, 2 October 1937; DDAFA minutes, 1931.

43. Information on the Cape is based on my interviews with Ben Malamba, Langa, 26 July 1995, Peter Sitsila, Langa, 27 July 1995; by Dr A.W. Crosse-Upcott with Mr Mahase, 11 October 1955 (transcript in the Monica Wilson Papers, University of Cape Town Manuscripts and

Archives Library); 'Conference Instead of Tournament', *Bantu World*, 10 October 1942. On Ndabeni and Langa see Molapo (1994); Musemwa (1993); and Saunders (1979a: 165–193; 1979b: 194–230).

44. Evidence of clubs in Langa/Ndabeni from interviews with Sitsila and Malamba; Crosse-Upcott interview with Mahase; *Bantu World*, 27 June 1936.

45. 'Fort Hare Soccer Team Tour', *Bantu World*, 23 June 1934; 'JBFA Visits the Cape Province', *Bantu World*, 26 June 1937; 'Fort Hare Soccer Touring Team', *Bantu World*, 13 July 1940.

46. White provincial teams competed for the Currie Cup, a competition that grew more popular during the inter-war period. For example, a 1946 Challenge Cup final between Boksburg and Rangers at Wanderers attracted 40 000 spectators (Nöthling, 1982: 31).

47. *Durban Mayor's Minute 1932*; 'Rival Associations: JBFA–WAFA', *Umteteli Wa Bantu*, 27 August 1932. Due to huge demand and scarce playing facilities, matches in Johannesburg, Durban, and Cape Town lasted 80 minutes rather than the regulation 90 minutes; see, for example, *Bantu World*, 16 April 1932. Shortened matches remained the norm until the 1950s.

48. *Bantu World*, 3 February 1934.

49. LKP: Transcript of interview by B. Magubane with Douglas Evans, 4 July 1960.

CHAPTER 5

1. More than 6 000 spectators attended the first of two matches between the Johannesburg Bantu Football Association and Transvaal Indians held in 1932. The teams tied 3-3 on 31 May, but the JBFA won 5-0 on 1 August; *Bantu World*, 4 June 1932 and 5 August 1932.

2. Rolfes was the brother of Herbert (H.I.E.) Dhlomo, perhaps the foremost African literary figure writing in English of this period and a keen left winger for Adams College Shooting Stars in Durban and Puur Vuur (Pure Fire) in Johannesburg in the 1930s (see Couzens, 1985: 49). Rolfes had started his journalistic career with *Ilanga Lase Natal* in the 1920s, to which he returned as editor in 1943. H.I.E. Dhlomo joined the *Bantu World* staff in 1935 and followed his brother to become an assistant editor with *Ilanga* in the 1940s. Described by Couzens as a 'shy and reserved man who preferred watching cricket and football to mixing in intellectual society', Rolfes Dhlomo was chief vice-president of the Johannesburg Bantu Football Association in the early 1940s (Couzens, 1985: 61). Couzens believed that R.R.R. Dhlomo 'really hit his stride' with the 'Roamer' column. 'Roamer', a 'pseudonym for the all-knowing chronicler of the African experience in South Africa . . . contained', according to Les Switzer, 'some of the finest examples of informal or familiar essay writing in African literature' (Switzer, 1997: 200–201). The two football pieces by R.R.R. Dhlomo were published in *Bantu World* on 9 April 1938 and 23 August 1941.

3. *Bantu World*, 23 August 1941.

4. LKP: Magubane interview with Evans. Witchcraft was, and continues to be, part of urban African football cultures; see Martin (1995: 121).

5. Scotch (1961: 72).

6. 'Muti and Sport', *Drum*, March 1959.

7. Interview with Peter Sitsila, Langa, 27 July 1995.

8. Webb and Wright (1982: 322).

9. Scotch (1961).

10. Scotch (1961: 72–73). Interview with Sitsila. On the role of magic in Zulu war preparations see Laband (1997: 26–27, 34–35).

11. Scotch (1961: 72).

12. 'Muti and Sport', *Drum*, March 1959.

13. Scotch (1961: 72).

14. Scotch (1961: 72). On war dancing and *ingoma* in Durban see Erlmann (1991: 95–111).

15. Interview with Moses Molelekoa, Khayelitsha, 26 July 1995.

16. Interestingly, Anne Leseth, an anthropologist from the University of Oslo, encountered similar recalcitrance in her investigation of the use of *juju* (or *uchawi*, meaning witchcraft) by football

teams in Dar es Salaam, Tanzania. One informant qualified his comments about the widespread use of witchcraft in local football by saying: 'Of course, it doesn't work, but this *juju* business has a psychological effect. Therefore I permitted it, even if I didn't believe it myself. Well, I think I have answered your question, madame,' as he ended the conversation (Leseth, 1997: 167).

17. Interview with Molelekoa. In the same vein, Joe Mthimka, the first African member of the unified, nonracial Western Province Soccer Association (1991–96), said this about magic and witchcraft: 'Those types of things are regarded as rural, as uncivilized if you are from here [Cape Town].' Personal Communication with J. Mthimka, Langa, 26 July 1995.

18. 'Are Ladies' Games Rough?', *Bantu World*, 22 October 1932.

19. 'History of Only Bantu Women Hockey Association in Union', *Bantu World*, 8 September 1934; 'Keen Interest Shown by Bantu People in All Forms of Sport', *Bantu World*, 18 August 1934.

20. Gunner and Gwala (1991). On the importance of audience participation in southern African performance cultures see Vail and White (1991). The interaction between audience and performers in black South African theatre has been examined by, among others, Gready (1994: 163–198); Kavanagh (1985); and Peterson (1990: 321–329).

21. Gunner and Gwala (1991: 3–4). *Izibongo* (praise poetry, praising) is an oral literary genre found in most southern African languages and cultures such as Xhosa, Ndebele, Sotho and Tswana. For a detailed bibliography on the subject see Gunner and Gwala (1991: 2). Gunner and Gwala mention *izibongo zebhola* (football praises) in their Introduction (1991: 7).

22. Maguire interview with Shabangu.

23. Interview with Sitsila. The half-moon is a difficult move: the attacking player touches the ball past one side of the defender while sprinting around the other side, disorienting the opponent for a split second, and regaining control of the ball.

24. Interview with Sitsila.

25. *Bantu World*, 22 May 1937.

26. 'Amalaita Attack Sportsmen', *Umteteli Wa Bantu*, 1 April 1933.

27. The first quote is from *Bantu World*, 9 April 1938; the second is from *Bantu World*, 23 August 1941.

28. Badenhorst (1992: 311); Erlmann (1996a: 91).

29. Referee's murder reported in 'Johannesburg African Football Association 1940 Annual Report', *Bantu World*, 8 March 1941. On contemporary crime and social dynamics on the Witwatersrand see Bonner (1993: 160–194, 1995: 115-129); Glaser (2000: 1–46); Stadler (1979: 93–123). In the Johannesburg metropolitan area, violent crime rose 20 per cent between 1944 and 1949 (Lodge, 1983: 100). For insight on gangs, leisure, and violence in inter-war Durban see La Hausse (1990: 79–111, 1996: 33–66). For a useful review of the literature on this topic see Beinart (1992: 455–486).

30. 'R. Roamer, Esq. On Football', *Bantu World*, 23 August 1941. Gambling on the outcome of matches was another cause for disorder; see discussion on football hooliganism in Chapter 8.

31. 'Annual Report of the 1935 JBFA Season', *Bantu World*, 4 April 1936; 'JAFA Annual Report for the Year 1935', *Bantu World*, 29 March 1936. A similar trend occurred in Durban; see Chapter 3.

32. 3/CT, 1/4/10/1/1/6: Minutes of the Native Affairs Committee (Cape Town City Council), 26 October 1932; *Bantu World*, 27 June 1936.

33. *Bantu World*, 2 October 1937. Bakers's football sponsorship was also linked to its drive to recruit a non-migrant labour force. In pursuit of this objective, for example, the Durban manufacturer showed films to its 300 workers at the company compound on Saturday nights (Vahed, 1998: 87).

34. 'Natal Beats Transvaal at Bantu Sports Ground in Brilliant Match', *Bantu World*, 12 August 1933.
35. *Bantu World*, 12 August 1933.
36. Lodge (1983: 13, 15).
37. 'Free State Meets Transvaal To-day At Bantu Sports Club', *Bantu World*, 4 August 1934. For the record, Natal and Free State drew 2-2 while Transvaal defeated Free State 2-0.
38. 'Natal Team Thanks Randites For Their Hospitality and Kindness', *Bantu World*, 25 August 1934.
39. Badenhorst and Mather (1997).
40. *Bantu World*, 25 August 1934.
41. Coplan (1985: 128–129). Self-consciously distinct from the lower-class *marabi* dances, the concert-and-dance became a central aspect of black urban popular culture. Coplan concluded that '[t]he universal format of middle-class African entertainment between the world wars was "concert-and-dance." Not only minstrel performances, but choir competitions, institutional functions, official receptions and meetings of political and other organizations were followed by a few hours of dancing to the music of jazz orchestras. [. . .] During the 1920s, the concert-and-dance pattern held for both working-class and middle-class entertainment' (1985: 120, 128–129).
42. M.L. Kumalo, 'Natal Team Thanks Randites For Their Hospitality and Kindness', *Bantu World*, 25 August 1934.
43. 'Who's Who in the News', *Bantu World*, 23 February 1935. BMSC Reds reportedly hosted a concert-and-dance party at the Communal Hall, Western Native Township, featuring the Merry Blackbirds Orchestra.
44. Coplan (1985: 131).
45. See photograph of Twala and the Rhythm Kings in Coplan (1985).
46. 'Natal Team Thanks Randites'.
47. 'Natal Team Thanks Randites'. My thanks to Ben Carton for help with translating this idiomatic expression from the original Zulu.
48. *Bantu World*, 22 August 1936. A report of the Cape Peninsula Bantu Football Association match between Pirates and Dangerous Points in Langa (or, possibly, Ndabeni) stated that 'both teams adopted kick-and-rush tactics'.
49. Numerical renditions of tactical formations indicate, in order, the number of defenders, midfielders, and forwards fielded by one team.
50. Gardner (1996: 187). For interesting comments on the social impact of the 1930 World Cup final in Uruguay and Argentina see Mason (1995: 39–43).
51. Gardner (1996: 183). For more observations of changes in football tactics see Orejan (1995).
52. 'Spectacular Soccer Final of Bakers Ltd Cup', *Bantu World*, 9 October 1937. On Samaniso's funeral see 'Passing Away of Enoch "Joko Tea" Samaniso', *Bantu World*, 14 June 1941.
53. 'Passing Away of Enoch "Joko Tea" Samaniso'; and 'Transvaal African Football Association, Annual Report for 1941', *Bantu World*, 4 April 1942.
54. *Bantu World*, 27 April 1935. In the interviews many former players referred to 'weak goal-keeping'.
55. Interview with Moses Molelekoa, Khayelitsha, 26 July 1995.
56. Maguire interview with Elliott Buthelezi, August 1991.
57. For a published account on this area see Field (2001: 211–224).
58. Interview with Conrad Stuurman, Factreton, 25 February 1998.
59. Coplan (1985: 267). The classic novel of this era is Dikobe, *The Marabi Dance* (1973).
60. Ballantine (1993: 28–29).
61. On liquor and leisure in southern Africa see Crush and Ambler (1992); La Hausse (1988, 1996: 33–66).

62. Ballantine (1993: 5).
63. Ndebele (1994: 46).
64. *Bantu World*, 23 June 1934. For example, a crowd of 16 000 people in Durban watched the 'test match' between Motherwell and (white) South Africa; see *Natal Mercury*, 1 March 1932. The Motherwell matches generated sizeable profits for cash-strapped white soccer organisations during the Depression.
65. Ndebele (1994: 48).
66. *Bantu World*, 8 July 1937. I am grateful to Richard Giulianotti for access to Webster (1990). In his account of Aberdeen's South African tours, Webster pointed out that the Scottish club fielded several white South Africans in the 1930s and early 40s, among them Herbert Currer, Billy Strauss, and Alfred Stanley Williams.
67. 'Learn Lessons From Others: Bantu Soccerites Should Emulate Those Who Know', *Bantu World*, 30 June 1934.
68. In some ways, these comments were typical of the 'New African' perspective, which Couzens described as the worldview of progressive, educated contemporary Africans. 'The whole exercise – the attempt to entrench the class – was legitimized', according to Couzens, 'in terms of "patriotism", the "patriot" being one who was working for the African people in general by improving the self *and* by working for others. Successful individualism would help the class' (1985: 16).
69. 'Learn Lessons From Others', *Bantu World*, 30 June 1934.
70. Thabe (1983: 3).
71. 'How Buccaneers were Born', *World*, 23 August 1963.
72. Giulianotti (1999: 143).
73. *Bantu World*, 30 June 1934.
74. *Bantu World*, 30 June 1934.
75. 'Highlanders Proud Holders of Four Cups', *Bantu World*, 7 December 1935. Highlanders's 'Motherwell' style also mentioned in *Bantu World*, 11 November 1933 and 25 November 1933. A photograph of the 1935 team appeared in Thabe (1983: 26). See also Badenhorst (1992: 146–150). South African social historians have tended to portray the Bantu Men's Social Centre as an arena for the playing out of 'petit bourgeois respectability' among elite Africans, but recent work suggests the former may be too narrow an interpretation; see Goodhew (2000: 241–266).
76. Mason (1998). My thanks to Tony Mason for sharing this material with me.
77. *Bantu World*, 15 July 1932.
78. 'The Town Council Refuses Association Use of Grounds', *Bantu World*, 23 February 1935.
79. *Bantu World*, 16 March 1935.
80. Blades (1998: 20–21). It is interesting to note that the majority of the All-India players were from Bengal, the only region in India where soccer competes with cricket in popularity. For a fuller examination of football in India see Dimeo and Mills (2001); and Mason (1990: 85–95).
81. 'Fort Hare Beaten By JAFA in Fast, Brilliant Match Last Week', *Bantu World*, 21 July 1934.
82. 'Rhod. Motherwell Soccer Team: Impression From 1937–1939 At Wemmer Ground', *Bantu World*, 26 August 1939.
83. Van Onselen (1982: 33).
84. Van Onselen (1982: 33).
85. Coplan (1985: 129).
86. 'Clumsy Tactics of Rhodesian Motherwells', *Bantu World*, 14 May 1938.
87. Giulianotti (1999: 143).
88. *Bantu World*, 9 September 1939. Transvaal's use of the WM system was mentioned in *Bantu World*, 1 October 1938. The WM developed in England as a response to the offside rule

change which lowered from three to two the number of defenders required to be between the forward-most attacker and the opponent's goal. In Chapman's Arsenal scheme the centre midfielder, Alex James, retreated to strengthen the backline and became known as the 'stopper' or 'third back'. To fill the gap left by the centre midfielder, Chapman withdrew the two inside forwards into midfield thus creating what was, essentially, a 3-2-2-3 formation. As Tony Mason has explained, Chapman's tactic 'invented' man-to-man (as opposed to zonal) marking and was based on a retreating, closely integrated defence and explosive counter-attacks (Mason, 1998: 3–4).

89. *Bantu World*, 10 June 1939.

90. Similar observations have been made with regard to the social and cultural roots of the Brazilian playing style; see, for example, Da Matta (1982); Giulianotti (1999: 140–141); Lopes (1997: 53–86). For more insight on tricksters and the ambiguities of everyday resistance in South Africa see La Hausse (1993: 195–228).

91. For nearly three decades (1932–59), the Bakers/Moroka-Baloyi Cup was the premier African football competition in the country. Statistics I have compiled suggest a shifting power of balance in African football during this period: Transvaal won the Cup seven times outright and shared it twice in the 1940s (the Orange Free State won in 1941), while Natal claimed seven titles in the 1950s. See *Golden City Post*, 9 August 1959. For further commentary on Baloyi's involvement in African soccer see Nauright (1997b: 111, 121–122).

92. National Archives of South Africa (NASA, Pretoria), Native Commissioner of Johannesburg files, KJB 406, N1/14/3 [50]: Transvaal African Football Association, 1945 Annual Report, 'African National Congress Match'. The £80 collected at the gate was probably directed at the ANC's expanding needs in 1944 due to the bus boycotts in Alexandra and the launch of the ANC Youth League.

93. 'National Congress Sport's Day', *Bantu World*, 19 August 1944; 'African National Congress Match', 2.

94. 'Playing for the Nation', *Bantu World*, 29 July 1944.

95. Lodge (1983: 25).

96. Anderson (1991).

97. Wagner (1989: 9).

98. Crush, Jeeves and Yudelman (1991: 9); Packard (1989: 34).

99. Monica Wilson Papers: Transcript of Dr Crosse-Upcott's interview with Mr Mahase, Langa football official, 11 October 1955.

100. 'Conference Instead of Tournament', *Bantu World*, 10 October 1942.

101. NTS 9684, 679/400: Copy of Letter by W.G. Stafford, Magistrate at Empangeni (Natal), 27 August 1942.

102. NTS 9684, 679/400: Chief Native Commissioner, Natal, to Secretary for Native Affairs, 17 September 1942.

CHAPTER 6

1. Maguire interviews with Skumbuzo Mthembu and Sidwell Mokgosinyane, August 1991, cited in Maguire (1991: 94).

2. Bonner and Segal (1998: 17–18).

3. Bonner and Segal (1998: 18); Carr (1990: 29).

4. In 1947 Leake Hall was incorporated into the Donaldson Orlando Community Centre where Nelson Mandela boxed and served on the board of trustees in the late 1940s. See National Archives of South Africa, Pretoria, Johannesburg Native Commissioner files, KJB 406, N1/14/3 [33]: Fourth Annual Report of the Donaldson Orlando Community Centre, 31 March 1949.

5. By the end of the Second World War, there were 32 Boys' and 22 Girls' Clubs on the Reef with 2 892 members who participated (at no direct cost) in boxing, weightlifting, table tennis (boys)

and needlework, dance, and gymnastics (girls). Initially, these clubs were funded by the Department of Social Welfare of the Johannesburg Non-European Department (established in 1937), the National Advisory Council for Physical Education, the mining companies, the Bantu Welfare Trust and various municipalities. After 1946, members had to pay a fee to gain access to the facilities (Archer & Bouillon, 1982: 124; Hellmann, 1940: 44–46).

6. Maguire interviews with Shabangu, and Rankus Maphisa, July 1991. For further details on rural South Africa see Beinart, Delius and Trapido (1986); Bundy (1979); Jeeves and Crush (1997); Keegan (1988); and Van Onselen (1996).

7. Maguire interview with Shabangu.

8. Maguire (1991: 2).

9. Maguire interview with Rankus Maphisa. Maphisa repeated this story in an interview for the documentary *In The Heart of Soweto* (part IV), 'Once a Pirate Always a Pirate' (R.M. Productions and V.N.S. Double Exposure 1, 1991).

10. Maguire interview with Shabangu, Sydney Mabuza, Willard Msomi, Elliott Buthelezi and Jimmy Sobi, August 1991.

11. Maguire interview with Elliott Buthelezi, August 1991; 'JBFA: Report of the Season 1939', *Bantu World*, 13 April 1940. The social anthropologist Ellen Hellmann gave evidence of the high demand for soccer in black townships on the Rand in the late 1930s and early 40s. According to Hellmann, teams in the Wednesday League were composed mostly of 'temporarily unemployed' adults rather than teenage students (Hellmann, 1948: 44–45).

12. Bonner (1995: 115–129); Nattrass (1993: 43); Posel (1991: 44–45).

13. 'How Buccaneers Were Born', *World*, 23 August 1963. In colonial Brazzaville the use of shoes in local football became a source of unexpected conflict between African players and colonial authorities (Martin, 1991: 56–71).

14. Pirates won fourteen, lost two, and drew two matches (30 points from eighteen matches), as reported in 'Johannesburg Bantu Football Association: Season 1940 Final Log', *Bantu World*, 22 February 1941. The 1940 official standings still listed Pirates under their old name of Orlando Boys' Club.

15. Pirates won twelve, lost six, and drew four matches (28 points from twenty-two matches), 'Johannesburg Bantu Football Association: Season 1941', *Bantu World*, 15 November 1941.

16. Maguire (1991: 8).

17. *World*, 23 August 1963.

18. Maguire interview with Maphisa.

19. Maguire interviews with Mike Tseka and Shabangu. According to SAIRR figures a man's average wage was £8.5s.6d., the wife's contribution was £1.9s.0d., and the children's was £1 (Sapire, 1993: 266). According to the Johannesburg Non-European Affairs Department's *Report on a Sample Survey of the Native Population Residing in the Western Areas of Johannesburg* (1951), Sophiatown's domestic workers earned £5.4s.4d. monthly, while a driver earned £16.5s.6d. (Lodge, 1983: 96). At Pirates, employed members paid a yearly fee of 3s. while students paid 1s.6d. In 1947 the fees were raised to 5s.6d. for workers and 3s.6d. for the unemployed and students; cited in the Minutes of Meetings of Orlando Pirates (hereafter MOP), 16 May 1947.

20. MOP, 16 June 1945.

21. Maguire interview with Tseka; Glaser (2000).

22. Maguire interview with Shabangu, Mabuza, Msomi, Buthelezi, and Sobi.

23. Biographical information on Mokgosinyane derived from Maguire's interviews with his grandson Sidwell Mokgosinyane, and Shabangu, Mabuza, Msomi, Buthelezi, and Sobi, 1991.

24. Maguire interviews with Shabangu, Mabuza, Msomi, Buthelezi, and Sobi; Minutes of Meetings of Orlando Pirates, 1945–61. Maguire interview with Fanyana Shiburi, August 1991.

25. 'How Buccaneers Were Born', *World*, 23 August 1963.
26. Maguire interviews with Buthelezi, Shabangu, and Mokgosinyane, July 1991.
27. Thabe (1983: 88). Maguire interview with Maphisa, July 1991.
28. Maguire interview with Shabangu, August 1991.
29. Maguire interviews with Buthelezi, Shabangu, and Mokgosinyane.
30. MOP, 1945–61.
31. Letter in MOP, 16 June 1945.
32. MOP, 13 June 1947.
33. 'Aid for Late Eddie Madlala', in MOP, June 1947.
34. Maguire interview with Shiburi.
35. MOP, 13 March 1946.
36. MOP, 14 September 1954.
37. MOP, 24 August 1950.
38. Field (1998: 72, 79).
39. MOP, 9 March 1946, 13 February 1952, 1 October 1952.
40. Maguire interview with Theo Mthembu, July 1991.
41. Maguire (1991: 58).
42. Maguire (1991: 7).
43. Maguire interview with Maphisa, and Maguire (1991: 10–11).
44. Maguire (1991: 8).
45. Maguire (1991: 10–11).
46. By 1916 education for whites in the Transvaal between the age of seven and fifteen was free and compulsory through Standard Five (Malherbe, 1977: 253). Education for blacks was neither free nor compulsory in the twentieth century. There was an exception in the Cape Province where 'Non-Europeans' (that is, Coloureds and Africans) received free education to Standard Six from 1920 until the enactment of the Bantu Education Act in 1953 (U.G. 29-1936 [Welsh Report]), *Report of the Interdepartmental Committee on Native Education, 1935–1936* (Pretoria, 1936), para.45. For more commentary on this topic see, for example, Kallaway (1984).
47. Hellmann (1940: 54–55).
48. Mothei (1983: 87).
49. Maguire interviews with Buthelezi, Shabangu, and Mokgosinyane. There was some confusion in the written and oral sources regarding this famous match. The oral history interviews with former Pirates contradict claims made by the black press nearly twenty years later in *World*, 23 August 1963. The *World* argued that the 1945 contest was part of an established tradition that pitted the winners of the JBFA's two top divisions to decide (a) the city champion, and (b) the promotion of the lower ranked club. Former player-manager and secretary of Pirates Isaac Mothei agreed with the oral testimony of his team-mates, stating that the 1945 Pirates vs African Morning Stars encounter was, in fact, a knock-out Cup final (Mothei, 1983: 87).
50. See 'How Buccaneers Were Born', *World*, 23 August 1963; Maguire interviews with Shabangu, Mabuza, Sobi, Msomi, and Buthelezi.
51. Lodge (1983: 101). For further analysis on the history of cultural dialogue and exchange between South Africa and the United States, see Nixon (1994) and Vinson (2000).
52. Maguire interviews with Shabangu, Mabuza, Sobi, Msomi, and Buthelezi, also cited in Maguire (1991: 7, 18). Information on Soweto slangs and class-consciousness derived from Bonner and Segal (1998: 58–59). For details on the role of Hollywood movies in Soweto youth gang culture see Glaser (2000: 69–70). For social histories of Sophiatown see Coplan (1985: 143–182); and Proctor (1979: 49–89).
53. Maguire interviews with Buthelezi and Shabangu. Also cited in Maguire (1991: 19).
54. Maguire (1991: 29–30).
55. Maguire interviews with Buthelezi, Shabangu, and Mokgosinyane.

56. MOP, 4 June 1952.
57. Maguire interview with Buthelezi, Shabangu, and Mokgosinyane.
58. Maguire interview with Shabangu.
59. Maguire (1991: 29).
60. 'Referee's Decision Mars Grand Game Between Pirates and Rovers', *African Sports*, December 1953.
61. 'Corrugated Rovers Beat Pirates in Re-Play of the Cup Final', *African Sports*, January 1954. The press reported that as late as 1955 South African teams were struggling in their application of the WM system; see *Golden City Post*, 24 July 1955.
62. Maguire (1991: 29).
63. Maguire (1991: 7); Mothei (1983: 88).
64. Maguire interview with Tseka (Maguire, 1991: 59).
65. MOP, 23 July 1952. Tseka became chairman of the club in the mid-1960s.
66. Maguire interview with Tseka.
67. Maguire (1991: 29).
68. Maguire interview with Shabangu, August 1991.
69. National Archives, Johannesburg Non-European Affairs Department, Welfare and Recreation Office (WRO) 138/8 v.1: Letter from JBFA president, H.P. Madibane, to NEAD Manager, 16 March 1950. Father T. Huddleston (1913–98) campaigned relentlessly against the forced removals and destruction of Sophiatown in the 1950s. He condemned the white government in his internationally acclaimed book *Naught for Your Comfort* (1956). Banned from South Africa, Father Huddleston became a leader of the anti-apartheid movement in Britain (see Denniston, 1999). On the Western Areas Removals see Coplan (1985: 143–181); Lodge (1983: 91–113); Proctor (1979); and Van Tonder (1993: 316–340).
70. WRO 138/40: Letter from E.P. Ngoqo to L.I. Venables, NEAD Manager, 20 January 1948.
71. WRO 138/40: 'Orlando Divisional Bantu Football Association', memo from J.G. Young to Senior Welfare Officer, 14 June 1948.
72. WRO 138/40: Letter from L.I. Venables, NEAD Manager, to The Secretary, JBFA, 16 January 1948.
73. MOP, 5 May 1949.
74. Bonner (1995: 120); Bonner and Segal (1998: 20–24); Couzens (1983); and Saunders (1994: 356). For more insight see French (1983).
75. James (1992: 4–5); Jeffrey (1992: 82–85); Nauright (1997b: 110–111).
76. Maguire (1991: 82).
77. Maguire interview with Tseka.
78. Couzens (1983: 210).
79. Maguire (1991: 81). According to Couzens, Mpanza was also known as 'Magebula' because 'it was he who "turned the sods" from which the houses of Orlando and Moroka [a neighbouring area of Soweto opened in 1947] "grew"' (Couzens, 1983: 210).
80. WRO 138/38: 'Johannesburg Municipal Townships Football Association', memorandum by J.G. Young, NEAD Recreation Officer, to NEAD Deputy Manager, 4 March 1949; 'Give JDFA a Chance', *Bantu World*, 20 December 1952; 'Amalgamation Must Not Be Thrown Overboard', and 'Mr. E.P. Ngoqo Discusses Soccer Amalgamation', both in *Bantu World*, 17 January 1953.
81. WRO 138/40: Letter from E.P. Ngoqo, Secretary JMTFA, to NEAD Manager, 25 February 1949.
82. Letter from E.P. Ngoqo to NEAD Manager, 25 February 1949. Ngoqo claimed that in 1949 the JMTFA had seventeen teams in Orlando, one in Pimville, and two in Kliptown; see WRO 138/38: 'Record of a Meeting between Officials of the NEAD, Representatives of the JBFA and the JMTFA', 4 August 1948.

83. Both the Board of Control and the JBFA/JAFA merger did not come to fruition. See WRO 138/38: 'Johannesburg Municipal Townships Football Association'; 'Record of a Meeting Between Officials of the NEAD, JBFA and JMTFA', 4 August 1948; 'Minutes of the Meeting in Connection with the Proposed Formation of a Sports Board of Control, 30 August 1948'. WRO 138/40: 'Minutes of Meeting in Connection with the Proposed Formation of a Sports Board of Control'.

84. 'Johannesburg Municipal Townships Football Association', and Maguire (1991: 82).

85. WRO 138/38: 'Johannesburg Municipal Townships Football Association', and 'Formation of Sports Board of Control', memorandum by L.I. Venables, NEAD Manager, 10 November 1949.

86. Jokl (1949: 456–457). It should be pointed out that thirteen of the thirty fields in question were on mine grounds. The survey concluded that Coloured and Indian sports were also greatly underserved.

87. NASA, Johannesburg Native Commissioner files, KJB 406, N1/14/3 [50]: Annual Report of the 1946 JAFA Season. WRO, 138/8 v.2: JAFA 1950 Annual Report.

88. WRO 138/40: Memorandum from D.T. Nicholas, Superintendent Orlando Township, to L.I. Venables, NEAD Manager, 25 May 1949. Unlike the freehold townships of Sophiatown and Alexandra, Orlando was a municipal township administered directly by the Non-European Affairs Department of the Johannesburg city council. The Orlando Native Advisory Board represented local residents but, as its name implies, this body had purely consultative powers.

89. WRO 138/38: Letter from E. Gwambe to Councillor J. Mincer, 22 August 1950.

90. Maguire (1991: 65).

91. WRO 138/38: Minutes of the Meeting between Representatives of the Orlando Sports Board of Control and Persons Interested in the Provision of Sports Facilities in Urban Native Areas of Johannesburg, 1 November 1950.

92. WRO 138/38: Letter from L.I. Venables, NEAD Manager, to Hon. Secretary, Johannesburg Joint Council of Europeans and Africans, 2 January 1951.

93. Another important consideration for the NEAD's opposition to the construction of Orlando Stadium was its renewed commitment to urban segregation under National Party rule. For evidence of the NEAD's hostility towards the OSBC see WRO 138/38: Letter from J.G. Young, Acting Senior Welfare Officer, to NEAD Manager, 4 August 1949; Record of Deputation from the Orlando Sports Board of Control received by the NEAD Manager, 5 October 1949; Memorandum from L.I. Venables, NEAD Manager, to Secretary, JAFA, and Secretary, JBFA, 'Formation of Sports Board of Control', 10 November 1949.

94. MOP, 14 April 1949.

95. MOP, 16 June 1949.

96. MOP, 23 June 1949. The two stars involved were Sobi and Shabangu; they were subsequently fined and warned not to engage in such conduct again.

97. Here I am obviously borrowing from Scott (1976).

98. MOP, 25 August 1949 and 1 September 1949. For this project, Mokgosinyane enlisted the help of a 'Mr Solomon'. This person may have been Justice S. Solomon, a patron of African football in Johannesburg since the 1930s. The club sheet first appeared late in 1950.

99. MOP, 11 May 1949.

100. MOP, 23 June 1949. An older supporter and associate (non-voting) member, Mr Khumalo, had first suggested the momentous move to the JAFA. Mokgosinyane's decisive support proved crucial to keeping Pirates's lower divisions in Orlando.

101. WRO 138/40: JAFA, List of teams falling within the Municipal area, attached to Letter from W.F. Nkosi, JAFA Hon. Secr., to NEAD Manager, 29 July 1951.

102. Pirates scored 78 goals and allowed 28. Pirates's 1949–50 Summer League results recorded in MOP, 1949–50. Crocodiles joined the JAFA in 1943 and immediately won the Championship division title; see 'JAFA Final Log, 1943 Season', *Bantu World*, 11 December 1943.

103. MOP, 27 June 1951, and 23 April 1952. 'Relatively lucrative' means that Pirates used the small income derived from challenge matches to pay for affiliation fees and other operational expenses. The club treasury held only £3.5s.0d. in 1952; MOP, 24 May 1952, and 2 July 1952.

104. WRO 138/8 v.2: JAFA Annual Report 1950; WRO 138/40: Letter from W.F. Nkosi, JAFA Hon. Secr., to NEAD Manager, 29 July 1951.

105. WRO 138/32: Proposed Use of a Portion of Wemmer Sports Ground as a Parking Area, Memorandum from NEAD Manager to JBFA, Witwatersrand Bantu Cycling Union, Transvaal Bantu Cricket Union, and Bantu Inter-Schools' League, 16 April 1948.

106. 'Soccer Crash Coming', *Drum*, January 1956.

107. Maguire (1991: 24–25). *Bantu World*, 12 March 1950.

108. 'Referee's Decision Mars Grand Game Between Pirates and Rovers', *African Sports*, December 1953; and 'Corrugated Rovers Beat Pirates in Re-Play of Cup Final', *African Sports*, January 1954.

109. Maguire interview with Mthembu.

110. 'Basotholand Holds Western Transvaal in Hard Game', *African Sports*, September 1953. 'Thrills Pile Up When Western Transvaal Beats Basutoland in Exhibition Soccer', *African Sports*, October 1953.

111. 'Pirates!', *Drum*, April 1953.

112. MOP, 14 September 1950, 17 January 1952, 13 February 1952.

113. MOP, 27 May 1951.

114. MOP, 6 June 1951.

115. MOP, 27 August 1952.

116. MOP, 1 September 1949, 22 September 1949.

117. MOP, 13 August 1952.

118. MOP, 2 April 1952, 9 July 1952, 13 August 1952.

119. Bonner (1995: 128).

120. Glaser (1998: 724).

121. Glaser (1998: 724).

122. Stadler (1979: 93–123). Data on violent crime cited in Lodge (1983: 100).

123. Bonner and Segal (1998: 27).

124. 'The Birds – Pride of Moroka', *World*, 16 August 1963; Nyamane (1997–98: 12–13); 'A History of Soccer in South Africa', supplement to *The Sowetan*, 29 May 1991.

125. Nyamane (1997–98: 12).

126. Nyamane (1997–98: 13); Thabe (1983: 100).

127. Maguire interview with Buthelezi. See also Maguire (1991: 7).

128. Bonner (1993: 169); Bonner and Segal (1998: 27).

129. Bonner and Segal (1998: 27, 64); Maguire (1991: 10). Maguire interview with Peter Mngomezulu, August 1991. Thanks to Philip Bonner for bringing the relationship between Ntoi and Swallows to my attention; personal communication, Johannesburg, 4 July 1995.

130. Bonner and Segal (1998: 64).

131. Maguire interview with Mngomezulu.

132. For a recent study of the Russians see Kynoch (2000: 267–290).

133. Guy and Thabane (1987: 441).

134. MOP, 13 April 1952.

135. Thabe (1983: 100)

136. See WRO 138/40: Minutes of meeting in connection with the proposed formation of a Sports Board of Control, 21 March 1949.

137.   WRO 138/8 v. 2: 1950 JAFA Annual Report. Once Kubheka left Swallows, his influential role in the club's early history went largely unrecognised. A club history published in the black press within a decade of his departure barely mentioned his name; see 'The Birds – Pride of Moroka'.

138.   1950 JAFA Annual Report.

139.   Maguire interviews with Shabangu, Mokgosinyane, and Buthelezi. Also see Couzens (1983: 210).

140.   The controversy stemmed from the referee's decision to award Pirates the game-winning penalty in suspicious circumstances. 'On the 18 yardsline of the Rovers, the referee blew his whistle for an out ball, and looking around, he noticed that a player belonging to Pirates was kicked. He changed his decision and ordered a penalty kick which J. Sobi sent through the net without any difficulty' ('Referee's Decision Mars Grand Game Between Pirates and Rovers', *African Sports*, December 1953).

141.   'Corrugated Rovers beat Pirates in Re-Play of Cup Final', *African Sports*, January 1954.

142.   For a biographical look at Eric 'Scara' Sono see Alegi (2000: 1–20).

143.   Maguire interview with Sam Shabangu, 23 July 1991.

144.   Posel (1991: 152–155).

145.   MOP, 30 January 1952. This campaign began in 1949 when Messrs. Nxumalo and Khumalo, two 'associate members', stayed away from meetings to protest their marginal position in the club. Nxumalo and Khumalo 'told some of our members that the Constitution was depriving them of their privileges as supporters of the club, and this was the main thing that made them not to attend meetings'. MOP, 15 September 1949.

146.   MOP, 27 January 1952 and 2 April 1952. This first supporters' club charged a substantial annual fee of 10s. that put it beyond the reach of most working-class people in Orlando.

CHAPTER 7

1.   Mokone (1980: 12).

2.   The Prohibition of Mixed Marriages Act (1949) and its corollary, the Immorality Act (1950), criminalised inter-racial relationships. The Population Registration Act (1950) classified all South Africans by race (white, Coloured, Asian [Indian], African); the Group Areas Act (1950) mandated residential racial segregation; the Suppression of Communism Act (1950) gave the regime broad powers to control movements opposed to apartheid. The Bantu Authorities Act (1951) replaced the Natives Representative Council (1936) with representation of Africans via appointed 'tribal' chiefs in reserves designed for future 'self-government' outside 'white' South Africa – the foundations for the homelands of the 'Grand Apartheid' of the 1960s. Pretoria created labour bureaus (supervised by the Department of Native Affairs) in 1951 to ensure a steady provision of cheap African labour to urban manufacturers and rural farmers, and the government took over African schools under the Bantu Education Act (Thompson, 1990: 190–199).

3.   Bonner (1993: 160–194, 1995: 115–129); Breckenridge (1990: 55–78); Glaser (2000); Guy and Thabane (1987: 436–456); Lodge (1983); Moodie (1994).

4.   Clingman (1998: 233).

5.   Morrell (1998: 625).

6.   Archer and Bouillon (1982: 93, 152–153).

7.   National Archives (NASA), Pretoria, Department of Native Affairs files, NTS 4562, 1047/311: Town Clerk, Durban, to Secretary for Native Affairs, 18 September 1952.

8.   *Golden City Post*, 28 July 1957, 4 August 1957 and 11 May 1958.

9.   Botto (1954: 48–49).

10.   Magubane (1963: 53).

11.   Magubane (1963: 53).

12.   Population figures cited in Maylam (1996: 16). Number of African football teams found in the Durban Archives Repository (DAR), Town Clerk files, 3/DBN, 4/1/2/1167, 30/352: Secretary,

DDAFA, to Town Clerk, 26 January 1934; and Durban Native Affairs Department, Annual Report for 1950, 127–128.

13. City of Durban, Minute of Mayor 1958–59, 22; Kuper (1965: 347).

14. For more details on the dearth of playing grounds available to black South Africans around this period see Cobley (1994: 212–230); Jokl (1949: 442–464).

15. Durban Native Affairs Department, Annual Report for 1950: 135. A similar ratio of three fields for 100 000 Africans existed in Pretoria in the mid-1940s (Jokl, 1949: 454).

16. City of Durban, Minute of Mayor 1950, 33.

17. Figures cited in City of Durban, Minute of Mayor 1957–58, 12. By comparison, the council gave £5 000 for the development of sports grounds for Indians at Springfield in 1952–53; cited in City of Durban, Minute of Mayor 1952–53, 17.

18. Merrett (1994: 97–122).

19. The Durban city council had already recognised the dire need for recreation and social welfare spending in the 1948 Broome Commission Report. Set up to investigate African housing, health, welfare, and recreational facilities in Durban, the Broome commission had included the 'provision of additional playing fields and facilities' among its recommendations; cited in Durban Native Affairs Department, Annual Report for 1948, 119. The 1949 African–Indian violence killed 142 people, wounded more than a thousand, and destroyed many Indian-owned buildings and shops (Davenport, 1987: 367–368).

20. Archer and Bouillon (1982: 149).

21. Durban Native Affairs Department, Annual Report for 1950, 127–128; City of Durban, Minute of Mayor 1952–53, 25.

22. Quoted in City of Durban, Minute of Mayor 1955–56, 32. It is unclear whether municipal spending on black sport was geared to benefit migrant workers or the settled urban African population since Somtseu Ground had been hosting both football and *ngoma* dancing since 1931. However, the authorities did view *ngoma* and football as serving different groups. For example, one official believed *ngoma* dances 'supply the vigourous recreation that the Tribal Native requires, just as Football does for the de-tribalised native' (Vahed, 1998: 92). In the end, it seems that the Durban authorities were neither willing nor able to implement this vision. In a related struggle, African migrants on the gold mines rejected the Chamber of Mines's attempts to force 'tribal' recreation upon them (Badenhorst & Mather, 1997: 473–489).

23. First quote is from City of Durban, Minute of Mayor 1953–54, 32; the second quote is from City of Durban, Minute of Mayor 1955–56, 32.

24. City of Durban, Minute of Mayor 1955–56, 32.

25. Collaborative Africana Microfilm Project, Center for Research Libraries (Chicago), LKP: Ngidi, 'History of the Bush Bucks Football Club' (hereafter, LKP: Ngidi).

26. Chapman (1989: 185).

27. LKP: Ngidi.

28. One newspaper story claimed that Durban Bush Bucks had an 'unbeaten football record which has been established since 1945'; cited in *Bantu World*, 27 October 1951. This winning streak is unlikely to have lasted six years, but, given the lack of statistics on black South African football, it is impossible to assess the report's credibility.

29. Mokone (1980: 14).

30. *Drum* reporter Lewis Nkosi wrote a piece for the magazine entitled 'The Fabulous Decade'. Transvaal won the Moroka-Baloyi Cup outright in 1940, and then consecutively from 1943 through 1949. In 1942 Natal and Transvaal shared the title, while the Orange Free State won in 1941. Natal's seven titles were in 1950–52, 1954–55, 1958–59. Western Transvaal interrupted the streak in 1953. In 1956 the Moroka-Baloyi was not completed and no data appeared about the 1957 competition. These statistics were gathered by me from the black press.

31. Mokone (1980: 22).

32. Telephone interview with Darius Dhlomo, 12 February 2003.
33. Dhlomo interview, 12 February 2003.
34. Mokone (1980: 14–15).
35. Dhlomo interview, 12 February 2003.
36. Scotch (1961: 71–72).
37. LKP: Ngidi.
38. LKP: Ngidi; *Drum*, July 1956.
39. The growth of football in Lesotho was connected to labour migrancy and school sport. Hugh Ashton's fieldwork in the 1930s revealed that 'organized sports, such as hockey, football and athletics, have been introduced, inter-school matches are played and an annual nation-wide competition is held. [. . .] Both sons of the late Paramount Chief Griffith were keen soccer players and encouraged the game' (Ashton, 1952: 59, 98).
40. *Golden City Post*, 12 August 1956; Beinart (1992: 476–477).
41. For example, see *Umteteli Wa Bantu*, 20 January 1923.
42. *Umteteli Wa Bantu*, 25 March 1933.
43. Bakers Limited also regularly showed films for its 300 workers at the company compound on Saturday nights (Vahed, 1998: 87).
44. Maguire interview with Mthembu. The most famous among the UTC men was dribbling maestro Difference 'City Council' Mbanya (see Chapter 8).
45. Skota (1966: 94).
46. Interview with John Esau, Cape Town, 29 March 1998. Mr Esau, a professional footballer in the early 1970s, worked as a salesman for BAT.
47. 'Africa's Leading Sportsmen Recommend Africa's Leading Cigarettes'; *Drum*, June 1958. For an interesting study on a similar topic see Burke (1996).
48. Interview with Sitsila.
49. 'Is it to be Professional Or Amateur Football?', *Bantu World*, 30 November 1935.
50. *Bantu World*, 30 November 1935.
51. The Native Urban Areas Act in 1923 required Africans not only to live in segregated urban areas (as long as suitable alternative housing was provided by the municipalities) but also to carry and produce passes upon request. As a result, 'an African entering a proclaimed urban area was obligated to report to an official within twenty-four hours and obtain a permit to seek work' (Thompson, 1990: 166–167).
52. Wilson and Mafeje (1963: 120–121).
53. *Post*, 12 July 1959 and 27 September 1959.
54. *World*, 1 April 1961.
55. Interview with Ben Malamba.
56. Jeffrey (1992: 70).
57. Kuper (1965: 347–364); Magubane (1963); Wilson and Mafeje (1963: 114–126, 145).
58. Dean (1978: 149).
59. *Ilanga Lase Natal*, 21 February 1953.
60. LKP: Magubane notes of interviews with J. Khambule and Edward C. Jali.
61. Kuper (1965: 347); *Bantu World*, 6 March 1954.
62. City of Durban, Minute of Mayor 1956–57, 21.
63. *African Sports*, August 1953; Kuper (1965: 347); *Ilanga Lase Natal*, 29 August 1953 and 18 September 1953. For a published account on African football in colonial Zimbabwe see Stuart (1996: 167–180). For further reading see Ranger (1987: 196–213); and Thompson (1976 [first published in 1935]).
64. 'South Africa Plays Impressive Soccer at Centenary Tournament', *African Sports*, August 1953.
65. *Golden City Post*, 11 November 1956; *Drum*, April 1958.

66. ' "Baby" With a Power Packed Kick!', *Drum*, July 1961. All quotes in this paragraph are from this source.
67. *African Sports*, August 1953.
68. *African Sports*, August 1953.
69. NASA, Johannesburg Non-European Affairs Department, Welfare and Recreation Office files (WRO) 138/8 v.3: Letter from the Office of the High Commissioner, Salisbury, to the Commissioner for Immigration and Asiatic Affairs, Pretoria, 31 July 1954.
70. Stuart (1996: 176–177).
71. City of Durban, Native Affairs Department Annual Report 1956–57, 105; NASA, NTS 4633, 503/313 (8): Team list for Grupo Desportivo Nova Alianca, 18 September 1957. For a memoir of football in Mozambique see De Oliveira (1998). On Maputo see Penvenne (1995).
72. *Golden City Post*, 19 May 1957.
73. *Golden City Post*, 23 June 1957.
74. *Golden City Post*, 22 September 1957.
75. Alegi (1999: 55–74).
76. *African Sports*, October 1953. *Drum* featured Gibson Makhanda as the only non-South African among the stars of the 1954 football season; see ' "54" 's Leading Soccerites', *Drum*, October 1954.
77. *Golden City Post*, 22 September 1957.
78. According to an Indian reporter, the quality of play of the Natal African side 'improved a hundredfold under ex-Arsenal and England player, Topper Brown' (*The Leader*, 24 June 1956).
79. Interview with Darius Dhlomo, 12 February 2003.
80. *The Leader*, 24 June 1956.
81. *Golden City Post*, 17 July 1955.
82. NASA, WRO 138/8 v. 2: South Africa African Football Association 1951 Biennial Report.
83. LKP: Report of the DDAFA Annual General Meeting, 15 February 1959; Report of the DDAFA Commission of Inquiry, 13 June 1959, 8–9. With regards to 'Catering and Provision Allowances' the report stated: 'Of the amount of £769 9s. 3d. which appears in the Auditor's Report under this heading, your executive committee, through its Treasurer, was only able to account for £87 15s 0d. The difference remains unexplained.'
84. DDAFA Commission of Inquiry, 9–13, 26–27.
85. LKP: Magubane interview with E.C. Jali; Magubane (1963: 40).
86. Magubane (1963: vii–viii).
87. Wilson and Mafeje (1963: 145).
88. Coplan (1985: 103–104).
89. DDAFA Commission of Inquiry.
90. *Golden City Post*, 1 December 1957.
91. *Golden City Post*, 16 February 1958.
92. For an illuminating study of the uses and manipulations of Shaka in history-writing see Hamilton (1998); and Wylie (2000).
93. *Golden City Post*, 30 November 1958. Eventually, Eastern Transvaal received the trophy.
94. LKP: Report of the DDAFA Meeting, 15 February 1959.
95. Report of the DDAFA Commission of Inquiry, 13 June 1959, 5.
96. For further discussion of Inanda's history see Hughes (1996: 299–309).
97. Report of the DDAFA Commission of Inquiry, 26–27.
98. Report of the DDAFA Commission of Inquiry.
99. Report of the DDAFA Commission of Inquiry, 37–39.
100. Magubane (1963: 38). Among the president's spurious charges were that the chairman of the commission had left only 1s.6d. at the end of his term in office.

101. LKP: DDAFA Annual General Meeting, February 1960; also cited in Kuper (1965: 355).
102. DDAFA Annual General Meeting, February 1960.
103. Magubane notes on the DDAFA Annual General Meeting, February 1960.
104. For analyses of sport, politics, and identities in apartheid South Africa see Archer and Bouillon (1982); Booth (1998); Brickhill (1976); De Broglio (1970); Draper (1963); Hain (1971); Jarvie (1985); Lapchick (1975); Nauright (1997b); and Ramsamy (1982).
105. Brutus (1971: 142–153); Nixon (1994: Ch.5).
106. Archer and Bouillon (1982: 150).
107. Archer and Bouillon (1982: 153).
108. Odendaal (1995: 30). The Cape District FA is located in the southern suburb of Wynberg. The first black football association organised in the Western Cape was the Western Province Football Union, a mostly Coloured body founded in 1904 in the Windermere-Kensington area north of the city centre.
109. 'Federation, Football of the Future', *Drum*, September 1952.
110. Quoted in WRO 138/8 v.2: South Africa African Football Association Biennial Report 1951. See also Couzens (1983: 211).
111. South Africa African Football Association Biennial Report 1951.
112. SAAFA Biennial Report 1951; University of the Western Cape, Mayibuye Archive, Papers of the Western Province Association Football Board (unsorted): 'South African Soccer Federation Public Relations document', (1988?); LKP: 'Memorandum to FIFA' by Charles M. Pillay for the SASF, 12 July 1960.
113. Couzens (1983: 211). Friendly matches between blacks and whites were an exception to the rule since the majority of white footballers did not support integration (Draper, 1963: 2).
114. 'Federation, Football of the Future', *Drum*, September 1952.
115. Chapman (1989: 196).
116. Conversation with Dennis Brutus, Tufts University (Medford, MA), 11 February 2000.
117. Korr (2000). For a preliminary account of the history of sport in Robben Island prison see Roberts (1994).
118. Lodge (1983: 109–110); Van Tonder (1993: 316–340).
119. Nicol (1991: 31–32).
120. Lodge (1983: Ch.2).
121. For further reading on Kajee see Calpin (ca.1950).
122. The combined circulation of the four monthlies aimed at an African audience, *Drum*, *Zonk*, *Highnote*, and *Africa*, was approximately 182 000 in 1954 according to the South African Institute of Race Relations (*Survey of Race Relations, 1953–54*. Johannesburg, 1954: 147). By 1959 circulation had increased to 82 000 for *Drum*; 80 000 for the new weekly *Golden City Post*; 58 000 for *Zonk*; and 39 000 for the bi-weekly (since 1955, then daily after 1962) *World*. It was estimated that each periodical purchased was read by at least six Africans (South African Institute of Race Relations, 1959: 293–294).
123. The Johannesburg city council allowed black people to use Wembley for high-profile matches until Pretoria vetoed the practice in the mid-1950s. The municipal policy was aimed at collecting substantial rental fees and entertainment taxes from the organisers.
124. 'The Prince of Soccer!', *Drum*, June 1953. Barney Samson's *Drum* story revealed that the 'hard training' Mabila smoked 40 cigarettes daily but did 'not believe heavy smoking is bad for his play'.
125. Lineups previewed in 'The Match of the Year!', *Drum*, October 1952. For more coverage of Makatelele see 'Beware Wolves, Danger Ahead', *Drum*, October 1957.
126. '"Khomo the Great" Considered Best All-Rounder', *African Sports*, July 1953, and 'Sporting Personalities: Grant Khomo', *Drum*, September 1952, are the sources for biographical information on Khomo contained in this paragraph.
127. 'The Match of the Year!', *Drum*, October 1952.

128. 'A Splendid Climax to a Fine Soccer Season!', *Drum*, November 1952.
129. *Drum*, November 1952; *African Sports*, July 1953.
130. 'Coloureds Trounce White Champions!', *Drum*, December 1955.
131. 'Pretoria Methodist beats European side', *Bantu World*, 8 May 1954; WRO 138/8 v.3: W.J.P. Carr, NEAD Manager, to Secretary Moroka-Jabavu Football League, 13 May 1954.
132. NEAD Manager, to Secretary Moroka-Jabavu Football League, 13 May 1954; a newspaper clipping in the same Welfare and Recreation section file noted the detectives' inquiries into this inter-racial soccer match.

CHAPTER 8

1. *World*, 8 April 1963.
2. Archer and Bouillon (1982: 187).
3. Collaborative Africana Microfilm Project, Center for Research Libraries (Chicago), Leo Kuper Papers (LKP): 'SASF Memorandum to FIFA', 12 July 1960.
4. FIFA executive committee findings cited in 'SASF Memorandum to FIFA'. For an insightful perspective on the broader significance of South Africa to football's international relations see Darby (2002: 70–81).
5. Nauright (1997b: 118).
6. Merrett (1996: 147).
7. Telephone interview with Dennis Brutus, 7 June 2001.
8. Lapchick (1975: 23).
9. *Golden City Post*, 22 January 1956.
10. Nöthling (1982: 33).
11. *The Leader*, 1 June 1956. The creation of All-Blacks was geared at bringing the smaller 'Bantu' group into Federation. After the 1956 FIFA Congress the black press revealed that: 'The two associations will maintain their autonomy as far as domestic matters are concerned but in representative matters the new body will take over' (*Golden City Post*, 2 September 1956).
12. 'Non-white Soccer Springboks – After FIFA Decides!' *Drum*, August 1958.
13. South African Institute of Race Relations, *Survey of Race Relations 1955–56* (Johannesburg, 1956: 226).
14. Darby (2002: 34).
15. It must be noted that government interference in black leisure had actually begun earlier. In 1953 the Department of Native Affairs conducted a survey of recreational facilities available to Africans employed in 'white' urban areas. Minister of Native Affairs H.F. Verwoerd and Secretary of Native Affairs W.W. Eiselen used this survey to argue that Africans (for example, gardeners, domestic servants, and others) working in 'white' areas would be required to practise their sport exclusively in the outlying black townships. While many white residents disagreed in principle with this idea, because they preferred that their servants indulge in sport in a restricted and controlled space rather than wander or gather at street corners in their neighbourhoods, hardly any white residents voiced support for permanent recreational facilities for blacks adjacent to their own residences. See Department of Native Affairs files, NTS 4562, 1047/311; and South African Institute of Race Relations, *Survey of Race Relations, 1953–54*: 148–149.
16. Booth (1998: 58); Draper (1963: 6). For an ethnographic history of apartheid bureaucracy in the 1950s and its role in routinising oppression see Evans (1997).
17. Jarvie (1985: 48).
18. Draper (1963: 6).
19. LKP: South African Sports Association (SASA) Memorandum to International Olympic Committee, May 1959.
20. University of Brighton, Falmer Library, Sir Stanley Rous Papers: 'Memorandum to the FIFA by the FASA', presented to the FIFA Commission, January 1963. My thanks to Alan Tomlinson for access to documents on South Africa in the Rous Papers.

21. Unconfirmed press reports indicated that white soccer officials in the Transvaal had approached the Johannesburg African Football Association with an offer of affiliated membership as early as July 1956; see *Golden City Post*, 12 August 1956.

22. Archer (1987: 236–237).

23. WRO 138/8 v.4: Record of Discussion between Representatives from the Southern Transvaal Football Association, the Johannesburg Bantu Football Association, and Officials of the Non-European Affairs Department, 17 February 1958. See also 'Soccer War May Start', *Golden City Post*, 4 May 1958.

24. Number of JBFA teams cited in City of Johannesburg, Minutes of the Native Affairs Committee, 31 July 1959. There were 80 teams affiliated to the southwestern townships and Pimville associations, approximately 60 teams in Orlando, and about 150 teams in JAFA. Thus, the total number of teams in greater Johannesburg, notwithstanding the mines, was about 543.

25. Record of Discussion, 17 February 1958.

26. 'JBFA Affiliation to White Soccer May Ruin FIFA Link-up', *Golden City Post*, 8 March 1959; 'JBFA Joins a White Organization', *World*, 7 March 1959.

27. City of Johannesburg, Minutes of the Native Affairs Committee, 31 July 1959.

28. Lapchick (1975: 27). SAIRR, *Survey of Race Relations: 1957–58* (Johannesburg, 1958: 217).

29. Draper (1963: 42). LKP: 'Sport in South Africa: The Soccer Challenge to FIFA', in SASA's Report to the IOC, May 1959.

30. Black (1998: 49).

31. Booth (1998: 75–76).

32. LKP: Minutes of the Meeting of National Sporting Bodies convened by the South African Sports Association, Durban, 10–11 January 1959. Figures confirmed by Magubane (1963: 93–94).

33. Minutes of SASA meeting, 10–11 January 1959. The other two authors of the SASA constitution were Dennis Brutus and R.S. Govender.

34. SASA, 'The Soccer Challenge to FIFA', 6.

35. LKP: Letter from A.J. Albertyn to Hon. Secr. SASF, 10 January 1960.

36. FIFA, *Minutes of the XXXIInd Ordinary Congress*, Rome, 22 August 1990, cited in Darby (2002: 73). Darby notes that this anti-discriminatory resolution 'represented a significant milestone in the struggle against the application of apartheid to sport'. It also became part of FIFA's constitution soon thereafter.

37. RP: Letter from Dr Helmut Kaeser, FIFA General Secretary, to FASA, 31 October 1961.

38. 'A History of Soccer in South Africa', supplement to *The Sowetan*, 29 May 1991; 'It's Pro Soccer Now at the Cape!' *Drum*, May 1961.

39. The pro soccer elders appointed R.K. Naidoo (Durban Indian Football Association, DIFA) president, Dan Twala (JAFA) vice-president, Ramhori Lutchman (DIFA) secretary, and Alfred Thango (Durban & County African Football Association) treasurer. The men established a 'Working Committee', which included I.J. Motholo (Durban and County), Louis Nelson (DIFA), Lucas Khoza (JAFA), E.I. Haffejee (DIFA), Louis Tangee (Blackpool United Football Club) and R. Mannar (Transvaal United Football Club) (Bansda, 1961).

40. See the case 'State vs Brandsma and Others', Supreme Court of South Africa (Natal Provincial Division), 19 October, 1962, cited in *South African Law Reports* (1963/1), 261–264. While no law prevented racially mixed team sports, the Boxing and Wrestling Control Act of 1954 prohibited inter-racial professional boxing matches and training. Even so, it was common practice for whites and blacks to train and spar together (see Draper, 1963: 90–91).

41. Draper (1963: 48, 50, 64–66). For more discussion of these issues see Darby (2002); and Sugden and Tomlinson (1998: 127–151).

42. For further insights on the role of patron-managers and the informal economy of soccer clubs in the southern Transvaal see Jeffrey (1992: 68–94).

43. For published contemporary accounts of the first years of the NFL see Granger (1961); Litchfield (1963, 1965).

44. Litchfield (1965: 122).

45. Nöthling (1982: 31).

46. Maguire interview with Theo Mthembu, August 1991.

47. For biographical information on Mokone see Mokone (1980). Until the early 1990s, the only three full-time pro clubs in Wales – Cardiff City, Swansea and Wrexham – played in the English league structures. It is interesting to note that the United Kingdom has maintained the separate representation of four nations (England, Scotland, Wales, and Northern Ireland) in FIFA. All other FIFA members are allowed only one association per nation-state. For more details on this topic see Duke (1996: 9–23).

48. Telephone interview with Darius Dhlomo, 26 February 2003.

49. *World*, 28 January 1961. Barney Gaffney, a Coloured high school teacher in Benoni, acted as mediator between Leeds and Johanneson, who became the first black South African to play in an English FA Cup final. Sadly, Johanneson died from alcoholism in a drab council home in Leeds in 1995 (Orakwue, 1998); and Blades (1998: 78–79). The entrepreneurial Barney Gaffney also set up a trial for Johanneson's team-mate Gerald Francis at Leeds in 1958–59. Joseph 'Carlton' Moloi of Moroka Swallows went for a trial to Cardiff in 1961. Moloi's failure led Mokone to take an anti-pro-league stance: 'Professional football isn't easy as people back home think . . . Yes, "Carlton", a real star in South Africa, just couldn't make it' (*World*, 18 March 1961).

50. Maguire interview with Mthembu.

51. The Group Areas Boards were local administrative units responsible for residential segregation under the Group Areas Act (1950). The SASL, unlike the South African Council of Sport (SACOS) in the 1970s, never believed in absolute non-cooperation with the state as a guiding principle. For analysis of conflicts within the sport boycott movement caused by the non-cooperation principle see Booth (1998: 153–160).

52. After 1960 the liberation movements adopted armed struggle and opened a sabotage campaign against military and state targets. Nelson Mandela, Walter Sisulu, and fifteen other leading members of the ANC underground were arrested by security forces at the Rivonia farm (Transvaal) in July 1963. The leaders were sentenced to life imprisonment on Robben Island. By the end of 1964 the apartheid state had succeeded in breaking down the underground resistance in South Africa (Thompson, 1990: 211).

53. Blades (1998: 58–59).

54. Interview with Vince Belgeums, Factreton, 27 March 1998; interview with Conrad Stuurman and Basil Jansen, Grassy Park, 18 May 1998.

55. 'Fans All Go for the Pros', *Drum*, November 1961.

56. *World*, 15 April 1961; *The Leader*, 14 April 1961.

57. Bansda (1961). *New Age*, 19 October, 1961; *World*, 21 October 1961; *Drum*, November 1961. The Green Point Track that hosted the 1961 Cup final is not to be confused with the neighbouring Green Point Stadium, a facility reserved for white sportsmen and women during apartheid.

58. *The Leader*, 1 February 1963.

59. Interview with Jansen and Stuurman; *Drum*, November 1961, 29. According to *New Age*, 13 July 1961, organisers made 'elaborate arrangements . . . to prevent scalers from seeing the [Transvaal United vs. Moroka Swallows] match from outside the sports ground' at Natalspruit in 1961.

60. Attendance data for the SASL's final season in 1965 are incomplete and were not included in the author's estimate.

61. For a fuller analysis of Scara Sono's playing career see Alegi (2000: 1–20).

62. Letter from D. Lomberg to the author, 19 February 1999.

63. On the South African press see, for example, Tomaselli, Tomaselli, and Muller (1987).

64. *The Leader*, 1 February 1963.

65. This figure was derived by dividing the number of black South Africans included in the 1960 Census (4 847 000) by the total SASL attendance (676 575); Population Census, 1960, cited in Van der Horst (1964: table 1, 19). The total does not take into account returning fans. It is interesting to note that, according to both newspaper sources and oral testimonies, a small number of white spectators attended SASL games.

66. Interview with Bernard Hartze, Cape Town, 29 January 1998.

67. SAIRR, *Survey of Race Relations: 1962* (Johannesburg, 1963): 218.

68. *Drum*, July 1962 and April 1963.

69. On the intriguing relationship between race, class, and football styles in the Brazilian context see Lopes (1997: 67–79).

70. *The Leader*, 6 July 1962.

71. Interview with Belgeums.

72. *World*, 9 August 1962. For further commentary about this memorable European match see Crawford (1992: 433–438).

73. For more insight on changing tactical developments see Gardner (1996: 198–201); and Giulianotti (1999: 127–145).

74. *Drum*, December 1961.

75. Goal averages for the World Cup tournaments in 1954, 1958 and 1962 were 5,38, 3,60, and 2,78, respectively (Gardner, 1996: 202). Data provided by the Association of Football Statisticians in England indicate that the goals-per-game average in the English First division declined from 3,78 in 1958 to 3,00 in 1967. A similar trend occurred in the (more defensive) Italian serie A; according to the *2001 Almanacco Illustrato del Calcio* (Modena, 2000) the average dropped from 2,93 in 1958–59 to 2,00 in 1966–67.

76. Interviews with Jansen and Stuurman; *Drum*, January 1962.

77. Wages by Sector and Racial Group, 1975 (rand per month) cited in Archer and Bouillon (1982: 161).

78. Scara Sono died in a car crash in May 1964 aged 27. On 6 June, over 30 000 people attended his funeral in Soweto (Alegi, 2000: 1, 14–15).

79. Interview with Belgeums.

80. The populist character of the SASL was well-established among township fans; see, by way of example, 'Leave the People's League alone, Uncle Dave Motsamai', letter to the editor by Johnny Vic Sono of Orlando West, *World*, 15 May 1964. An undated article written by Mecro Zwane and published in *Elethu* [1962?] also described the SASL as 'The People's League'. My thanks to Cape Ramblers veteran Doug Lomberg for sharing this clipping from his personal archive.

81. For further discussion of sport and sociability see Holt (1989: 368–377).

82. Gaitskell (1982: 338–357).

83. Maguire (1991: 6).

84. Maguire (1991: Ch.5). *World*, 12 July 1962, 30 October 1962, 23 May 1963, 21 October 1964; *The Leader*, 9 March 1962.

85. *The Leader*, 23 March 1963.

86. *World*, 30 January 1964.

87. 'Results of Real Fighters Draw', *World*, 23 May 1963.

88. *World*, 12 July 1962 and 30 October 1962. The cost of a round-trip bus fare for Blackpool and Pirates supporters travelling to Durban in 1962 was R7. See also Mr Cele's announcement for Moroka Swallows fans going to Durban in *World*, 21 October 1964.

89. I am grateful to Laura Fair and Jean Hay for specific comments that encouraged a deeper consideration of women's role in football culture.

90. Mrs Montgomery, wife of Berea president and founder George Montgomery, was the first president; Mrs G.N. Naidoo the vice-president; and Mrs Numise Naidoo the secretary. 'First Pro supporter club started', *The Leader*, 25 August 1961.

91. *The Leader*, 25 August 1961.

92. Maguire (1991: 90).

93. Maguire (1991: 90–91).

94. These women asked Scara Sono to help them with their football activities. 'Now Women's Soccer for the Rand', *World*, 12 September 1962.

95. Saavedra (2003: 243).

96. For more information on Pottier see *Cape Herald*, 15 March 1963, and *Post*, 25 August 1963. As of 2004, no South African woman had refereed a men's professional match.

97. For a rare published account of South African women's sport see Hargreaves (1997: 191–209).

98. In this respect, football clubs differed from the co-operative *stokfel marabi* parties described by Coplan (1985: 104).

99. *World*, 1 November 1962; *Sunday Times*, 26 August 1962; *Die Transvaler*, 28 August 1962. For further documentation on this tragedy see the South African police files at the National Archives, Pretoria: SAP 665, 15/27/62.

100. For a fascinating study see Shirts (1988: 97–112).

101. Kuper (1965: 347–364); Magubane (1963: 39); Wilson and Mafeje (1963: 145).

102. *New Age*, 7 June 1961.

103. 'Non-white' support was the key to Durban City's popularity, providing as much as 50 per cent of the league-best average attendance of 12 477 at New Kingsmead Stadium in 1964 (Litchfield, 1965: 54–55).

104. The NPSL was resurrected in 1967–68. Thanks to the backing of municipalities, the state, and corporate sponsors, the NPSL rose to dominance in 1971–72, though purged of its Coloured and Indian members (see Epilogue).

105. Glaser (2000: 105).

106. Maguire interview with Boy Shogwe, Johannesburg, September 1991.

107. Bale (1993: 64–76).

108. Maguire interview with Shogwe.

109. *World*, 19 July 1964.

110. Maguire interview with Shogwe. All quotes in this paragraph are culled from this interview. The incident was widely reported in the black press; see, for example, 'Pirates Equalize with Easthorpe "Under Fire"', *Post*, 31 May 1964.

111. Beckles (1998); Burton (1996: 89–106); Patterson (1996: 141–147).

112. Letter by 'Fullback' from Soweto in *World*, 14 November 1965.

113. Archer and Bouillon (1982: 196).

114. For more details on soccer's struggles in the 1960s see Archer and Bouillon (1982: 194–198); Draper (1963: 40–67).

115. 'Our Soccer Fights for Survival', *Drum*, November 1962; SAIRR (1964: 292); Brickhill (1976: 57).

116. Minutes of the Johannesburg city council, Management Committee, 'Allocation of Football Stadia and Fields', 9 October 1962, copy in City of Johannesburg, Non-European Affairs Department, 376/62.

117. See, for example, the *Post* of 25 August 1963.
118. 'State vs Brandsma and Others', Supreme Court of South Africa (Natal Provincial Division), 19 October 1962; cited in *South African Law Reports* (1963/1), 261–264.
119. The number of white players in the SASL seems to have been small, perhaps no more than a dozen in the 1961–65 period; see 'Luckless Lincoln Score Off-Field Victory', *Drum*, July 1962; SAIRR (1963: 218). The 1962 court decision explains why the great Indian golfer Papwa Sewgolum – having obtained an official permit to compete – received his 1963 Natal Open Golf Championship trophy outside of the clubhouse, in the pouring rain.
120. While no law existed in team sports, the Boxing and Wrestling Control Act of 1954 prohibited inter-racial professional boxing matches and training. Even so, many white and black fighters continued to train and spar together (Draper, 1963: 90–91).
121. Quotes are from a 1964 South African Soccer Federation 'Memorandum to all FIFA Members on racial discrimination in South Africa Soccer' and relating to '(1) Expulsion/Suspension of FASA' and '(2) Our Application for Membership in FIFA', copies in the Rous Papers. A 1959 letter from SASF asking FASA its intentions with regard to racial integration was forwarded by the white association to the Minister of the Interior. Cited in Leo Kuper Papers: SASF Biennial Report 1959–60, 9. The black press also provided extensive coverage of the 'war of attrition'.
122. Rous Papers, 1964 Memorandum to FIFA Members. Police harassment of whites playing for black teams also occurred. For example, police warned Joseph Biasi, a 24-year-old miner from Venice, Italy, not to continue his stint as goalkeeper for African Morning Stars in 1961. Apparently, Biasi's 'daringly acrobatic saves won the hearts of the crowd'. Cited in *World*, 14 January and 21 January 1961.
123. Data collected by the author from official SASL figures published in *The Leader*, 1 February 1963 and 17 January 1964.
124. *Drum*, November 1963.
125. The SASL leased the ground from the Johannesburg Indian Sports Ground Association. For details on the case see the Supreme Court case, Johannesburg Indian Sports Ground Association vs Johannesburg City Council, 28 August and 21 September 1964, in *South African Law Reports* (1964/4), 779–785.
126. Clingman (1998: 233).
127. *The Leader*, 26 November 1965. This was the only League loss suffered by Swallows in 1965; *World*, 22 November 1965
128. Personal communication with Rob Allingham, 13 June 2000.
129. 'New Shock Facing Fans: Bid to Close Kliptown, Group Areas Board Notice Owners', *World*, 22 October 1964.

EPILOGUE

1. For an overview of these changes see Giulianotti (1999); and Murray (1996: 129–151). For discussion of Africa's role in global football politics, see Darby (2002); and Sugden and Tomlinson (1998: 127–151).
2. Lapchick (1975: 144). 'Big Swazi Game Off!' *World*, 18 August 1969.
3. According to one account, Johnson and Khoza were thrown out after going to Botswana to play challenge matches for an undisclosed sum of money. While Mokgoatleng's expulsion was largely the result of his close friendship with Johnson and Khoza, Nene's widespread popularity seemed to pose a threat to Pirates officials like Mike Tseka and women in the so-called 'development committee' (Sello, 1991: 19–25).
4. Kaizer Motaung's successful NASL career spanned five seasons (105 matches), in which he scored 43 goals and recorded 18 assists. For useful sources on this league and soccer in the

United States in general, see Allaway et al. (2001); Jose (2003); and Markovits and Hellerman (2001).

5. Motaung's comments are reported in a brief history of the club posted on its official website: http://www.kaizerchiefs.com (accessed on 7 October 2003).

6. North (1985: 147); Sello (1991: 5–25).

7. De Broglio (1970: 24).

8. See 'Success After a Brave Start', *African Soccer Mirror*, May 1972.

9. Interview with Bernard Hartze, Cape Town, 29 January 1998.

10. Interview with Hartze. The colours of world champions Brazil, led by Pelé, inspired the Sundowns's choice of gold and blue. On loan from Sundowns, Hartze made his professional debut with Berea in the SASL in 1965. In the late 1960s, Hartze has a successful trial with Leeds United, then one of the top clubs in England. He trained with the first team and was well-regarded by manager Don Revie, but life in England for a young black South African was very difficult; ultimately, 'home-sickness' motivated him to return to South Africa.

11. According to Hartze, he earned about R500 monthly at Pirates, but this figure changed depending on bonuses paid and matches played (interview with Hartze). For more details on the early years of Cape Town Spurs, see Mayibuye Centre Archive, University of the Western Cape (unsorted) *Papers of the Western Province Association Football Board* (WPAFB): Box 5. The Western Province Association Football Board sold Cape Town Spurs to Ronnie Martin in 1982 for R20 000, cited in *Sharpshoot Soccer Mirror*, April 1983.

12. Statistics corroborated by *SASFPL Newsletter*, August 1972, in WPAFB.

13. A first league called the NPSL was launched in 1962 to counter the successful SASL, but collapsed rather quickly. In 1967 the NPSL was resurrected as the professional arm of SABFA. The 1971 Keg League was sometimes called the 'airborne league' because of teams' frequent use of air travel.

14. According to a confidential memorandum from Marais to Sir Stanley Rous, president of FIFA, the 'FASA has already made extensive inquiries and found that worthwhile sponsorships for prize-money are readily available and, provided the main municipalities in the country and the Department of Bantu Affairs give the move solid backing, financially and otherwise, there is no reason why a national league for Africans should not prove an enormous success from *every* point of view, including the financial aspect'. Marais added that he and W.J.P. Carr (NEAD) 'would take a personal interest in the scheme, if only in the initial stages' and would actively seek the 'tacit approval of the Non-White press'. Cited in Rous Papers, 'Proposed National Football League for Bantus' (1967).

15. Gleeson (2003). I am indebted to Mark Gleeson for sending me his invaluable statistical account of South African professional leagues during the 1971–89 period.

16. For further commentary on 'multinationalism' see Archer and Bouillon (1982: 206–227, 250–259); Booth (1998: 99–109); and Merrett (1996: 146–165). For deeper insights on the international politics of football see Darby (2002).

17. Archer and Bouillon (1982: 250–259).

18. Doug Cress, 'Color Blind', *Los Angeles Times*, 3 July 2000.

19. Doug Cress, 'Color Blind', *Los Angeles Times*, 3 July 2000.

20. Hellenic took the first game 4-0 at Hartleyvale Ground in Cape Town. Chiefs won the return match 2-1. As runners-up they received R7 000. Englishman Jack Taylor, who had officiated the 1974 World Cup final in Munich, West Germany, refereed the controversial second game.

21. *African Soccer Mirror*, August 1977: 7.

22. On 16 June 1976, security forces shot pupils marching peacefully in the streets of Orlando in Soweto to protest the use of Afrikaans as a medium of instruction in African schools. As the protest spread to townships nationwide, the government's brutal repression killed 575 and

wounded 2 389 people (Lodge, 1983: 330). According to Lodge, the official estimates of the casualties were 'highly conservative'.

23. The creation of the Football Council was part of Pretoria's broader attempt to 'reform apartheid' in the late 1970s. This process brought about the legalisation of African trade unions in 1979 and led to a new tricameral constitution in 1983 granting token political representation to Coloureds and Indians, but not Africans. The members of the Football Council were: FASA, SANFA, SASA (Indian) and SAFA (Coloured).

24. 'Black Fans are Keeping the NPSL Turnstiles Clicking', *Sharpshoot*, July 1979.

25. Archer and Bouillon (1982: 253).

26. Stellenbosch Farmers Wineries also sponsored black cricket in the 1970s (Odendaal, 2003: 220).

27. *African Soccer Mirror*, August 1977: 4. See also *African Soccer Mirror*, April 1977: 21, 24. 'Mainstay believes firmly that S.A. is on the verge of a sporting breakthrough that may well usher this country back into international soccer' ('Announcing the Mainstay League Cup' in ASM, April 1977: 21).

28. Archer and Bouillon (1982: 254).

29. Archer and Bouillon (1982: 253).

30. SACOS expelled the FPL for violating its 'double-standards resolution', which mandated that 'Any person, whether . . . a player, administrator, or a spectator, committed to the nonracial principle in sport, shall not participate in, nor be associated with, any code of sport which practices, perpetrates or condones, racialism or multiracialism' (Booth, 1998: 150). The controversy had a personal dimension, since Norman Middleton, SACOS's first president and SASF chief, was a member of the Coloured Labour Party, an organisation which operated within apartheid structures.

31. Archer and Bouillon (1982: 257–258).

32. Gleeson (2003: 36, 62). *Goal!*, 31 January 1982.

33. Gleeson (2003: 28, 38, 54, 68).

34. Alan Paton Centre (PC), University of KwaZulu-Natal, Pietermaritzburg, Papers of the Football Association of Natal and KwaZulu, PC 114/1/8/1: Operations Review of the National Professional Soccer League, August 1983, 11–13. It should be noted how SAB and UTC also sponsored the anti-apartheid FPL through competitions such as the FPL Benson & Hedges Cup.

35. PC 114/1/1/6: Report of the Auditors to the Members of the South African National Football Association, 23 July 1984.

36. Gleeson (2003: 51); Sello (1991: 33).

37. Gleeson (2003: 56, 94).

38. PC 114/1/1/6: National Professional Soccer League Annual Report for 1983; and PC 114/1/8/ 1, 'Operations Review of the NPSL'.

39. 'Operations Review': 14.

40. Gleeson (2003: 67). 'The End of an Era?' *Sharpshoot Soccer Mirror*, November 1983: 5. The name stemmed from Sono's experience playing with Pelé for the 1977 NASL champions New York Cosmos.

41. Interview with Mark Gleeson, Cape Town, 20 August 2003.

42. 'Operations Review': 20–25.

43. *Sharpshoot Soccer Mirror*, May 1981: 13.

44. Gleeson (2003: 82–83). PC 114/1/1/7: 'Events Leading to the Breakaway of some NPSL Clubs'. Moroka Swallows eventually joined the Castle League. Additional evidence presented in this paragraph draws from Gleeson (2003: 83–84, 91).

45. WPAFB: 'The SASF and the Road Ahead in Relation to Alignment with Progressive Organisations' (March 1988?): 8.

46. Perhaps the most troubling example of violence in the 1980s resulted from a traumatic split within Orlando Pirates. On 23 March 1985 two different Pirates teams took the field against Jomo Cosmos at Johannesburg's Ellis Park Stadium. Before a national television audience, a knife-wielding attacker repeatedly stabbed a 'rebel' Pirates official on the pitch. According to Mark Gleeson, this televised display of violence marked a turning-point for South African soccer (interview with Gleeson, 20 August 2003). The evidence appears to confirm this view. For example, S.S.T. Nkwalo, president of the Transvaal Football Association, discussed how hooliganism frightened people away from the grounds. 'Soccer had become the Townships' religion. Alas, all of a sudden, all that enthusiasm has evaporated into thin air. The paying customer[s] have shown their disapproval with the present set-up by staying away from matches.' Cited in PC 114/1/1/7: South African National Football Association Annual General Meeting Report for 1985, 'Transvaal Football Association 1985 Presidential Address'.

47. WPAFB: 'Pursuing Unity in Football: Challenges and Constraints in the Way to Unity', by SASF Public Relations, 1988.

48. WPAFB: Joint Communique of African National Congress, the National Soccer League, and the Soccer Association of South Africa, Lusaka, Zambia, 19 October 1988.

49. Gleeson (2003: 103–104).

50. WPAFB: Report on the meeting of the South African Soccer Federation and the African National Congress, Lusaka, Zambia, 5–6 November 1988.

51. For a critical perspective on the 'unity' process see Booth (1995: 105–124).

52. South Africa and Cameroon played two more matches: Cameroon won 2-1 on 9 July at the Goodwood racecourse in Cape Town; the teams drew 2-2 on 11 July at the Rand Stadium in Johannesburg.

53. Interview with Vince Belgeums, Factreton, 27 March 1998.

APPENDIX

1. Akyeampong and Ambler (2002: 1–22). See also Eckert and Jones (2002: 5–16). For additional insights on African leisure see Akyeampong (1996, 2002); and Ambler (2001: 81–105).

2. For a useful overview see Barber (1997). For time-sensitive analyses of music and theatre in West Africa see Barber (2000); Barber, Collins and Ricard (1997); Collins (1994); and Waterman (1990). On Congolese popular theatre and painting see Fabian (1990, 1998); as well as Jewsiewicki (1996: 334–355). For eastern Africa see Fair (1998: 63–94); Mitchell (1956); and Ranger (1975). On clothing in general see Hendrickson (1996).

3. Coplan (1985); Erlmann (1991); Harries (1994); and La Hausse (1988). Among other such studies see, for example, Gunner (1994).

4. Minkley and Rassool (1998: 90). Among the many discussions on this topic see Bonner (1994: 977–985); and Bozzoli and Delius (1990: 13–45). For a sharply critical view see Maloka (2001: 16–19).

5. For discussion of the development of social history in the broader context of South African historiography see Saunders (1988: 184); Smith (1988: 214). For a recent essay see Cobley (2001: 613–625). *Laduma!* tries to avoid a tendency among some social historians to overgeneralise, downplay, or 'ventriloquise' individual actions and ideas, marginalise non-economic forces such as race, religious and spiritual beliefs, and emphasise trivial detail. For more commentary on these issues see Bonner (1997); Minkley and Rassool (1998); and Saunders (1997: 307–315). For a South African social historian's poignant reflection on postmodernism's influence on history writing see Maylam (2000: 121–135).

6. Couzens (1983: 198–214).

7. Jeffrey (1992: 68–94).

8. Martin (1995).

9. Atkins (1993); Cooper (1983: 7–50, 1992: 209–245); Thompson (1967). For further comments see Giles-Vernick (2000: 135–141).

10. Couzens (1982: 314–337)

11. Alegi (1999: 73).

12. For a useful review essay, see Maylam (1995: 19–38). For important regional perspectives see Crush and Ambler (1992). For more details see, for example, Bonner (1989); Maylam and Edwards (1996); Nasson (1989: 285-309); and Van Onselen (1982). For a Zambian case study see Ambler (1990: 295–313).

13. Badenhorst (1982); Cobley (1994: 212–230); Vahed (1998: 67–123). See also Badenhorst and Mather (1997: 473–489). For an older, incisive monograph see Jarvie (1985). On mine sport and ethnic divisions in the Northern Province see Malunga (2000: 465–482). For studies north of the Limpopo, see Martin (1995); and Ranger (1987: 196–213).

14. Merrett (1994: 97–122).

15. Maylam (1995: 21).

16. For publications by the History Workshop see Bonner et al. (1989); Bonner et al. (1993); and Bozzoli (1979, 1983, 1987). For published studies on Cape Town, see Bank and Minkley (1998/99: 4–16); Bickford-Smith (1995); Bickford-Smith, Van Heyningen and Worden (1999); Saunders et al. (1984); Western (1981); and Worden, Bickford-Smith and Van Heyningen (1998). On Durban, by way of example, see Freund (2002); and Maylam and Edwards (1996).

17. Paths to comparative approaches suggested in Cobley (1999: 133–155, 2001); and Greenstein (1994: 641–661).

18. Holt (1989); Mangan (1986, 1988); Morrell (1996); Stoddart (1988: 649–673).

19. On cultural hegemony see Cashman (1988: 258–272); Guttmann (1994); and Hargreaves (1986). On 'weapons of the weak' see Klein (1991). For a different approach see Stoddart and McD Beckles (1996).

20. Greenstein (1998); Miller (1999: 1–32).

21. Van der Merwe (1983: 40–42).

22. Tony Mason's (1980) pioneering use of newspapers in his social history of football in England before the First World War and Les Switzer's (1997) extensive work on the black press in South Africa were both sources of inspiration and guidance in the research and writing process. See also Switzer and Switzer (1979).

23. Mason (1981: 248).

24. The circulation of Drum in March 1954 was 70 000 copies (Chapman, 1989: 194).

25. Switzer (1997: 1–53, 189–212). The revamped sport sections helped the black daily World raise its circulation to 90 000 copies in 1968; see Tomaselli, Tomaselli, and Muller (1987: 47).

26. Van Onselen (1996: 10).

27. The oral history component of this study was limited by both time considerations and extraordinary amounts of archival work. For analyses of oral history in South African history-writing see La Hausse (1991: 342–350); and Rassool (1997).

28. For further discussions of these issues, see Cahn (1994: 594–609); and Hill (1996: 1–19).

29. Conversation with I. Zuma, Langa, 9 February 1998. For a fascinating published account of the black slum of Windermere see Field (2001: 211–224).

30. Ndebele (1994: 56–57).

Select Bibliography

PRIMARY SOURCES

Manuscript sources

Alan Paton Papers (University of KwaZulu-Natal, Pietermaritzburg)
Bantu Men's Social Centre Papers (University of the Witwatersrand)
AWG Champion Papers (University of South Africa)
J. Howard Pim Papers (University of the Witwatersrand)
Leo Kuper Papers (Center for Research Libraries, Chicago)
Monica H. Wilson Papers (University of Cape Town)
Orlando Pirates Football Club minutes of meetings, 1945–61 (in the possession of R. Maguire, Cape Town)
Papers of the American Board of Commissioners for Foreign Missions (Harvard University)
Papers of the Western Province Association Football Board (University of the Western Cape)
Phillips Papers (University of the Witwatersrand)
SAIRR records (University of the Witwatersrand)
Sir Stanley Rous Papers (University of Brighton)

Official publications

Governmental

GOV 367. Report of the Inter-Departmental Committee on the *Social, Health and Economic Conditions of Urban Natives* (Smit Commission). Pretoria: Dept. of Native Affairs, 1942.
U.G. 22-32. *Report of the Native Economic Commission.* Pretoria: Government Printers, 1932.
U.G. 29-36. *Report of the Interdepartmental Committee on Native Education, 1935–1936* (Welsh Report). Pretoria: Government Printers, 1936.
U.G. 34-14. *Report of the Tuberculosis Commission.* Cape Town: Government Printers, 1914.

Municipal

City of Cape Town, 'Minutes of the Meetings of Cape Town Town Council'
City of Durban, 'Minutes of the Mayor', Durban Town Council
City of Johannesburg, 'Minutes of the Meetings of Johannesburg City Council'

Oral sources

Interviews with Peter Alegi:
Vince Belgeums, Factreton, 27 March 1998
Dennis Brutus, 7 June 2001 (via telephone)
Darius Dhlomo, 12 February and 26 February 2003 (via telephone)
John Esau, Kensington, 29 March 1998
Mark Gleeson, Cape Town, 20 August 2003
Bernard Hartze, Cape Town, 29 January 1998
Basil Jansen, Grassy Park 18 May 1998
Ben Malamba, Langa, 26 July 1995

Moses Molelekoa, Khayelitsha, 26 July 1995
Joe Mthimka, Langa, 27 July 1995
Peter Sitsila, Langa, 27 July 1995
Conrad Stuurman, Factreton and Langa, 9 February 1998; Factreton, 25 February 1998; Grassy
    Park, 18 May 1998

Interviews with Richard Maguire:
Elliot Buthelezi, August 1991
Sydney Mabuza, August 1991
Rankus Maphisa, July 1991
Peter Mngomezulu, August 1991
Sidwell Mogkosinyane, August 1991
Willard Msomi, August 1991
Skumbuzo Mthembu, August 1991
Theo Mthembu, August 1991
Sam Shabangu, 23 July 1991 and August 1991
Fanyana Shiburi, August 1991
Boy Shogwe, September 1991
Jimmy Sobi, August 1991
Mike Tseka, August 1991

Notes of interviews with Dr A.R.W. Crosse-Upcott (Monica Wilson Papers):
Bishop Fassie, Langa, 10 January 1956
Mr Gallo, Langa, 22 February 1956
Mr Mahase, Langa, 11 October 1955
Mr Mahase and Mr Smous, Langa, 5 December 1955
S. Matshiqi, Langa, 16 and 22 August, 30 September 1955, 15 and 28 November 1955
Mr Mgijima, Langa, 25 January 1956
Mr Rogers, Langa, 19 August 1955
Mr Sello, Langa, 21 October 1955, 2 and 5 December 1955

Notes of Interviews with Bernard Magubane, Durban 1960 (Leo Kuper Papers):
Edward C. Jali, John Khambule, I.J. Motholo. Reggie Ngcobo, J. Thambisa, Douglas Evans.

Audio/Visual
'Once a Pirate Always a Pirate', *In The Heart of Soweto*, part IV. Produced by R.M. Productions and
    V.N.S. Double Exposure 1 (1991).

Serials

Newspapers
African Soccer Mirror/Sharpshoot
African Sports
Bantu World/World
Business Day
Cape Argus
Cape Herald
Cape Standard
Cape Times
Fed Fan
Golden City Post/Post
The Guardian/New Age
Ilanga Lase Natal

Natal Mercury
Rand Daily Mail
South African Outlook
The Leader
The Sowetan
The Star
The Workers' Herald
Umteteli Wa Bantu

Scholarly journals
Africa
African Studies
American Historical Review
Canadian Journal of the History of Sport (now *Sport History Review*)
Comparative Studies in Society and History
Historia
History in Africa
International Journal of African Historical Studies
International Journal of the History of Sport
Journal of African History
Journal of American History
Journal of Natal and Zulu History
Journal of Southern African Studies
Journal of Sport History
Kleio
Kronos
Leisure Studies
Past and Present
Race & Class
Radical History Review
Sporting Traditions
Soccer and Society
South African Historical Journal
Transafrican Journal of History
Twentieth-Century British History

SECONDARY SOURCES

Aguilar, Mario (ed.). *The Politics of Age and Gerontocracy in Africa*. Trenton, NJ: Africa World Press, 1998.

Akyeampong, Emmanuel K. 'Bukom and the Social History of Boxing in Accra, Ghana', *International Journal of African Historical Studies* 35, 1 (2002): 39–60.

———. *Drink, Power, and Cultural Change: A Social History of Alcohol in Ghana, c.1800 to Recent Times*. Portsmouth, NH: Heinemann, 1996.

———. 'What's in a Drink? Class Struggle, Popular Culture and the Politics of *Akpeteshie* (Local Gin) in Ghana, 1936–67', *Journal of African History* 37 (1996): 215–236.

Akyeampong, E.K., and Charles Ambler. 'Leisure in African History', *International Journal of African Historical Studies* 35, 1 (2002): 1–16.

Alegi, Peter. 'Playing to the Gallery: Sport, Cultural Performance, and Social Identity in South Africa, 1920s–1945', *International Journal of African Historical Studies* 35, 1 (2002): 17–38.

————. '"All Work and No Play Makes Jack a Dull Boy": Black Power, Zuluness, and Chief Albert Luthuli's Sporting Life, 1920–1946'. Paper presented at the annual meeting of the North American Society for Sport History. French Lick, IN, 26 May 2002.

————. *Amathe Nolimi* (It is Saliva and the Tongue): Contracts of Joy in South African Football, *c.* 1940–1976', *International Journal of the History of Sport* 17, 4 (2000): 1–20.

————. ' "Feel the Pull in Your Soul": Local Agency and Global Trends in South Africa's 2006 World Cup Bid', *Soccer and Society* 2, 3 (2001): 1–21.

————. 'Katanga v Johannesburg: A History of the First Sub-Saharan African Football Championship, 1949–50', *Kleio* 31 (1999): 55–74.

————. 'Umdlalo Wabantu: A Social History of Soccer in Urban Black South African Communities, 1886–1956'. M.A. thesis, Yale University, 1995.

Allaway, Roger, Colin Jose, and David Litterer. *The Encyclopedia of American Soccer History*. Lanham, MD: Rowman and Littlefield, 2001.

Ambler, Charles. 'Alcohol, Racial Segregation, and Popular Politics in Northern Rhodesia', *Journal of African History* 31, 2 (1990): 295–313.

————. 'Popular Film and Colonial Audiences: The Movies in Northern Rhodesia', *American Historical Review* 106, 1 (2001): 81–105.

Anderson, Benedict. *Imagined Communities: Reflections on the Origin and Spread of Nationalism*. London: Verso, 1991.

Appaduraj, Arjun. 'Playing with Modernity: The Decolonization of Indian Cricket'. In A. Appaduraj, *Modernity at Large: Cultural Dimensions of Globalization*. Minneapolis and London: University of Minnesota Press, 1996: 89–113.

Archer, Robert. 'An Exceptional Case: Politics and Sport in South Africa's Townships'. In W.J. Baker and J.A. Mangan (eds.), *Sport in Africa: Essays in Social History*, 1987: 229–249.

Archer, Robert, and Antoine Bouillon. *The South African Game: Sport and Racism*. London: Zed Press, 1982.

Armstrong, Gary, and Richard Giulianotti (eds.). *Entering the Field: New Perspectives in World Football*. Oxford and New York: Berg, 1997.

————. *Football Cultures and Identities*. London: MacMillan, 1999.

Ashton, Hugh. *The Basuto*. London: Oxford University Press for the International African Institute, 1952.

Atkins, Keletso. *The Moon is Dead! Give Us Our Money! The Cultural Origins of an African Work Ethic, Natal, South Africa, 1843–1900*. Portsmouth, NH: Heinemann, 1993.

Atkinson, T. 'Recreation for Urban Natives', *South African Outlook*, 2 October 1933: 197.

Badenhorst, Cecile. 'Mines, Missionaries, and the Municipality: Organized African Sport and Recreation in Johannesburg, *c.*1920–1950'. Ph.D. dissertation, Queen's University, 1992.

Badenhorst, C., and Charles Mather. 'Tribal Recreation and Recreating Tribalism: Culture, Leisure and Social Control on South Africa's Gold Mines, 1940–1950', *Journal of Southern African Studies* 23, 3 (1997): 473–489.

Bailey, Peter. 'Leisure, Culture and the Historian: Reviewing the First Generation of Leisure Historiography in Britain', *Leisure Studies* 8 (1989): 107–127.

Baker, William J. 'Political Games: The Meaning of International Sport for Independent Africa'. In W.J. Baker and J.A. Mangan (eds.), *Sport in Africa*, 1987: 272–294.

Baker, W.J., and J.A. Mangan (eds.). *Sport in Africa: Essays in Social History*. New York: Africana, 1987.

Bale, John. 'Capturing "The African" Body? Visual Images and Imaginative Sports', *Journal of Sport History* 25, 2 (1998): 234–251.

————. *Sport, Space and the City*. London: Routledge, 1993.

Bale, J., and Joe Sang. *Kenyan Running: Movement Culture, Geography and Global Change*. London: Frank Cass, 1996.

Ballantine, Christopher. *Marabi Nights: Early South African Jazz and Vaudeville*. Johannesburg: Ravan Press, 1993.

Bank, Andrew, and Gary Minkley. 'Genealogies of Space and Identity in Cape Town', *Kronos: Journal of Cape History* 25 (1998–99): 4–16.

Bansda, D.N. (ed.). *Official Program of the SASL R2000 United Tobacco Co. Knock-Out Cup Final.* Cape Town: Western Province Soccer League, 1961.

Barber, Karin. *The Generation of Plays: Yoruba Popular Life in Theater.* Bloomington and Indianapolis: Indiana University Press, 2000.

———. 'Introduction'. In Barber, K. (ed.), *Readings in African Popular Culture.* Bloomington and Oxford, 1997: 1–12.

———. 'Popular Arts in Africa', *African Studies Review* 30, 3 (1987): 1–78.

Barber, K., J. Collins, and A. Ricard. 'Three West African Popular Theater Forms: A Social History'. In Barber, Collins, and Ricard, *West African Popular Theater.* Bloomington and Indianapolis: Indiana University Press, 1997.

Bates, Robert, V.Y. Mudimbe, and Jean O'Barr (eds.). *Africa and the Disciplines: The Contributions of Research in Africa to the Social Sciences and Humanities.* Chicago: University of Chicago Press, 1993.

Beckles, Hilary McD. (ed.). *A Spirit of Dominance: Cricket and Nationalism in the West Indies.* Kingston: Canoe Press, 1998.

Beinart, William. 'The Origins of the *Indlavini*: Male Associations and Migrant Labour in the Transkei', *African Studies* 50, 1 (1991): 103–128.

———. 'Political and Collective Violence in Southern African Historiography', *Journal of Southern African Studies* 18, 3 (1992): 455–486.

Beinart, W., and S. Dubow (eds.). *Segregation and Apartheid in Twentieth-Century South Africa.* London: Routledge, 1995.

Beinart, W., P. Delius, and S. Trapido (eds.). *Putting a Plough to the Ground: Accumulation and Dispossession in Rural South Africa, 1885–1930.* Johannesburg: Indiana University Press, 1986.

Bickford-Smith, Vivian. *Ethnic Pride and Racial Prejudice in Victorian Cape Town.* Cambridge: Cambridge University Press, 1995.

———. 'Leisure and Social Identity in Cape Town, British Cape Colony, 1838–1910', *Kronos* 25 (1998/99): 103–128.

Bickford-Smith, V., Elizabeth Van Heyningen, and Nigel Worden. *Cape Town in the Twentieth Century: An Illustrated Social History.* Claremont: David Philip, 1999.

Black, David, and John Nauright. *Rugby and the South African Nation.* Manchester: Manchester University Press, 1998.

Blacking, John. 'Games and Sport in Pre-Colonial African Societies'. In W.J. Baker and J.A. Mangan (eds.), *Sport in Africa*, 1987: 3–22.

Blades, Jack (comp. & ed.). *The Rainbow Game: A Random History of South African Soccer.* Lanseria: Bailey's African History Archives, 1998.

Bonner, Philip. 'African Urbanisation on the Rand Between the 1930s and 1960s: Its Social Character and Political Consequences', *Journal of Southern African Studies* 21, 1 (1995): 115–129.

———. 'Backs to the Fence: Law, Liquor, and the Search for Social Control in an East Rand Town, 1929–1942'. In J. Crush and C. Ambler (eds.), *Liquor and Labor in Southern Africa*, 1992: 269–305.

———. *Holding Their Ground: Class, Locality and Culture in 19th- and 20th-century South Africa.* Johannesburg: Ravan Press and Witwatersrand University Press, 1989.

———. *Kings, Commoners and Concessionaires: The Evolution and Dissolution of the Nineteenth-Century Swazi State.* Cambridge: Cambridge University Press, 1982a.

———. 'New Nation, New History: The History Workshop in South Africa, 1977–1994', *Journal of American History* 81, 3 (1994): 977–985.

————. 'The Transvaal Native Congress, 1917–1920: The Radicalisation of the Black Petty Bourgeoisie on the Rand'. In S. Marks and R. Rathbone (eds.), *Industrialisation and Social Change in South Africa*, 1982b: 270–313.

————. 'The Russians on the Reef, 1947–1957: Urbanisation, Gang Warfare and Ethnic Mobilization'. In P. Bonner et al. (eds.), *Apartheid's Genesis*, 1993: 160–194.

————. 'The University of the Witwatersrand History Workshop: A Retrospect'. Paper for the conference 'Problematising History and Agency', University of Cape Town, Centre for African Studies, October 1997.

Bonner, P., and Lauren Segal. *Soweto: A History*. Cape Town: Maskew Miller Longman, 1998.

Bonner P., Peter Delius, and Deborah Posel (eds.). *Apartheid's Genesis: 1935–1962*. Johannesburg and Braamfontein: Ravan Press and Witwatersrand University Press, 1993.

Bonner, P., I. Hofmeyr, D. James, and T. Lodge (eds.). *Holding Their Ground: Class, Locality and Culture in 19th and 20th Century South Africa*. Johannesburg: Ravan Press, 1989.

Booth, Douglas. *The Race Game: Sport and Politics in South Africa*. London: Frank Cass, 1998.

————. 'South Africa's "Autonomous Sport" Strategy: Desegregation Apartheid Style', *Sporting Traditions* 6, 2 (1990): 155–179.

————. 'United Sport: An Alternative Hegemony in South Africa?', *International Journal of the History of Sport* 12, 3 (1995): 105–124.

Bose, Mihir. *A History of Indian Cricket*. London: Deutsch, 1990.

Botto, Remo. 'Some Aspects of the Leisure Occupations of the African Population of Cape Town'. M. Soc. Sci. thesis, University of Cape Town, 1954.

Bozzoli, Belinda (ed.). *Class, Community and Conflict*. Johannesburg: Ravan Press, 1987.

Bozzoli, B. *Labour, Townships and Protest*. Johannesburg: Ravan Press, 1979.

————., (ed.). *Town and Countryside in the Transvaal*. Johannesburg: Ravan Press, 1983.

Bozzoli, B., and Peter Delius. 'Radical History and South African Society', *Radical History Review* 46, 7 (1990): 13–45.

Bradford, Helen. *A Taste of Freedom: The ICU in Rural South Africa, 1924–1930*. New Haven and London: Yale University Press, 1987.

Breckenridge, Keith. 'Migrancy, Crime and Faction Fighting: The Role of the Isithozi in the Development of Ethnic Organizations in the Compounds', *Journal of Southern African Studies* 16, 1 (1990): 55–78.

Brickhill, Joan. *Race against Race: South Africa's 'Multinational' Sport Fraud*. London: International Defence and Aid Fund, 1976.

Bromberger, Christian. 'Football as World-View and as Ritual', *French Cultural Studies* 6 (1995): 293–311.

Brown, Joshua, Patrick Manning, Karin Shapiro, Jon Wiener, Belinda Bozzoli, and Peter Delius (eds.). *History from South Africa: Alternative Visions and Practices*. Philadelphia: Temple University Press, 1991.

Brutus, Dennis. 'The Sportsman's Choice'. In Alex La Guma (ed.), *Apartheid: A Collection of Writings on South African Racism by South Africans*. New York and London: Seven Seas, 1971: 142–153.

————. 'Room for All Sportsmen', *Golden City Post*, 5 August 1956.

Bryant, Alfred T. *The Zulu People*. Pietermaritzburg: Shuter & Shooter, 1949.

Bundy, Colin. *The Rise and Fall of the South African Peasantry*. London: Heinemann, 1979.

Burke, Timothy. *Lifebuoy Men, Lux Women: Commodification, Consumption, and Cleanliness in Modern Zimbabwe*. Durham, NC: Duke University Press, 1996.

Burton, Richard D.E. 'Cricket, Carnival and Street Culture in the Caribbean'. In B. Stoddart and H. McD. Beckles (eds.), *Liberation Cricket: West Indies Cricket Culture*, 1996: 89–106.

Cahn, Susan K. '"Sports Talk": Oral History and Its Uses, Problems, and Possibilities for Sport History', *Journal of American History* 81, 2 (1994): 594–609.

Calpin, G.H. *A.I. Kajee: His Work for the South African Indian Community*. Durban: ca.1950.

Campbell, J.D. ' "Training for Sport is Training for War": Sport and the Transformation of the British Army, 1860–1914', *International Journal of the History of Sport* 17, 4 (2000): 21–58.

Carr, William J.P. *Soweto: Its Creation, Life and Decline*. Johannesburg: SAIRR, 1990.

Carton, Benedict. *Blood from Your Children: The Colonial Origins of Generational Conflict in South Africa*. Pietermaritzburg: University of Natal Press, 2000.

———. 'Locusts Fall from the Sky: Manhood and Migrancy in KwaZulu'. In R. Morrell (ed.), *Changing Men in Southern Africa*, 2001: 129–140.

Cashman, Richard. 'Cricket and Colonialism: Colonial Hegemony and Indigenous Subversion'. In J.A. Mangan (ed.), *Pleasure, Profit, and Proselytism*, 1988: 258–272.

Chapman, Michael. *The 'Drum' Decade: Stories from the 1950s*. Pietermaritzburg, University of Natal Press, 1989.

Chehabi, Houchang. 'Football'. *Encyclopedia Iranica*. Vol.X. London and Boston: Routledge & Kegan Paul.

Clayton, Anthony. 'Sport and African Soldiers: The Military Diffusion of Western Sport throughout Sub-Saharan Africa'. In W.J. Baker and J.A. Mangan (eds.), *Sport in Africa*, 1987: 114–137.

Clegg, Jonathan. '*Ukubuyisa Isidumbu* – "Bringing Back the Body": An Examination into the Ideology of Vengeance in the Msinga and Mpofana Rural Locations, 1882–1944'. In P. Bonner (ed.), *Working Papers in Southern African Studies, Vol. 2*. Johannesburg: African Studies Institute University of the Witwatersrand, 1981: 164–198.

Clingman, Steven. *Bram Fischer: Afrikaner Revolutionary*. Amherst, MA: University of Massachusetts Press, 1998.

Cobley, Alan Gregor. *Class and Consciousness: The Black Petty Bourgeoisie in South Africa, 1924–1950*. Westport, CT: Greenwood Press, 1990.

———. 'Does Social History Have a Future? The Ending of Apartheid and Recent Trends in South African Historiography', *Journal of Southern African Studies* 27, 3 (2001): 613–625.

———. 'Forgotten Connections, Unconsidered Parallels: A New Agenda for Comparative Research in Southern Africa and the Caribbean', *African Studies* 58, 2 (1999): 133–155.

———. 'A Political History of Playing Fields: The Provision of Sporting Facilities for Africans in the Johannesburg Area to 1948', *International Journal of the History of Sport* 11, 2 (1994): 212–230.

———. *The Rules of the Game: Struggles in Black Recreation and Social Welfare Policy in South Africa*. Westport, CT: Greenwood Press, 1997.

Coleman, James S. *Foundations of Social Theory*. Cambridge, MA: Harvard University Press, 1990.

Coles, Robert W. 'Football as a "Surrogate" Religion?'. In Michael Hill (ed.), *A Sociological Yearbook of Religion in Britain 8*. London: SCM Press, 1975.

Collins, John [E.J.]. *Highlife Time*. Accra: Anansesem Publications, 1994.

Cook, Peter Allan Wilson. *Social Organization and the Ceremonial Institutions of the Bomvana*. Cape Town and Johannesburg: Juta, 1931.

Cooper, Frederick. 'Back to Work: Categories, Boundaries and Connections in the Study of Labour'. In P. Alexander and R. Halpern (eds.), *Racializing Class, Classifying Race*. New York: St. Martin's Press, 2000: 213–235.

Cooper, F. 'Colonizing Time: Work Rhythms and Labor Conflict in Colonial Mombasa'. In Nicholas B. Dirks (ed.), *Colonialism and Culture*. Ann Arbor: University of Michigan Press, 1992: 209–245.

———. 'Conflict and Connection: Rethinking Colonial African History', *American Historical Review* 99 (1994): 1516–1545.

———. 'Urban Space, Industrial Time, and Wage Labor in Africa'. In F. Cooper (ed.), *Struggle for the City: Migrant Labor, Capital and the State in Urban Africa*. Beverly Hills, CA: Sage, 1983: 7–50.

Cope, Richard. *Ploughshare of War: The Origins of the Anglo-Zulu War of 1879*. Pietermaritzburg: University of Natal Press, 1999.

Cope, Trevor (ed.). *Izibongo: Zulu Praise-Poems*. Oxford: Clarendon Press, 1968.

Coplan, David. 'The African Performer and the Johannesburg Entertainment Industry: The Struggle for African Culture on the Witwatersrand'. In B. Bozzoli (ed.), *Labour, Townships and Protest*, 1979.

———. 'The Emergence of an African Working-Class Culture'. In S. Marks and R. Rathbone (eds.), *Industrialisation and Social Change in South Africa*, 1982: 358–375.

———. *In the Time of Cannibals: The Word Music of South Africa's Basotho Migrants*. Chicago: University of Chicago Press, 1994.

———. *In Township Tonight! South Africa's Black City Music and Theater*. New York: Longman, 1985.

Couzens, Tim. 'An Introduction to the History of Football in South Africa'. In B. Bozzoli (ed.), *Town and Countryside in the Transvaal*, 1983: 198–214.

———. 'Moralizing Leisure Time: The Transnational Connection and Black Johannesburg, 1918–1936'. In S. Marks and R. Rathbone (eds.), *Industrialisation and Social Change in South Africa*, 1982: 314–337.

———. *The New African: A Study of the Life and Work of H.I.E. Dhlomo*. Johannesburg: Ravan Press, 1985.

Cox, Richard, Dave Russell, and Wray Vamplew (eds.). *Encyclopedia of British Football*. London: Frank Cass, 2002.

Crawford, Scott A.G.M. 'A Speculative Paradigm on the Birth of the Modern Sport Spectacular: The Real Madrid and Eintracht Frankfurt European Cup Final of 1960', *International Journal of the History of Sport* 9, 3 (1992): 433–438.

Creek, F.N.S. *A History of the Corinthians Football Club*. London: Longmans, Green and Co., 1933.

Crush, Jonathan, and Charles Ambler (eds.). *Liquor and Labor in Southern Africa*. Athens, OH: Ohio University Press, 1992.

Crush, J., Alan Jeeves, and David Yudelman. *South Africa's Labor Empire: A History of Black Migrancy to the Gold Mines*. Boulder, CO: Westview Press, 1991.

Cunningham, Anne (comp.). J. Howard Pim Papers, *Inventory of Collection*. Johannesburg: University of the Witwatersrand, 1976: v.

Da Matta, Roberto. 'Notes Sur le Football Brésilien', *Le Débat* 19 (1982).

Darby, Paul. *Africa, Football and FIFA: Politics, Colonialism and Resistance*. London: Frank Cass, 2002.

Davenport, T.R.H. *South Africa: A Modern History*. Toronto: University of Toronto Press, 1987.

De Broglio, Chris. *South Africa: Racism in Sport*. London: Christian Action Publications, 1970.

De Kiewiet, Cornelius W. *A History of South Africa: Social & Economic*. London: Oxford, 1941.

De Oliveira, Angelo. *Isto de Futebóis*. Maputo: Ndjira, 1998.

Dean, D. Shirley. *Black South Africans: A Who's Who, 57 Profiles of Natal's Leading Blacks*. Oxford: Oxford University Press, 1978.

Delius, Peter. *The Land Belongs to Us: The Pedi Polity, the Boers and the British in the Nineteenth-Century Transvaal*. Johannesburg: Ravan Press, 1983.

Denniston, Robin. *Trevor Huddleston: A Life*. New York: St. Martin's Press, 1999.

Desai, Ashwin, Vishnu Padayachee, Krish Reddy, and Goolam Vahed. *Blacks in Whites: A Century of Cricket Struggles in KwaZulu-Natal*. Pietermaritzburg: University of Natal Press, 2002.

Dikobe, Modikwe. *The Marabi Dance*. London: Heinemann, 1973.

Dimeo, Paul, and James Mills (eds.). *Soccer in South Asia: Empire, Nation, Diaspora*. London: Frank Cass, 2001.

Dobson, Paul. *Rugby in South Africa*. Cape Town: South African Rugby Board, 1989.

Draper, Mary. *Sport and Race in South Africa*. Johannesburg: SAIRR, 1963.

Dubow, Saul. 'The Elaboration of Segregationist Ideology'. In W. Beinart and S. Dubow (eds.), *Segregation and Apartheid in Twentieth Century South Africa*, 1995: 145–175.

Duke, Vic. *Football, Nationality and the State*. Essex, UK: Addison Wesley Longman, 1996.

Dyreson, Mark. 'Regulating the Body and the Body Politic: American Sport, Bourgeois Culture, and the Language of Progress, 1880–1920'. In S.W. Pope (ed.), *The New American Sport History*, 1997: 121–144.

Eckert, Andreas, and Adam Jones. 'Historical Writing about Everyday Life', *Journal of African Cultural Studies* 15 (2002): 5–16.

Edgar, Robert R., and Luyanda ka Msumza (eds.). *Freedom in Our Lifetime*. Athens, Ohio: Ohio University Press, 1996.

Edwards, Iain. 'Cato Manor, June 1959: Men, Women, Crowds, Violence, Politics and History'. In P. Maylam and I. Edwards (eds.), *The People's City*, 1996: 102–142.

———. 'Swing the Assegai Peacefully? "New Africa", Mkhumbane, the Co-operative Movement and Attempts to Transform Durban Society in the Late 1940s'. In P. Bonner et al. (eds.), *Holding Their Ground*, 1989: 59–104.

Eldredge, Elizabeth. *A South African Kingdom: The Pursuit of Security in Nineteenth-Century Lesotho*. Cambridge: Cambridge University Press, 1993.

Elphick, Richard, and Herman Gilliomee. *The Shaping of South African Society, 1652–1820*. Middletown, CT: Wesleyan University Press, 1989 (first published in 1979).

Erlmann, Veit. *African Stars: Studies in Black South African Performance*. Chicago and London: University of Chicago Press, 1991.

———. 'But Hope Does Not Kill: Black Popular Music in Durban, 1913–1939'. In P. Maylam and I. Edwards (eds.), *The People's City*, 1996a: 67–101.

———. *Nightsong: Performance, Power, and Practice in South Africa*. Chicago and London: University of Chicago Press, 1996b.

Etherington, Norman. *Preachers, Peasants and Politics in South East Africa, 1835–1880*. London: Royal Historical Society, 1978.

Evans, Ivan. *Bureaucracy and Race: Native Administration in South Africa*. Berkeley: University of California Press, 1997.

Fabian, Johannes. *Moments of Freedom: Anthropology and Popular Culture*. Charlottesville and London: University Press of Virginia, 1998.

———. 'Popular Culture in Africa: Findings and Conjectures', *Africa* 48, 4 (1978): 315–334.

———. *Power and Performance: Ethnographic Explorations through Proverbial Wisdom and Theatre in Shaba, Zaire*. Madison, WI: University of Wisconsin Press, 1990.

Fair, Laura. 'Dressing Up: Clothing, Class and Gender in Post-Abolition Zanzibar', *Journal of African History* 39, 1 (1998): 63–94.

———. 'Kickin' it: Leisure, Politics and Football in Colonial Zanzibar, 1900s–1950s', *Africa* 67, 2 (1997): 224–251.

———. *Pastimes and Politics: Culture, Community, and Identity in Post-Abolition Urban Zanzibar, 1890–1945*. Athens, OH: Ohio University Press, 2001.

Feierman, Steven. 'African Histories and the Dissolution of World History'. In Bates, Mudimbe, and O'Barr (eds.), *Africa and the Disciplines*. Chicago: University of Chicago Press, 1993: 167–212.

Field, Sean. 'Disappointed Men: Masculine Myths and Hybrid Identities in Windermere'. In R. Morrell (ed.), *Changing Men in Southern Africa*, 2001: 211–224.

———. 'From the "Peaceful Past" to the "Violent Present": Memory, Myth and Identity in Guguletu'. In D.R. Howarth and A.J. Norval (eds.), *South Africa in Transition*. New York and London: St. Martin's Press, 1998: 72–92.

Fishwick, Nicholas. *English Football and Society, 1910–1950*. Manchester: Manchester University Press, 1989.

French, K. 'James Mpanza and the Sofasonke Party in the Development of Local Politics in Soweto'. M.A. thesis, University of the Witwatersrand, 1983.

Freund, Bill. 'Durban: Towards a Structural Analysis of a South African City'. In D.A. Anderson and R. Rathbone (eds.), *Africa's Urban Past*. Portsmouth, NH: Heinemann, 2000: 144–161.

————. *Insiders and Outsiders: The Indian Working Class of Durban, 1910–1990*. Portsmouth, NH: Heinemann, 1995.

————. *The Making of Contemporary Africa*. Boulder, CO: Lynne Rienner, 1998.

Freund, Bill, and Vishnu Padatachee (eds.). *(D)urban Vortex: South African City in Transition*. Pietermaritzburg: University of Natal Press, 2002.

Gaitskell, Deborah. 'Upward All and Play the Game: The Girl Wayfarers' Association in the Transvaal 1925–1975'. In P. Kallaway (ed.), *Apartheid and Education*, 1984: 222–264.

————. '"Wailing for Purity": Prayer Unions, African Mothers and Adolescent Daughters, 1912–1940'. In S. Marks and R. Rathbone (eds.), *Industrialisation and Social Change in South Africa*, 1982: 338–357.

Galeano, Eduardo. *Soccer in Sun and Shadow*. New York and London: Verso, 1998.

Gardner, Paul. *The Simplest Game*. New York: MacMillan, 1996.

Gibson, Alfred, and William Pickford. *Football and the Men Who Made It*. Cape Town: D.E. McConnell & Co., 1906.

Giles-Vernick, Tamara. 'Workers, Football Players, Musicians, and Painters: Remaking Conventional Narratives of Africa's Colonial Past', *Radical History Review* 77 (2000): 135–141.

Giulianotti, Richard. *Football: A Sociology of the Global Game*. Cambridge: Polity, 1999.

Glaser, Clive. *Bo-Tsotsi: The Youth Gangs of Soweto, 1935–1976*. Portsmouth, NH: Heinemann, 2000.

————. 'Swines, Hazels and the Dirty Dozen: Masculinity, Territoriality and the Youth Gangs of Soweto, 1960–1976', *Journal of Southern African Studies* 24, 4 (1998): 719–736.

Gleeson, M. 'History of the Castle League'. Manuscript, 2003.

Gluckman, Max. *The Ideas in Barotse Jurisprudence*. New Haven: Yale University Press, 1965a.

————. (ed). *Ideas and Procedures in African Customary Law*. Oxford: Oxford University Press, 1969.

————. *Politics, Law and Ritual in Tribal Society*. Chicago: Aldine, 1965b.

Gluckman, Mary, and Max Gluckman. 'On Drama, and Games and Athletic Contests'. In J.C. Harris and R.J. Park (eds.), *Play, Games, and Sports in Cultural Contexts*, 1983: 191–209.

Goodhew, David. 'Working-Class Respectability: The Example of the Western Areas of Johannesburg, 1930–55', *Journal of African History* 41, 2 (2000): 241–266.

Goulstone, John. 'The Working-Class Origins of Modern Football', *International Journal of the History of Sport* 17, 1 (2000): 135–143.

Granger, Vivian. *The World's Game Comes to South Africa*. Cape Town: Howard Timmins, 1961.

Gready, Paul. 'Political Autobiography in Search of Liberation: Working-Class Theater, Collaboration and the Construction of Identity'. In Liz Gunner (ed.), *Politics and Performance: Theater, Poetry and Song in Southern Africa*. Johannesburg: Witwatersrand University Press, 1994: 163–198.

Greenstein, Ran. *Comparative Perspectives on South Africa*. New York: St. Martin's Press, 1998.

————. 'The Study of South African Society: Towards a New Agenda for Comparative Historical Inquiry', *Journal of Southern African Studies* 20, 4 (1994): 641–661.

Grundlingh, Albert, André Odendaal, and Burridge Spies. *Beyond the Tryline: Rugby and South African Society*. Johannesburg: Ravan Press, 1995.

Gunner, Liz (ed.). *Politics and Performance: Theatre, Poetry and Song in Southern Africa*. Johannesburg: University of the Witwatersrand Press, 1994.

Gunner, L., and Mafika Gwala (eds.). *Musho! Zulu Popular Praises*. East Lansing, MI: Michigan State University Press, 1991.

Guttmann, Allen. *From Ritual to Record: The Nature of Modern Sports*. New York: Columbia University Press, 1978.

————. *Games and Empires: Modern Sports and Cultural Imperialism*. New York: Columbia University Press, 1994.

Guy, Jeff. *The Destruction of the Zulu Kingdom: The Civil War in Zululand, 1879–1884*. London: Longman, 1979.

Guy, J., and Motlatsi Thabane. 'The Ma-Rashea: A Participant's Perspective'. In B. Bozzoli (ed.), *Class, Community and Conflict*, 1987: 436–456.

Hain, Peter. *Don't Play with Apartheid*. London: George Allen & Unwin, 1971.

Halisi, C.R.D. *Black Political Thought in the Making of South African Democracy*. Bloomington and Indianapolis: Indiana University Press, 1999.

Hall, Donald E. (ed.). *Muscular Christianity: Embodying the Victorian Age*. Cambridge: Cambridge University Press, 1994.

Hamilton, Carolyn (ed.). *The Mfecane Aftermath: Reconstructive Debates in Southern African History*. Johannesburg: Witwatersrand University Press, 1995

Hamilton, C. *Terrific Majesty: The Powers of Shaka Zulu and the Limits of Historical Invention*. Cambridge, MA: Harvard University Press, 1998.

Hanna, Judith Lynne. 'African Dance and the Warrior Tradition'. In Ali A. Mazrui (ed.), *The Warrior Tradition in Modern Africa*, 1977: 111–133.

Hardy, Stephen. 'Entrepreneurs, Structures, and the Sportgeist: Old Tensions in a Modern Industry'. In D.G. Kyle and G.D. Stark (eds.), *Essays on Sport History and Sport Mythology*. College Station, TX: Texas A&M Press, 1990: 45–82.

Hargreaves, Jennifer. *Sport, Power and Culture*. Cambridge: Polity Press, 1986.

———. 'Women's Sport, Development, and Cultural Diversity: The South African Experience', *Women's Studies International Forum* 20, 2 (1997): 191–209.

Harries, Patrick. *Work, Culture and Identity: Migrant Laborers in Mozambique and South Africa, c.1860–1910*. Portsmouth, NH: Heinemann, 1994.

Harris, Janet C., and Roberta J. Park (eds.). *Play, Games, and Sports in Cultural Contexts*. Champaign, IL: Human Kinetics, 1983.

Hattersley, Alan F. *Pietermaritzburg Panorama: A Survey of One Hundred Years of an African City*. Pietermaritzburg: Shuter and Shooter, 1938.

———. *Portrait of a City*. Pietermaritzburg: Shuter and Shooter, 1951.

———. *Portrait of a Colony*. Cape Town: Cambridge University Press, 1940.

Hellmann, Ellen. *Problems of Urban Bantu Youth*. Johannesburg: SAIRR, 1940.

———. *Rooiyard: A Sociological Survey of an Urban Native Slumyard*. Cape Town: Oxford University Press, 1948.

Hemson, David. 'In the Eye of the Storm: Dock-workers in Durban'. In P. Maylam and I. Edwards (eds.), *The People's City*, 1996: 145–173.

Hendrickson, Hildi (ed.). *Clothing and Difference: Embodied Identities in Colonial and Post-Colonial Africa*. Durham, NC: Duke University Press, 1996.

Hill, Jeffrey. 'British Sports History: A Post-modern Future?' *Journal of Sport History* 23, 1 (1996): 1–19.

Hindson, Doug. *Pass Controls and the Urban African Proletariat*. Johannesburg: Ravan Press, 1987.

Hobsbawm, Eric, and Terence Ranger. *The Invention of Tradition*. Cambridge: Cambridge University Press, 1983.

Holt, Richard. 'Ideology and Sociability: A Review of New French Research into the History of Sport under the Early Third Republic (1870–1914)', *International Journal of the History of Sport* 6, 3 (1989): 368–377.

———. 'Sport and History: The State of the Subject in Britain', *Twentieth-Century British History* 7, 2 (1996): 231–252.

———. *Sport and the British: A Modern History*. Oxford: Clarendon Press, 1989.

———. 'Working-Class Football and the City: The Problem of Continuity', *British Journal of Sport History* 3, 1 (1986): 5–17.

Hopkins, Charles H. *History of the YMCA in North America*. New York: Association Press, 1951.

Horton, J.W. 'South Africa's Joint Councils: Black-White Co-operation between the Two World Wars', *South African Historical Journal* 4 (1972): 29–44.

Huddleston, Trevor. *Naught for Your Comfort*. Garden City, NY: Doubleday, 1956.

Hughes, Heather. 'The City Closes In: The Incorporation of Inanda into Metropolitan Durban'. In P. Maylam and I. Edwards (eds.), *The People's City*, 1996: 299–309.

Hunter, Monica. *Reaction to Conquest: Effects of Contact with Europeans on the Pondo of South Africa*. London: Oxford University Press, 1961 (first published in 1936).

James, C.L.R. *Beyond A Boundary*. London: Hutchinson, 1963.

James, Deborah. 'Urban Life and the Struggle for Autonomous Culture in Some Transvaal Communities', *African Studies* 51, 1 (1992): 1–9.

Jarvie, Grant. *Class, Race and Sport in South Africa's Political Economy*. London and Boston: Routledge & Kegan Paul, 1985.

Jeeves, Alan, and Jonathan Crush (eds.). *White Farms, Black Labour: Agrarian Transition in Southern Africa, 1910–1950*. Portsmouth, NH: Heinemann, 1997.

Jeffrey, Ian. 'Street Rivalry and Patron-Managers: Football in Sharpeville, 1943–1985', *African Studies* 51, 1 (1992): 68–94.

Jewsiewicki, Bogumil. 'Zairian Popular Painting as Commodity and as Communication'. In M.J. Arnoldi, et al. (eds.), *African Material Culture*. Bloomington and Indianapolis: Indiana University Press, 1996: 334–355.

Johns, Sheridan. *Raising the Red Flag: The International Socialist League & the Communist Party of South Africa, 1914–1932*. Belville: Mayibuye Books, 1995.

Johnstone, Frederick A. *Class, Race, and Gold*. London: Routledge & Kegan Paul, 1976.

Jokl, Ernst. 'Physical Education, Sport and Recreation'. In E. Hellmann (ed.), *Handbook on Race Relations in South Africa*. Cape Town: Oxford University Press, 1949: 442–464.

Jones, Stephen G. *Sport, Politics and the Working Class: Organized Labor and Sport in Inter-War Britain*. Manchester: Manchester University Press, 1988.

Jose, Colin. *North American Soccer League Encyclopedia*. Haworth, NJ: Saint Johann Press, 2003.

Kaeppler, Adrienne L. 'Dance'. In Richard Baumann (ed.), *Folklore, Cultural Performances, and Popular Entertainments*. New York and Oxford: Oxford University Press, 1992: 196–203.

Kallaway, Peter (ed.). *Apartheid and Education: The Education of Black South Africans*. Johannesburg: Ravan Press, 1984.

Kavanagh, Robert. *Theater and Cultural Struggle in South Africa*. London: Zed Books, 1985.

Keegan, Timothy. *Colonial South Africa and the Origins of the Racial Order*. Charlottesville, VA: University Press of Virginia, 1996.

———. *Facing the Storm: Portraits of Black Lives in Rural South Africa*. Athens, OH: Ohio University Press, 1988.

Klein, Alan. *Sugarball: The American Game, the Dominican Dream*. New Haven: Yale University Press, 1991.

Korr, Charles P. 'The Makhanya Football Association: Sport in Robben Island Prison'. Paper for the conference 'Global Games: Sports, Politics, and Society', Tufts University, February 2000.

———. 'West Ham United Football Club and the Beginnings of Professional Football in East London, 1895–1914', *Journal of Contemporary History* 13, 2 (1978): 211–232.

Krige, Eileen J. *The Social System of the Zulus*. Pietermaritzburg: Shuter & Shooter, 1965 (first edition, 1936).

Kuper, Leo. *An African Bourgeoisie: Race, Class, and Politics in South Africa*. New Haven and London: Yale University Press, 1965.

Kynoch, Gary. 'Politics and Violence in the "Russian Zone": Conflict in Newclare South, 1950–57'. *Journal of African History* 41 (2000): 267–290.

Laband, John. *The Rise and Fall of the Zulu Nation*. London: Arms and Armour, 1997.

La Hausse de Lalouvière, Paul. *Brewers, Beerhalls, and Boycotts: A History of Liquor in South Africa*. Johannesburg: Ravan Press, 1988.

———. ' "The Cows of Nongoloza": Youth, Crime and Amalaita Gangs in Durban, 1900–1936', *Journal of Southern African Studies* 16, 1 (1990): 79–111.

———. 'Drink and Cultural Innovation in Durban: The Origins of the Beerhall in South Africa, 1902–1916'. In J. Crush and C. Ambler (eds.), *Liquor and Labor in Southern Africa*, 1992: 78–114.

———. 'The Message of the Warriors: The ICU, the Laboring Poor and the Making of a Popular Political Culture in Durban, 1925–1930'. In P. Bonner et al. (eds.), *Holding Their Ground*, 1989: 19–58.

———. 'Oral History and the South African Historian'. In J. Brown et al. (eds.), *History from South Africa*, 1991: 342–350.

———. *Restless Identities: Signatures of Nationalism, Zulu Ethnicity and History in the Lives of Petros Lamula (c.1881–1948) and Lymon Maling (1889–c.1936)*. Pietermaritzburg: University of Natal Press, 2000.

———. 'So who was Elias Kuzwayo? Nationalism, Collaboration and the Picaresque in Natal'. In P. Bonner et al. (eds.), *Apartheid's Genesis*, 1993: 195–228.

———. 'The Struggle for the City: Alcohol, the Ematsheni and Popular Culture in Durban, 1902–1936'. In P. Maylam and I. Edwards (eds.), *The People's City*, 1996: 33–66.

Lambert, John. *Betrayed Trust: Africans and the State in Colonial Natal*. Pietermaritzburg: University of Natal Press, 1995.

Lapchick, Richard E. *The Politics of Race and International Sport: The Case of South Africa*. Westport, CT: Greenwood Press, 1975.

Legassick, Martin. 'The Sotho-Tswana Peoples before 1800'. In L. Thompson (ed.), *African Societies in Southern Africa*, 1969: 86–125.

Leseth, Anne. 'The Use of *Juju* in Football: Sport and Witchcraft in Tanzania'. In G. Armstrong and R. Giulianotti (eds.), *Entering the Field*, 1997: 159–174.

Lever, Janet. *Soccer Madness*. Prospect Heights, IL: Waveland Press, 1995 (first published 1983).

Lewsen, Phyllis. *John X. Merriman: Paradoxical South African Statesmen*. New Haven and London: Yale University Press, 1982.

Lipton, Merle. *Capitalism and Apartheid*. Totowa, NJ: Rowman & Allanheld, 1985.

Litchfield, Eric. *Eric Litchfield's Book of Soccer*. Johannesburg: Hugh Keartland, 1965.

———. *Goals in the Sun*. Johannesburg: Simondium-Uitgewers, 1963.

Lodge, Tom. *Black Politics in South Africa since 1945*. London and New York: Longman, 1983.

Lopes, Josè Sergio Leite. 'Successes and Contradictions in "Multiracial" Brazilian Football'. In G. Armstrong and R. Giulianotti (eds.), *Entering the Field*, 1997: 53–86.

Luthuli, Albert. *Let My People Go*. New York: McGraw-Hill, 1962.

Maasdorp, Gavin, and A.S.B. Humphreys (eds.). *From Shantytown to Township: An Economic Study of African Poverty and Rehousing in a South African City*. Cape Town: Juta, 1975.

MacClancy, Jeremy (ed.). *Sport, Identity and Ethnicity*. Oxford: Berg, 1996.

Mager, Anne Kelk. *Gender and the Making of a South African Bantustan*. Portsmouth, NH: Heinemann, 1999.

———. 'Youth Organizations and the Construction of Masculine Identities in the Ciskei and Transkei, 1945–1960', *Journal of Southern African Studies* 24, 4 (1998): 653–667.

Magubane, Bernard. 'Sport and Politics in an Urban African Community: A Case Study of African Voluntary Organizations'. M. Soc. Sci. thesis, University of Natal, 1963.

Maguire, Joseph, and Grant Jarvie. *Sport and Leisure in Social Thought*. London and New York: Routledge, 1994.

Maguire, Richard. 'The People's Club: A Social and Institutional History of Orlando Pirates Football Club, 1937–1973'. B.A. Hons. thesis, University of the Witwatersrand, 1991.

Mahjoub, Faouzi. *Le Football Africain: Trente Ans de Coupe D'Afrique Des Nations, 1957–1988*. Paris: Groupe Jeune Afrique, 1988.

Mahlmann, Peter. 'Sport as a Weapon of Colonialism in Kenya: A Review of the Literature', *Transafrican Journal of History* 17 (1988): 172–185.

Malherbe, Ernst Gideon. *Education in South Africa, v.2: 1923–75*. Cape Town: Juta, 1977.

Maloka, Eddy. 'Writing for Them: "Radical" Historiography in South Africa and the "Radical" Other', *Codesria Bulletin* 1–2 (2001): 16–19.

Malunga, Felix. 'Sports and Ethnicism: Instruments of Labour Control at the Messina Copper Mines, 1920–1960', *Historia* 45, 2 (2000): 465–482.

Mamdani, Mahmood. *Citizen and Subject: Contemporary Africa and the Legacy of Late Colonialism*. Princeton: Princeton University Press, 1996.

Mancoe, J.B. *The Bloemfontein Bantu and Coloured People's Directory*. Bloemfontein: 1934.

Mandela, Nelson. *Long Walk to Freedom*. London: Little, Brown and Company, 1994.

Mangan, James Anthony. *Athleticism in the Victorian and Edwardian Public School: The Emergence and Consolidation of an Educational Ideology*. London: Cambridge University Press, 1981.

———. *The Games Ethic and Imperialism Aspects of the Diffusion of an Ideal*. London: Viking, 1986.

———., (ed.). *Pleasure, Profit, and Proselytism: British Culture and Sport at Home and Abroad*. London: Frank Cass, 1988.

Manyoni, W.E.G. 'Attitude of Soccer Enquiry Committee Puzzles Enthusiasts', *Bantu World*, 25 March 1933.

Marable, W. Manning. 'African Nationalist: The Life of John Langalibalele Dube'. Ph.D. dissertation, University of Maryland, 1976.

Markovits, Andy, and Steven L. Hellerman. *Offside: Soccer and American Exceptionalism*. Princeton, NJ: Princeton University Press, 2001.

Marks, Shula. *The Ambiguities of Dependence in South Africa: Class, Nationalism, and the State in Twentieth-Century Natal*. Johannesburg: Ravan Press, 1986.

———. 'The Traditions of the Natal "Nguni": A Second Look at the Work of A.T. Bryant'. In L. Thompson (ed.), *African Societies in Southern Africa*, 1969: 126–144.

Marks, S., and Anthony Atmore (eds.). *Economy and Society in Pre-Industrial South Africa*. London: Longman, 1980.

Marks, S., and Richard Rathbone, (eds.). *Industrialisation and Social Change in South Africa: African Class Formation, Culture and Consciousness, 1870–1930*. London: Longman, 1982.

Martin, Phyllis M. 'Colonialism, Youth and Football in French Equatorial Africa', *International Journal of the History of Sport* 8, 1 (1991): 56–71.

———. *Leisure and Society in Colonial Brazzaville*. Cambridge: Cambridge University Press, 1995.

Mason, Tony. *Association Football and English Society: 1863–1915*. London: Harvester Press, 1980.

———. 'Football and the Historian', *International Journal of the History of Sport* 5, 1 (1988): 136–141.

———. 'Football on the Maidan: Cultural Imperialism in Calcutta', *International Journal of the History of Sport* 7, 1 (1990): 85–95.

———. 'Football and the Workers in England, 1880–1914'. In Richard Cashman and Michael McKernan (eds.), *Sport: Money, Morality, and the Media*. New South Wales: New South Wales University Press, 1981.

———. 'Kick and Rush or Revolt into Style? Football Playing among English Professionals from Great Power to Image of Decline'. Manuscript, 1998.

———. *Passion of the People? Football in South America*. London and New York: Verso, 1995.

Mayer, Philip. *Black Villagers in an Industrial Society*. Cape Town: Oxford University Press, 1980.

————. *Townsmen or Tribesmen: Conservatism and the Process of Urbanisation in a South African City*. Cape Town: Oxford University Press, 1971 (first published 1961).

Mayer, P., and Iona Mayer. 'Self-Organization by Youth amongst the Xhosa-speaking Peoples of the Ciskei and Transkei (2 vols.)'. Institute of Social and Economic Research, Rhodes University, 1972.

————. 'Socialization by Peers: The Youth Organization of the Red Xhosa'. In P. Mayer (ed.), *Socialization: The Approach from Social Anthropology*. London: Tavistock, 1970: 159–189.

Maylam, Paul. 'Aspects of African Urbanization in the Durban Area before 1940'. In Richard Haines and Gina Buijs (eds.), *The Struggle for Social and Economic Space: Urbanization in Twentieth-Century South Africa*. Durban: Institute for Social and Economic Research University of Durban-Westville, 1985: 41–62.

————. '"Dead Horses, the Baby and the Bathwater": "Post-Theory" and the Historian's Practice', *South African Historical Journal* 42 (2000): 121–135.

————. 'Explaining The Apartheid City: 20 Years of South African Urban Historiography', *Journal of Southern African Studies* 21, 1 (1995): 19–38.

————. 'Municipal Fraud: The Operation of Durban's Native Revenue Account, 1908–1953', *Journal of Natal and Zulu History* 11 (1988): 69–92.

————. 'The Struggle for Space in Twentieth-Century Durban'. In P. Maylam and I. Edwards (eds.), *The People's City*, 1996: 1–30.

Maylam, P., and Iain Edwards (eds.). *The People's City: African Life in Twentieth-Century Durban*. Pietermaritzburg and Portsmouth, NH: University of Natal Press and Heinemann, 1996.

Mazrui, Ali A. (ed.). *The Warrior Tradition in Modern Africa*. Leiden: E.J. Brill, 1977.

McAllister, Patrick A. 'Resistance To "Betterment" in the Transkei: A Case Study From Willowvale District', *Journal of Southern African Studies* 15, 2 (1989): 346–368.

McAllister, P., and Dumisani Deliwe. 'Youth in Rural Transkei: The Demise of "Traditional" Youth Associations and the Development of New Forms of Association and Activity: 1975–1993', Working Paper No. 61, Grahamstown: Rhodes University Institute of Social and Economic Research, 1996.

McCabe, Thomas. 'An Attempt to Create Space: The Fate of Soccer in American Colleges, 1869–1906', Manuscript, 1999.

McHugh, R.J. *The Siege of Ladysmith*. London: Chapman & Hall, 1900.

Merrett, Christopher. '"In Nothing Else are the Deprivers so Deprived": South African Sport, Apartheid and Foreign Relations, 1945–71', *International Journal of the History of Sport* 13, 2 (1996): 146–165.

————. 'Sport, Racism and Urban Policy in South Africa: Pietermaritzburg, a Case Study', *Sporting Traditions* 10, 2 (1994): 97–122.

————. 'Sports Historians are a Motley Bunch', *South African Historical Journal* 33 (1995): 178–181.

Messner, Michael A. *Power at Play: Sports and the Problem of Masculinity*. Boston: Beacon Press, 1992.

Messner, M.A., and Donald F. Sabo (eds.). *Sport, Men, and the Gender Order: Critical Feminist Perspectives*. Champaign, IL: Human Kinetics, 1990.

Miller, Joseph. 'History and Africa/Africa and History', *American Historical Review* 104 (1999): 1–32.

Minkley, Gary, and Ciraj Rassool. 'Orality, Memory, and Social History in South Africa'. In S. Nuttall and C. Coetzee (eds.), *Negotiating the Past: The Making of Memory in South Africa*. Oxford: Oxford University Press, 1998.

Mitchell, J. Clyde. *The Kalela Dance: Aspects of Social Relationships among Urban Africans in Northern Rhodesia*. Manchester: Manchester University Press, 1956.

Mokone, Stephen. *The Life and Times of a Soccer Player*. Pretoria: De Jager-Haum, 1980.

Molapo, Rachidi Richard. 'Sports, Festivals and Popular Politics: Aspects of the Social and Popular Culture in Langa Township, 1945–1970'. M.A. thesis, University of Cape Town, 1994.

Moodie, Dunbar T. *Going For Gold: Men, Mines, and Migration*. Johannesburg: University of Witwatersrand Press, 1994.

Moore, Sally Falk. *Anthropology and Africa: Changing Perspectives on a Changing Scene*. Charlottesville: University Press of Virginia, 1994.

Morrell, Robert (ed.). *Changing Men in Southern Africa*. Pietermaritzburg and London: University of Natal Press and Zed Press, 2001.

———. 'Of Boys and Men: Masculinity and Gender in Southern African Studies', *Journal of Southern African Studies* 24, 4 (1998): 605–630.

———. 'Forging a Ruling Race: Rugby and White Masculinity in Colonial Natal, *c.*1870–1910'. In J. Nauright and T.J.H. Chandler (eds.), *Making Men: Rugby and Masculine Identity*, 1996: 91–120.

Mothei, Isaac. 'Pirates'. In George Thabe (ed.), *It's a Goal!*, 1983: 87–88.

Murray, Bill. *The World's Game: A History of Soccer*. Chicago: University of Illinois Press, 1996.

Murray, Bruce. 'Politics and Cricket: The D'Oliveira Affair of 1968', *Journal of Southern African Studies* 27, 4 (2001): 667–684.

———. 'The Sports Boycott and Cricket: The Cancellation of the 1970 South African Tour of England', *South African Historical Journal* 46 (2002): 219–249.

Musemwa, Muchaparara. 'Aspects of the Social and Political History of Langa Township, Cape Town, 1927–1948'. M.A. thesis, University of Cape Town, 1993.

Nasson, Bill. '"She Preferred Living in a Cave with Harry the Snake-catcher": Towards an Oral History of Popular Leisure and Class Expression in District Six, Cape Town, *c.*1920–1950'. In P. Bonner et al. (eds.), *Holding Their Ground*, 1989: 285–309.

Nattrass, Nicoli. 'Economic Aspects of the Construction of Apartheid'. In P. Bonner et al. (eds.), *Apartheid's Genesis*, 1993: 42–64.

Nauright, John. 'Masculinity, Muscular Islam and Popular Culture: 'Coloured' Rugby's Cultural Symbolism in Working-Class Cape Town *c.*1930–70', *International Journal of the History of Sport* 14, 1 (1997a): 184–190.

———. '"The Mecca of Native Scum" and "A Running Sore of Evil": White Johannesburg and the Alexandra Township Removal Debate, 1935–1945', *Kleio* 30 (1998): 64–88.

———. *Sport, Cultures and Identities in South Africa*. London: Leicester University Press, 1997b.

Nauright, J., and Timothy J.H. Chandler (eds.). *Making Men: Rugby and Masculine Identity*. London: Frank Cass, 1996.

Ndebele, Njabulo S. *South African Literature and Culture*. Manchester: Manchester University Press, 1994.

Nicol, Mike. *A Good-looking Corpse: The World of Drum – Jazz and Gangsters, Hope and Defiance in the Townships of South Africa*. London: Secker & Warburg, 1991.

Nixon, Rob. *Homelands, Harlem, and Hollywood: South African Culture and the World Beyond*. London: Routledge, 1994.

Nkwi, Paul Nchoji, and Bea Vidacs. 'Football: Politics and Power in Cameroon'. In G. Armstrong and R. Giulianotti (eds.), *Entering the Field*, 1997: 123–140.

North, James. 'Sports: The Kaizer Chiefs'. In J. North, *Freedom Rising*. New York: Macmillan, 1985: 144–157.

Nöthling, F.J. 'Soccer in South Africa (A Brief Outline)', *Kleio* 14 (1982): 28–41.

Nuttall, Tim. 'The Leaves in the Trees are Proclaiming Our Slavery: African Trade Union Organization, 1937–1949'. In P. Maylam and I. Edwards (eds.), *The People's City*, 1996: 174–201.

Nyamane, Phil. 'Reaching Back'. In *The Birds: The Official Magazine of Moroka Swallows FC*, 2 (November 1997–January 1998): 12–13.

Odendaal, André. *Cricket in Isolation: The Politics of Race and Cricket in South Africa*. Cape Town: Odendaal, 1977.

———. 'South Africa's Black Victorians: Sport and Society in South Africa in the Nineteenth Century'. In J.A. Mangan (ed.), *Pleasure, Profit, Proselytism*, 1988: 193–214.

———. *The Story of an African Game: Black Cricketers and the Umasking of One of Cricket's Greatest Myths, South Africa, 1850–2003*. Cape Town: David Philip, 2003: 220.

———. 'The Thing That is Not Round: The Untold History of Black Rugby in South Africa'. In A. Grundlingh, A. Odendaal, and B. Spies, *Beyond the Tryline*, 1995: 24–63.

Omo-Osagie, Anthony I. *African Unity through Sports*. Benin City: Ambik Press, 1987.

Orakwue, Stella. *Pitch Invaders: The Modern Black Football Revolution*. London: Victor Gollancz, 1998.

Orejan, Jaime W. 'A Descriptive History of Tactics Used in Football Assn. from 1863 to the Present'. Ph.D. dissertation, University of Southern Mississippi, 1995.

Packard, Randall. *White Plague, Black Labor: Tuberculosis and the Political Economy of Health and Disease in South Africa*. Berkeley: University of California Press, 1989.

Park, Roberta J., and Janet C. Harris (eds.). *Play, Games, and Sports in Cultural Contexts*. Champaign, IL: Human Kinetic Publishers, 1983.

Parker, G.A. *South African Sports*. London: Sampson Low, Marston & Co., 1897.

Patterson, Orlando. 'The Ritual of Cricket'. In B. Stoddart and H. McD. Beckles (eds.), *Liberation Cricket*, 1996: 141–147.

Paul, Sigrid. 'The Wrestling Tradition and Its Social Functions'. In W.J. Baker and J.A. Mangan (eds.), *Sport in Africa*, 1987: 23–46.

Peires, Jeffrey B. 'The Central Beliefs of the Xhosa Cattle-Killing', *Journal of African History* 28 (1987): 43–63.

———. *The House of Phalo: A History of the Xhosa People in the Days of Their Independence*. Berkeley and Los Angeles: University of California Press, 1981.

Penvenne, Jeanne M. *African Workers and Colonial Racism: Mozambican Strategies and Struggles in Lourenço Marques, 1877–1962*. Portsmouth, NH: Heinemann, 1995.

Perkin, Harold. 'Teaching the Nations How to Play Sport in the Empire and Commonwealth', *International Journal of the History of Sport* 6, 2 (1989): 41–48.

Peterson, Bheki. 'Performing History Off the Stage: Notes of Working-Class Theater', *Radical History Review* 46, 7, (1990): 321–329.

Phillips, Ray. *The Bantu in the City: A Study of Cultural Adjustment on the Witwatersrand*. Lovedale: Lovedale Press, 1936.

———. *The Bantu Are Coming*. Edinburgh: Edinburgh Press, 1930.

Plaatje, Sol T. *Mafeking Diary: A Black Man's View of a White Man's War*. Cambridge, U.K.: Meridor Books, 1990.

———. *Native Life in South Africa*. Johannesburg: Ravan Press, 1982 (first published 1916).

Pope, Stephen W. 'Sport History: Into the 21st Century', *Journal of Sport History* 25, 2 (1998): i–x.

———. (ed.). *The New American Sport History: Recent Approaches and Perspectives*. Urbana and Chicago: University of Illinois Press, 1997.

Posel, Deborah. *The Making of Apartheid, 1948–1961: Conflict and Compromise*. Oxford: Clarendon Press, 1991.

Proctor, André. 'Class Struggle, Segregation and the City: A History of Sophiatown, 1905–1940'. In B. Bozzoli (ed.), *Labour, Townships and Protest*, 1979: 49–89.

Putnam, Robert D. *Making Democracy Work: Civic Traditions in Modern Italy*. Princeton, NJ: Princeton University Press, 1994.

Ramsamy, Sam. *Apartheid, The Real Hurdle: Sport in South Africa and the International Boycott.* London: International Defence & Aid Fund for Southern Africa, 1982.

Ranger, Terence. *Dance and Society in Eastern Africa 1890–1970: The Beni Ngoma.* London: Heinemann, 1975.

———. 'Pugilism and Pathology: African Boxing and the Black Urban Experience in Southern Rhodesia'. In W.J. Baker and J.A. Mangan (eds.), *Sport in Africa*, 1987: 196–213.

Rassool, Ciraj. 'Local Resistance, Collective Identities and Ordinary Experience: Social History and the Production of Lives in South Africa'. Paper for the conference 'Problematizing History and Agency', University of Cape Town, 1997.

Rich, Paul. *White Power and the Liberal Conscience: Racial Segregation and South African Liberalism, 1921–1960.* Johannesburg: Ravan Press, 1984.

Richards, Paul. 'Soccer and Violence in War-Torn Africa: Soccer and Social Rehabilitation in Sierra Leone'. In G. Armstrong and R. Giulianotti (eds.), *Entering the Field*, 1997: 141–158.

Roberts, Cheryl. *Against the Grain: Women and Sport in South Africa.* Cape Town: Township Publishing Co-operative, 1992.

———. *Sport in Chains.* Cape Town: Township Publishing Co-operative, 1994.

Rycroft, David K., and A.B. Ngcobo. *The Praises of Dingana (Izibongo ZikaDingana).* Pietermaritzburg: University of Natal Press, 1988.

Saavedra, Martha. 'Football Feminine – Development of the African Game: Senegal, Nigeria and South Africa', *Soccer and Society* 4, 2/3 (2003): 225–253.

Sammons, Jeffrey A. '"Race" and Sport: A Critical Historical Examination', *Journal of Sport History* 21, 3 (1994): 203–278.

———. 'Sports History? Why? What? How? Methodological Suggestions for Research, Writing, and Teaching in the South African Context'. Collected Paper no.4, Centre for African Studies, University of Cape Town, 1986.

Samuelson, Robert C.A. *Long, Long Ago.* Durban: Knox, 1929.

Sapire, Hilary. 'African Political Organization in Brakpan in the 1950s'. In P. Bonner et al. (eds.), *Apartheid's Genesis*, 1993: 252–274.

Sarro, Ramon. 'The Generation Game: Football among the Baga of Guinea'. In G. Armstrong and R. Giulianotti (eds.), *Football Cultures and Identities*, 1997: 141–153.

Saunders, Christopher. 'The Creation of Ndabeni: Urban Segregation and African Resistance in Cape Town'. In C. Saunders (ed.), *Studies in the History of Cape Town, vol. I*, 1979a: 165–193.

———. 'From Ndabeni to Langa'. In C. Saunders (ed.), *Studies in the History of Cape Town, vol. I*, 1979b: 194–230.

———. *The Making of the South African Past.* Totowa, NJ: Barnes & Noble, 1988.

———. 'More Protest and Challenge', *South African Historical Journal* 36 (1997): 307–315.

———. (ed.). *Reader's Digest Illustrated History of South Africa.* 3rd ed. Cape Town: Reader's Digest, 1994.

———. *Studies in the History of Cape Town*, vols.1–5. Cape Town: Department of History, University of Cape Town, 1984.

Saunders, C., and Nicholas Southey. *A Dictionary of South African History.* Cape Town: David Philip, 1998.

Scotch, N.A. 'Magic, Sorcery, and Football among Urban Zulus', *Journal of Conflict Resolution* 5 (1961): 70–74.

Scott, James. *The Moral Economy of the Peasant: Rebellion and Subsistence in Southeast Asia.* New Haven: Yale University Press, 1976.

———. *Seeing Like a State: How Certain Schemes to Improve the Human Condition Have Failed.* New Haven: Yale University Press, 1998.

Sello, Sekola. *Chiefs: 21 Glorious Years: The Official History of SA's Glamour Football Club.* Johannesburg: Skotaville, 1991.

Shirts, Matthew. 'Socrates, Corinthians, and Questions of Democracy and Citizenship'. In J. Arbena (ed.), *Sport and Society in Latin America*. Westport, CT: Greenwood Press, 1988: 97–112.

Sithole, Frank. 'African Wanderers'. In G. Thabe (ed.), *It's a Goal!*, 1983: 95.

Skota, T.K. Mweli. *The African Who's Who: An Illustrated Classified Register and National Biographical Dictionary of the African in the Transvaal*. Johannesburg: Central News Agency, 1966.

Smith, Ken. *The Changing Past: Trends in South African Historical Writing*. Athens, OH: Ohio University Press, 1988.

Soga, John Henderson. *The Ama-Xosa: Life and Customs*. Lovedale: Lovedale Press, 1932.

Spies, Burridge. 'The Imperial Heritage'. In A. Grundlingh, A. Odendaal, and B. Spies, *Beyond the Tryline*, 1995: 66.

Stadler, Alf. '"Birds in the Cornfield": Squatter Movements in Johannesburg, 1944–47', *Journal of Southern African Studies* 6, 1 (1979): 93–123.

Stoddart, Brian. 'Sport, Cultural Imperialism, and Colonial Response in the British Empire', *Comparative Studies in Society and History* 30, 4 (1988): 649–673.

Stoddart, B., and Hilary McD. Beckles (eds.). *Liberation Cricket: West Indies Cricket Culture*. Manchester: Manchester University Press, 1996.

Struna, Nancy. *People of Prowess: Sport, Leisure, and Labor in Early Anglo-America*. Urbana, IL: University of Illinois Press, 1996.

Stuart, Ossie. 'The Lions Stir: Football in African Society'. In S. Wagg (ed.), *Giving the Game Away*, 1995: 24–51.

———. 'Players, Workers and Protestors: Social Change and Soccer in Colonial Zimbabwe'. In J. MacClancy (ed.), *Sport, Identity and Ethnicity*, 1996: 167–180.

Sugden, John, and Alan Tomlinson. *FIFA and the Contest for World Football: Who Rules the People's Game?* Cambridge: Polity Press, 1998.

Swanson, Maynard. '"The Durban System": Roots of Urban Apartheid in Colonial Natal', *African Studies* 35 (1976): 159–176.

Switzer, Les (ed.). *South Africa's Alternative Press: Voices of Protest and Resistance, 1880s–1960s*. Cambridge: Cambridge University Press, 1997.

Switzer, L., and D. Switzer. *The Black Press in South Africa and Lesotho: A Descriptive Bibliographic Guide to African, Coloured, and Indian Newspapers, Newsletters, and Magazines, 1836–1976*. Boston: Hall, 1979.

Telchin, Robert. 'The Game of the People in The People's City: Soccer, Integration and African Empowerment in Durban, South Africa, 1916–1965'. B.A. Hons. thesis, Carleton College, 1999.

Thabe, George A.L. (ed.). *It's a Goal! 50 Years of Sweat, Tears and Drama in Black Soccer*. Johannesburg: Skotaville, 1983.

Thirty-fourth Annual Report of the Transvaal Chamber of Mines: Year 1923. Johannesburg, 1924.

Thompson, Edward P. 'Time, Work-Discipline, and Industrial Capitalism', *Past and Present* 38 (1967): 56–97.

Thompson, J. de L. *The Story of Rhodesian Sport: vol. 1, 1889–1935*. Bulawayo: Books of Rhodesia, 1976 (first published 1935).

Thompson, Leonard (ed.). *African Societies in Southern Africa*. New York and Washington: Praeger, 1969.

———. *A History of South Africa*. New Haven: Yale University Press, 1990.

Thompson, Paul. 'Schools, Sport and Britishness: Young White Natal, 1902–1961', *South African Historical Journal* 45 (2001): 223–248.

Thompson, Richard. *Race and Sport*. London: Oxford University Press, 1964.

Tomaselli, Keyan, Ruth Tomaselli, and Johan Muller (eds.). *Narrating the Crisis: Hegemony and the South African Press*. Johannesburg: Richard Lyon & Co., 1987.

Torr, Louise. 'Lamontville'. In P. Maylam and I. Edwards (eds.), *The People's City*, 1996: 245–273.

Tracey, Hugh. *African Dances of the Witwatersrand Gold Mines*. Johannesburg: African Music Society, 1952.

Vahed, Goolam. 'Control of African Leisure Time in Durban in the 1930s', *Journal of Natal and Zulu History* 18 (1998): 67–123.

Vail, Leroy (ed.). *The Creation of Tribalism in Southern Africa*. Berkeley: University of California Press, 1989.

Vail, L., and Landeg White. *Power and the Praise Poem: Southern African Voices in History*. Charlottesville: University Press of Virginia, 1991.

Van der Horst, Sheila. *African Workers in Town: A Study of Labour in Cape Town*. Cape Town: Oxford University Press, 1964.

Van der Merwe, Floris J.G. '"Athletic Sports" and the Cape Town Society, 1652–1900', *Canadian Journal of the History of Sport* 19, 1 (1988): 28–39.

———. 'Ernst Franz Jokl as the Father of Physical Education in South Africa'. In *North American Society for Sport History Proceedings*. Iowa City, IA: NASSH, 1990: 81.

———. 'Sport and Games in Boer Prisoner of War Camps during the Anglo-Boer War, 1899–1902', *International Journal of the History of Sport* 9, 1 (1992): 439–457.

———. 'The State of Sport Historiography and Information in South Africa'. In *North American Society for Sport History Proceedings*. Iowa City, IA: NASSH, 1983: 40–42.

Van Onselen, Charles. *Chibaro: African Mine Labor in Southern Rhodesia, 1900–1933*. London: Pluto Press, 1976.

———. *The Seed is Mine: The Life of Kas Maine, a South African Sharecropper, 1894–1985*. New York: Hill & Wang, 1996.

———. *Studies in the Social and Economic History of the Witwatersrand, 1886–1914*. Vol. I: *New Babylon;* Vol. II: *New Nineveh*. Johannesburg: Ravan Press, 1982.

Van Tonder, Deon. '"First Win the War, then Clear the Slums": The Genesis of the Western Areas Removal Scheme, 1940–1949'. In P. Bonner et al. (eds.), *Apartheid's Genesis*, 1993: 316–340.

Vasili, Phil. 'Colonialism and Football: the First Nigerian Tour of Britain', *Race and Class* 36, 4 (1995): 55–70.

Vinson, Robert Trent. 'Uncertain Hegemony: The Garvey Movement in Segregationist South Africa, 1920–1940'. Ph.D. dissertation, Howard University, 2000.

Vundla, Kathleen. *P.Q.: The Story of Philip Vundla of South Africa*. Johannesburg: Moral Re-Armament, 1973.

Wagg, Stephen (ed.). *Giving the Game Away: Football, Politics, and Culture on 5 Continents*. London: Leicester University Press, 1995.

Wagner, Eric (ed.). *Sport in Asia and Africa: A Comparative Handbook*. Westport, CT: Greenwood Press, 1989.

Walshe, Peter. *The Rise of African Nationalism in South Africa: The African National Congress, 1912–1952*. Berkeley and Los Angeles: University of California Press, 1971.

Walvin, James. *The People's Game: A History of Football Revisited*. Edinburgh: Mainstream Publishing, 1994.

Warwick, Peter. *Black People and The South African War: 1899–1902*. London: Cambridge University Press, 1983.

Waterman, Christopher A. *Jùjú: A Social History and Ethnography of an African Popular Music*. Chicago and London: University of Chicago Press, 1990.

Webb, Colin de B., and John Wright (eds.). *The James Stuart Archive of Recorded Oral Evidence Relating to the History of the Zulu and Neighboring People*. 5 vols. Pietermaritzburg: Killie Campbell, 1976, 1979, 1982, 1986, 2001.

Webster, Jack. *The Dons: The History of Aberdeen Football Club*. London: S. Paul, 1990.

Western, John. *Outcast Cape Town*. Berkeley: University of California Press, 1996 [first published in 1981].

Whitson, David. 'Sport in the Social Construction of Masculinity'. In M.A. Messner and D.F. Sabo, *Sport, Men, and the Gender Order*, 1990: 19–29.

Willan, Brian. *Sol Plaatje: South African Nationalist, 1876–1932*. Berkeley and Los Angeles: University of California Press, 1984.

Williams, Donovan. *Umfundisi*. Lovedale: Lovedale Press, 1978.

Wilson, Francis. *Labour in the South African Gold Mines*. Cambridge: Cambridge University Press, 1972.

Wilson, Monica, and Archie Mafeje. *Langa: A Study of Social Groups in an African Township*. Cape Town: Oxford University Press, 1963.

Worden, Nigel, Vivian Bickford-Smith, and Elizabeth Van Heyningen. *Cape Town – The Making of a City: An Illustrated Social History*. Claremont: David Philip, 1998.

Worger, William H. *South Africa's City of Diamonds: Mine Workers and Monopoly Capitalism in Kimberley, 1867–1895*. New Haven and London: Yale University Press, 1987.

Wright, Harrison. *The Burden of the Present: Liberal-Radical Controversy over Southern African History*. Cape Town: David Philip, 1977.

Wright, John. 'A.T. Bryant and "The Wars of Shaka"', *History in Africa* 18 (1991): 409–425.

———. *Bushman Raiders of the Drakensberg, 1840–1870: A Study of Their Conflict with Stockkeeping Peoples of Natal*. Pietermaritzburg: University of Natal Press, 1971.

Wylie, Dan. *Savage Delight: White Myths of Shaka*. Pietermaritzburg: University of Natal Press, 2000.

Wylie, Diana. *Starving on a Full Stomach: Hunger and the Triumph of Cultural Racism in Modern South Africa*. Charlottesville and London: University Press of Virginia, 2001.

Yudelman, David. *The Emergence of Modern South Africa: State, Capital, and the Incorporation of Organized Labor on the South African Gold Fields, 1902–1939*. Westport, CT and London: Greenwood Press, 1983.

Index